BLACK GOLD

Black Gold

Britain and Oil in the
Twentieth Century

Charles More

continuum

Continuum UK, The Tower Building, 11 York Road, London SE1 7NX
Continuum US, 80 Maiden Lane, Suite 704, New York, NY 10038

www.continuumbooks.com

First published 2009

British Library Cataloguing-in-Publication Data
A catalogue record for this book is available from the British Library.

ISBN 978 1 84725 043 8

Typeset by Pindar NZ, Auckland, New Zealand
Printed and bound by MPG Books Ltd, Cornwall, Great Britain

Contents

Preface

In 1900 the internal combustion engine was about to start its conquest of the world's highways, and worldwide oil consumption was poised to begin a period of rapid growth which would last until the oil crises of the 1970s. There was only one major international oil company in 1900 – the US-based Standard Oil – but by 1914 there were several. Most were American, but two which have lasted to the present day were European. One was the Royal Dutch/Shell group, part Dutch and part British, and one the wholly British Anglo-Persian Oil Company, later to become BP. So Britain, which then had practically no known oil, fostered two companies which are still world leaders in the industry.

This book is about why and how that happened and how Britain and the British government have interacted with oil and oil companies over the twentieth century. Britain's troubled relationship with the Middle East is part of the story. The role oil played in wars is another. The power of oil companies *vis-à-vis* governments and markets a third. And the changes brought about by the oil crises of the 1970s a fourth. The discovery and exploitation of oil and gas in the North Sea is covered, and the book also looks at the social history of oil and its products during the century – their uses, their marketing and their impact. The conclusion ends with a brief look at the future.

There are plentiful secondary sources and the book is mainly based on these, but I have consulted primary sources where there are gaps. Books of particular value include the official histories of Royal Dutch/Shell and BP, referred to in notes as *RDS* and *BP*. Full references are given in the bibliography. Both histories are, so far as I can tell, admirably objective – certainly neither hesitates to criticize their company. I owe a particular debt to the BP history. Unfortunately the fourth volume of this, from 1975, has not yet been published. Two other books which were very valuable were Geoffrey Jones, *The State and the Emergence of the British Oil Industry*, on the British industry's early years, and Daniel Yergin's *The Prize*, a history of the international oil industry. Statistics, if not otherwise attributed, are likely to come from the extremely useful *BP Statistical Review of World Energy*, accessible on the company's website. North Sea oil lacks a comprehensive history and Professor Alexander Kemp's book in the UK government's Official History series will be of great value when it is published. I should also mention the oral history archive 'Lives in the Oil Industry'. I only listened extensively to three interviews out of nearly two hundred, but the archive is clearly important not just for the history of North Sea oil and gas but also for British – especially Scottish – social history.

A few words are needed about terminology. 'Oil' encompasses vegetable and mineral oil, but most people will take it to mean the latter, and it has been used in that sense in the book. Mineral oil is also known as petroleum. Before petroleum is refined it is commonly known as crude oil, or crude. 'Upstream' refers to exploration for and production of crude, and 'downstream' to its refining and marketing. I have used the British 'petrol' rather than the American 'gasoline' for one of oil's main products. However, I have preferred 'kerosene' to the traditional British 'paraffin'. As people become less familiar with paraffin stoves and lighting, kerosene – now mainly used for jet fuel – is becoming the accepted usage. The familiar measure of oil, a barrel, never actually used for physical storage today, contains about 35 Imperial gallons (42 US gallons). There are about seven to eight barrels per ton depending on the specific gravity of the oil. 'bpd' means 'barrels per day' – a standard measure of output; 'oe' in that context means 'oil equivalent' and includes gas. I have specified metric tons (tonnes) where I know that to be the measurement but have not been exact about 'tons and 'metric tons' – the former is actually 1.016 of the latter. Finally, I should apologize to Dutch readers for sometimes abbreviating references to Royal Dutch Shell so that it may appear as if it was wholly British, when it is and was both Dutch and British.

I would like to acknowledge the assistance of the BP Archive. I would also like to acknowledge help from the following: Professor Bernard Alford; Joanne Burman; Michael Greenwood; Valerie Johnson; Tony Morris, who thought of the book in the first place; Suzanne Richards; Professor Hew Strachan; and, most of all, my wife Hilary.

1

Coming of Age: Oil 1900–18

CAPITALISTS AND CONCESSIONS

In 1884 word began to spread in Rockhampton, a port in Queensland, Australia, of a big gold discovery in the hills inland. The land beneath which the discovery lay was owned by the Morgan family and the gold mine became Mount Morgan. Like so many Australian mines, however, Mount Morgan after a brief flurry seemed to be 'a jeweller's shop on top and a blacksmith's shop below'. The mine still yielded gold, but not much, and the Morgans were glad to sell their holding to various local speculators, the largest proportion being acquired by William Knox D'Arcy, who already had an interest in the mine. D'Arcy's father, a solicitor, had emigrated from England and William had followed the paternal profession in Australia. He fitted well into the family's new home. He was keen on sport, particularly horse-racing, and speculation. He was also lucky. By 1886, Mount Morgan had turned out to be a jeweller's shop all the way down. It was one of the richest gold mines ever and D'Arcy's fortune was made. In its best year the company paid over one million pounds in dividends – and D'Arcy had over one-third of the capital. In 1889 D'Arcy returned to England where he lived the plutocratic lifestyle typical of the wealthy in late Victorian and Edwardian England.[1]

By 1900 Mount Morgan's falling yield was not enough to finance D'Arcy's colossal spending, and he needed another bonanza. An ex-ambassador to Persia, Sir Henry Drummond Wolff, introduced him to the possibilities of another type of gold – black gold. It would come in the form of Persian oil. Persia, the modern-day Iran, had long been seen as a potential oil producer, but the uncertainties of the country's politics frightened off investors. The country's nominally autocratic ruler, the Shah, was in reality weak. Local leaders or khans held much of the real power while the Shah was buffeted by Russian pressure from the north and British from the south. However, the Shah needed money and was anxious for a deal. D'Arcy, used to speculating deeply and still with plenty of capital in the form of Mount Morgan shares, was willing to take the risk. The concession, to search for and exploit oil over a large proportion of the country, was granted for 60 years in return for a lump sum payment and 16 per cent of the annual profits. 'Profits' being a moveable feast, the vagueness of this was to prove a hostage to fortune. But although the rate seemed low by later standards, the risks to D'Arcy were extreme: not only Persia's political vagaries but the fact that, as yet, no oil besides surface seepages had been found. Drummond Wolff's description of D'Arcy as a 'capitalist of the highest order' seems fair comment.[2]

The concession was signed in 1901, and its eventual importance to Britain's oil industry makes this as good a date as any to start its history. But there are a number of alternatives. The first internal combustion-engined car in Britain was Daimler's of 1897. In the same year, an existing fleet of oil tankers was incorporated as the "Shell" Transport and Trading Company. A decade earlier, the dawn of British oil multinationals had been heralded by the Burmah Oil Company, incorporated in 1886, only 27 years after the founding of the modern industry by Colonel Drake, who in 1859 struck oil at Titusville in Pennsylvania. Furthermore some aspects of the industry before 1900 were well developed. There were already oil tankers and pipelines, and the industry already tended towards oligopoly, that is the dominance of a few large companies, manifested in this period by the pre-eminence of Rockefeller's Standard Oil.

But in spite of some modern characteristics the industry in 1900 was still tiny and specialized. Numerous products can be extracted from crude oil, and in 1900 the only one consumed in quantity in Britain was kerosene, better known in this country as paraffin. (Technically paraffin is a waxy solid, distinct from paraffin oil, but British English usually refers to the latter simply as 'paraffin'.) Nowadays kerosene is mainly used as a fuel for jet engines, although it is also used for heating. But in 1900 its main use was for lighting, for the millions of homes which had progressed beyond candles but for whose owners or tenants gas lighting was too expensive or unavailable – electric lighting still being very rare. In other words, most oil consumed in Britain was used for a purpose which is now practically defunct. For practically every other use with which we now associate oil or natural gas, Britain like most countries used coal. Heating was mainly by coal – traditionally in Britain burnt on inefficient open fires – and likewise cooking in ranges was usually coal fired. The main alternative for these was gas, produced from coal. Railways were powered by steam which was raised by burning coal, as was most sea transport apart from the few remaining sailing ships. Most industry was also powered by steam engines. Where electricity was making inroads it, too, was mainly generated by coal-fired steam engines. To produce this heat and power, Britain in 1900 mined 225 million tons of coal each year, 44 million tons of which were exported.[3] And where steam engines were impracticable due to their weight in relation to power produced, as in road transport, the horse still reigned supreme.

One other event makes the beginning of the century an apt time to start. In 1901 the Admiralty started serious trials of oil to raise steam in warship boilers. Its relatively rapid adoption was not predestined. Oil had obvious benefits – higher thermal efficiency per ton of fuel, reduced labour costs and much easier fuelling. But Britain had plentiful supplies of Welsh steam coal which was considerably cheaper than oil. Nevertheless the Royal Navy, as well as being the largest navy in the world, had by 1905 also become the leader in the use of oil as a fuel, although the quantities used were still small.[4] The development was to prove of great importance to D'Arcy's Persian speculation.

The D'Arcy Concession's first exploration wells were drilled in the west of the country, where there were surface seepages of oil. Later this was to become an important oil producing area, but at the time drilling technology and geological understanding were limited. The Concession used old-fashioned pole drilling which hammered the drill bit into the ground. Attempts to shift to cable drilling – more efficient although it still relied on percussion, by raising and lowering a chisel-shaped bit – were stymied by the need to avoid offending the Russian drillers who were used to the pole method.[5] There were other difficulties. Hauling drilling materials in the virtually roadless landscape meant that some sort of infrastructure had to be created, and the necessary labour force housed and fed. But the local workers were quite unused to modern, or even pre-modern, methods. Progress became easier only when they were introduced to wheelbarrows. With limited central government control, local leaders 'seemed very keen on receiving a substantial present from us, especially in the shape of some shares of our Company'. By 1903 D'Arcy was running short of money. He had discussions with potential investors, including the Paris Rothschilds, but they were fruitless. An oil strike in 1904 was encouraging but the flow soon reduced to a trickle. He was saved by Burmah Oil (henceforth Burmah; the company produced oil in Burma but always spelt its name with an 'h'), a relatively wealthy company. Burmah's share in the Concession was finalized in 1905 and at the same time drilling moved to the south-west of Persia. There were more years of heat, difficulty and frustration to come. But on 20 May 1908, oil was struck at Masjid-I-Suleiman, about 120 miles from the Persian Gulf.[6]

A happy myth, promulgated in early accounts of the discovery, has Burmah sending a letter to George Reynolds, the stalwart supervisor of operations, instructing him to stop work, but this not being received until after oil was discovered. The reality is that there was a letter, but it instructed him to stop work after two more wells had been drilled to 1,600 feet, and oil was in fact struck by the first at a depth of 1,180 feet.[7] In the words of Burmah Oil's historian, 'Reynolds's drillers had just uncovered the most extensive oilfield thus far known to man ... and had taken the first step towards transforming the economies of the near and middle east'.[8] They had also saved D'Arcy's and Burmah's financial bacon, established the basis for what was to become one of the world's great oil companies, and ensured that, 30 years later, Britain would be able to fuel her armed forces in the Middle East and India in the Second World War.

How far was this an imperial adventure and how far a commercial speculation? Ernest Pretyman, an Admiralty minister, had introduced Burmah to D'Arcy. Bolstering British investment in Persia as an antidote to Russia was also a factor in the British government's attitude. But a later statement by Burmah's chairman made it clear that, although he believed that Imperial interests were served by investing in Persia, Burmah had primarily been interested in the commercial prospects.[9]

The key to the Concession's success was a vast oilfield, although it was years before its full extent was realized. Aeons ago marine algae and bacteria in long-gone seas died and sunk to the bottom. Their remains were buried under later rock formations and were transmuted by pressure and the earth's heat into oil and gas, which migrated upwards through porous rock until trapped. Therefore oil is likely to be found where non-porous rocks overlie porous ones – sandstone or some limestones. One would like to imagine Styx-like rivers flowing into sunless underground seas of oil, but in fact the oil, mixed with varying amounts of gas, is contained under pressure in the interstices of the rock itself. This simple description encompasses huge variations in the extent and nature of each field. Compared to any earlier discovery, the Masjid-I-Suleiman field was remarkable in its extent and its uniformity, since the field comprised one huge underlying dome of limestone through which the oil could flow freely, if slowly.

The next step, in 1909, was to float a company, which enabled D'Arcy to realize his investment and further cash to be raised to finance a pipeline and refinery. The new company was called the Anglo-Persian Oil Company – APOC – and so it remained until 1935. It was only in 1954 that it took the name British Petroleum, usually known as BP. APOC's refinery was established at Abadan, an area of swampland on the Persian Gulf. Refining at that time was by the long established method of distillation: as the product flowed through a series of increasingly hotter retorts 'fractions' of the oil were drawn off, the most volatile first. The residue was fuel oil. Persian crude posed problems: it was a sulphurous product which was difficult to refine. In addition the company had no distribution network save in a limited area around the Persian Gulf. By 1912 they were again in financial difficulties and had to conclude an agreement for Shell to take some of their crude oil and kerosene. This necessary arrangement was a very sore point to the APOC directors. Shell was widely unpopular, an attitude which owed itself partly to envy and, in APOC's case, a reasonable desire to stand on their own two feet. Furthermore, the APOC directors were imperially-minded – a fact which they used shamelessly in their subsequent negotiations with the British government but also reflected genuine beliefs. So they did not want to be seen simply as a subcontractor for another company.[10]

The obvious solution to their problems was the sale of the fuel oil which was largely going to waste. There were two sizeable potential markets, Indian railways and the Royal Navy. For merchant vessels, coal was still the predominant fuel since it could be shipped cheaply to ports around the world; on railways, where cheap coal was not always available, steam locomotives frequently burnt fuel oil. However, sales to the Indian railways were not forthcoming. This left the Navy. After 1905 there had been a brief period of retrogression to coal-firing, for economy reasons, but from 1909 they renewed their commitment to fuel oil and incorporated it in increasing amounts of new construction. This process had been given further impetus by Winston Churchill, who as an up-and-coming member of the Liberal government became First Lord of the Admiralty, that is its political head, in 1911.[11] The acceleration posed its own major problem – supply. Hitherto the Admiralty had met its oil needs from short-term contracts and one small longer term one with Burmah. But in 1913, under the pressure of demand, fuel oil prices began to rise. In addition there were already fears – premature as it turned out – that the USA, the world's largest producer, would in future have a declining surplus to sell overseas.[12]

At the same time, APOC was still having difficulties refining its oil and was in desperate financial straits. A bargain was struck. The government in 1914 subscribed for a large new issue of APOC shares, becoming the owner of two-thirds of the company. In return, APOC entered into a long-term supply contract for fuel oil. The bargain seemed unprecedented. This was a government formed from the party once committed to free trade and hostile to government interference. In reality, the Liberals had changed and the world had changed, and these changes are dealt with later in the chapter.

ENTREPRENEURS IN OIL

APOC and Burmah were not the only large British-owned oil companies in the 1900s. At the turn of the century, and indeed for the century to come, the largest was Shell. The origins of Shell lay in a London-based trading company owned by the Samuel family, whose merchandise included exotic sea-shells, popular for ornamentation in mid-Victorian Britain. Its diverse trading interests led to the firm developing strong Far Eastern connections. The commercial *coup* which established the family as a major player in the oil world came in 1892, when their first oil tanker – larger and safer than any previous one – was launched. The tanker was part of a complex plan which had had its foundations in Far Eastern sales of kerosene originating in Russia. This was shipped via a railway, financed by the Paris branch of the Rothschild banking family, from Baku on the Caspian to the Black Sea. The Baku oil producing region had already made Russia the second oil producer after the USA, and the Rothschilds had spotted the potential to export kerosene to the Far East.[13] But on its long passage from the Black Sea to the East it was inefficiently transported in wooden 'cases', each of which held two five-gallon cans. It was the Samuel brothers, Marcus and Sam, who devised the scheme for bulk export, developed a distribution network and took the risk of ordering a number of tankers, all the time keeping the plan under wraps to head off counter-action from Standard Oil. An important part was also played by a less well-known figure, Fred Lane, a shipbroker who had chartered the first bulk oil tanker to arrive in Britain in 1885.

The first tanker was rapidly followed by others and in 1897 the syndicate, headed by the Samuels, which owned the tankers formed a limited company, The "Shell" Transport and Trading Company. The capital of £1.8 million should be multiplied by at least 50 to arrive at some approximation to present-day values.[14] (The apostrophes around Shell were in the original title. For many years the company, and later the group which it joined, were familiarly referred to as 'the Shell', but I will use the now standard 'Shell' or 'the Shell group'.)

Shell's conception and, for a few early years its execution, were brilliantly successful. But Marcus Samuel, the prime mover, was carried away by his early triumphs. Shell expanded its tanker fleet too fast while Standard Oil effectively stymied its efforts to put together an adequate distribution network. By 1907 Shell was running out of money. It was forced into a shotgun marriage with a producing and marketing company, Royal Dutch.

Royal Dutch and Shell had been associated almost since Shell's foundations. Royal Dutch had suffered vicissitudes but, by the mid-1900s, it had become a very prosperous concern with producing interests in Sumatra and Romania.

The 1907 agreement preserved the two companies but merged their assets. Royal Dutch took 60 per cent of the profits, Shell 40 per cent, and in addition Royal Dutch bought a significant proportion of Shell's shares. So Shell was very much a minority partner and the ownership of the group was at first predominantly Dutch. But Henri Deterding, the moving force behind Royal Dutch, believed that Shell provided an invaluable *entrée* to the vast potential resources, and market, of the British Empire. Therefore the group was run as a genuine multinational in that its management was split between London and The Hague, whilst of course its operations were worldwide. Not immediately but in time the main holding companies underneath the two parent companies all had 'Shell' in their names and Shell became the name by which most knew the group.[15]

The union in 1907 also marked the beginning of a new phase of growth. The petrol market was now expanding rapidly. Shell had found it difficult to break into the British market due to Standard Oil's dominance but an agreement with British Petroleum gave it outlets in Britain. In spite of its name, British Petroleum at that time was predominantly German owned and had no connection with APOC, which was eventually to take it over. Also in 1907 Shell was allowed to bring tankerloads of petrol through the Suez Canal, which had hitherto refused their passage as petrol was more inflammable than kerosene. (Refining at that time was largely carried out near the source of production, so far more product was transported than crude oil.) The group expanded in Russia, purchasing the Rothschild interest there, while discovering new oilfields in Borneo and Egypt.[16] In 1911 it became the world's largest oil company when American anti-trust actions dissolved Standard Oil. The latter had been so large that its offshoots still constituted three of the world's seven largest oil companies with the largest, Standard Oil of New Jersey (now Exxon), vying with Shell for supremacy. But the old Standard Oil's ability to stymie others' growth was now diminished. Indeed the Shell group itself also expanded into the USA, buying wells in Oklahoma and California. Deterding's policy was to undercut the American companies, largely dependent on American production, in other parts of the world by applying the 'principle that each market must be supplied with products emanating from the fields which are most favourably situated geographically'. By the eve of the First World War, while Burmah remained a localized producer and APOC struggled with its production and marketing problems, the British arm of Royal Dutch/Shell seemed to bestride the British oil world.[17]

It had, however, one major rival whose connection with oil is now largely forgotten except by historians: Weetman Pearson. Pearson's name lives on in the media giant which owns the *Financial Times* and Penguin books. But the family started as civil engineering contractors, building drainage systems, docks and railways all over the world. Their success in this owed much to Pearson's character, which combined a willingness to take risks and ability to perceive the big picture with attention to detail. He had a more winning personality than many powerful people, possessing the ability to command without its frequent accompaniment, arrogance. His interest in social justice made him politically a Liberal, supporting old age pensions and other relatively advanced social programmes.[18]

In some ways Pearson's friendship with the Mexican leader Porfirio Diaz is paradoxical, given that Diaz ruled through a mixture of force and corruption. But Pearson may have been attracted by Diaz's genuine concern with the economic development of Mexico, which he had achieved with considerable success, although only limited benefits trickled down to the rural masses. Pearson had gained his first practical experience of civil engineering when only 21, on the main drainage of Southport. Diaz set him a bigger problem – the main drainage of Mexico City. Pearson solved it and seems to have gained Diaz's respect by his honest dealing. Then throughout the 1900s he rebuilt the ramshackle railway across the Tehuantepec isthmus. Soon after starting work on this, in 1901, he was travelling from Mexico to New York on business and stopped overnight in Laredo, in Texas. There everyone was talking about Spindletop, a huge nearby oil discovery. Before the discovery surface oil pools had been observed and – the story goes – Pearson remembered seeing similar ones near the Tehuantepec railway. He telegraphed to J. C. Body, his trusted assistant, 'to secure options . . . on . . . all land for miles around . . . move sharply'.[19] Pearson's involvement with oil had begun.

During the 1900s Pearson acquired vast acreages of oil concessions elsewhere in Mexico. Subsoil rights in Mexico were not the property of the state so no royalties were payable to the government – a source of irritation to later nationalists. When Pearson did obtain state lands for oil exploration, as in Vera Cruz, the royalty was low. But Diaz's argument was that foreign capital was needed and therefore it should be encouraged, not hindered. In this he was supported by most 'advanced' Mexican opinion.[20] Letting civil engineering contracts or oil concessions to Pearson was to a large part a studied policy of not becoming too dependent on American capital. (Diaz is supposed to have once remarked: 'Poor Mexico, so far from God and so close to the United States').[21] Because of this and because Pearson represented real competition in the oil market, American oil interests accused him of corruption. As noted, Pearson seems to have initially recommended himself to Diaz because of his honesty. The firm certainly greased the wheels once they were rolling, giving valuable *objets d'art* to members of Diaz's government and subsidising favourable press coverage.[22] But there was probably little chance of any progress in such a regime without some grease.

For many years, in fact, Pearson poured money into Mexican oil rather than sucking it out of the country. The Tehuantepec field and other concessions were disappointing. By 1910 Pearson had a large share of Mexican sales and a sales organization in Britain, but was importing US oil to supply them. He had spent £5 million, a colossal sum. But in that year he finally struck lucky at Potrero de Llano, where the No. 4 well gushed at 100,000 barrels a day.[23] By December 1918 it had yielded 100 million barrels of oil. Pearson perceived the importance of local involvement and was already reorganizing his subsidiary interests. Eventually his group included Mexican Eagle (*El Aguila*), in which Mexican interests were represented, and which controlled Mexican production and distribution; Eagle Tankers; and Anglo-Mexican which controlled the distribution of products outside Central America. Pearson's qualities as a manager were evident in Anglo-Mexican which 'was a model of a well-run oil company, and was markedly different in this respect from many of its British contemporaries'.[24] It was a long way from Southport's main sewer.

Pearson's problems were not over, however. In 1911 revolution broke out in Mexico and a period of chaos and civil war ensued, with Mexican Eagle's oilfields in the middle. Pearson's earlier competition with American interests came back to haunt him. The American company was owned by Henry Clay Pierce, who instigated newspaper attacks on Pearson repeating the corruption allegations. When Woodrow Wilson took up the office of President in February 1913, he immediately launched the USA into one of its periodic campaigns to export democracy – the intended target not being the Middle East, as 90 years later, but Central America and particularly the new Mexican dictator, Victoriano Huerta. Given his reputation in America, Pearson was inevitably a subsidiary target. His rascality in American eyes was exacerbated by the British government's recognition of Huerta. This convinced Wilson that it, and Pearson, were in each other's pockets, were propping up Huerta at the expense of other contenders for power, and were thus conspiring to thwart the Monroe Doctrine that European states should not intervene politically in the Americas. Wilson's perception was fantasy. Far from supporting Pearson, the British government initially did nothing about attacks on Mexican Eagle's properties precisely because it feared that a hostile US reaction might prevent the successful conclusion of negotiations over access to the Panama canal. *El Aguila* itself, like the American oil companies, was in reality taking sides as little as possible but trying to make the best of a bad job.[25] The companies sometimes had to pay levies to armed groups who controlled the areas in which they worked, which fuelled suspicions that they were attempting to influence the outcome of the revolution. But as Alan Knight points out, 'the companies did not finance revolutionary outbreaks; rather successful revolutionaries won the right to extract cash from the companies'.[26] Not surprisingly, by 1914 Pearson, now ennobled as Lord Cowdray, was thinking of selling his interest in Mexican Eagle and was starting to prospect for oil elsewhere.

Joseph Schumpeter, an early twentieth-century economist whose writings on economic growth are still classics, attached great importance to the role of the entrepreneur. Schumpeter saw entrepreneurs not as the suppliers of money but as those with the energy and foresight to promote new technology, open up hitherto untouched or neglected natural resources, or exploit other economic discontinuities. They thus made it possible to reap profits above the normal rate. This, in turn, promoted economic growth by attracting new capital to an industry. How far were the leading protagonists of the early British oil industry entrepreneurs in the Schumpeterian sense?[27]

D'Arcy was clearly a capitalist, as Drummond Wolff described him, in that he possessed wealth and took risks with it, rather than investing it cautiously as a mere *rentier* would do. His active role beyond that was very limited, however, and he hardly fits the entrepreneurial model. Marcus Samuel was very different. He too started with wealth, but not nearly as much; and devising and implementing the tanker scheme required all the qualities of an entrepreneur – although he was assisted by others such as his brother Sam, who provided organizational input, and Fred Lane.[28] Marcus Samuel's failures which led Shell to the verge of bankruptcy are sometimes put down to his neglect of basic management. They can also be attributed to an excess of entrepreneurial zeal leading to overchartering of tankers, and other errors. Deterding, not British but playing a large part in the history of British oil, was above all an effective manager although the high stakes of the early oil world meant that no one could survive who could not also take risks, which Deterding did. Charles Greenway, managing director of APOC, was primarily a shrewd and unscrupulous negotiator – useful characteristics in the early oil industry, but hardly entrepreneurial. By far the greatest entrepreneur of all was Pearson. He had capital on D'Arcy's scale but also entrepreneurial ability of a high calibre. He added to this greater managerial ability than Marcus Samuel as well as the famous Pearson luck – luck which he made, by his attention to detail and by never, even at the height of his spending, overreaching himself financially. Pearson also exemplified another of the traits Schumpeter discerned in entrepreneurs – that they were not primarily motivated by money. In the draft of a valedictory speech – he died before he could make it – Pearson wrote, 'Success is sweet ... but the joy is in the doing'.[29]

How far the early British oil industry was uniquely dependent on the entrepreneurial abilities of a few individuals is a question left until the end.

GOVERNMENTS AND OIL

It is easy to think of the British Empire at its peak as monolithic, and government attitudes to it as only shifting with political changes. In fact the Empire was diverse, ranging from the quasi-independent 'White Dominions' such as Canada and Australia, to tiny almost forgotten West Indian islands. After Joseph Chamberlain's expansive imperialism came to grief in the Boer War, British governments reverted to the view that this diverse Empire, while of considerable economic and moral value, was also expensive and the potential source of unwanted foreign policy entanglements. Chamberlain's campaign for tariff reform in the 1900s, whilst imperial, was also instrumental in keeping the Conservative party out of office, thus reducing his influence still further. So after 1900 departmental views, always important, came once more to the forefront. The Colonial Office, the India Office, the Admiralty and the Foreign Office, four departments which were all concerned with imperial policy or imperial defence, had different perspectives and the responsible ministers usually followed the departmental line unless political pressures were particularly strong. So far as there was a common view, it was that oil companies were commercial concerns and like other commercial concerns were out to make as much money as possible. Since governments took the capitalist order for granted, this was regarded as perfectly reasonable. But it did not mean that governments had a bias in favour of oil companies. Thus departmental and local attitudes became paramount, and these were more likely to be concerned with saving money or with beneficial economic development than with oil companies' welfare. Indeed oil companies, being regarded as profit-maximizing concerns, were seen as fair game for bargaining over price or concessions.

Some of these attitudes are illustrated by the history of Burmah Oil. Production rose gratifyingly after it had been set up in 1886 to develop deposits long known about and exploited in a small way by the Burmese. Parts of Burma were already British ruled and the rest had been appropriated by Britain after King Thibaw had been overthrown in 1885 (the appropriation had little or nothing to do with oil, and was more connected with fears of encroaching French influence).[30] Burma came under the Government of India, which had considerable autonomy although it was ultimately responsible to the India Office. Burmah Oil's royalties were set relatively low and a small tariff on kerosene imported into India from elsewhere was established, in order to encourage oil development. But the company was not otherwise favoured. Its frequent requests for a higher tariff and the extension of its concession area were turned down as the Government of India wanted to encourage competition and keep down kerosene prices. However, another department's concerns were to provide an opening for Burmah. By 1904 the Admiralty's growing interest in fuel oil led to concern about its supply, which at that time came from diverse sources including Anglo-American, Standard Oil's British marketing firm. One of the Admiralty's advisers, Boverton Redwood, argued strongly that it should buy oil from Burmah.

Redwood was one of the leading figures of the early British oil industry, his consulting firm serving most of the oil companies at one time or another, as well as advising government departments. Described as 'immaculately attired, with an orchid in his buttonhole, speaking in a slightly affected but impressive manner with a provincial accent', he seems an unlikely oilman but in fact possessed genuine technical expertise and wrote a standard textbook on the industry.[31] He also shared the standard assumptions of upper-middle-class Englishmen (and Scotsmen) about the desirability of imperial defence and therefore recommended that the Admiralty should establish an imperial source for some of its oil supply. The Admiralty accordingly supported Burmah in various ways in its less-than-harmonious relationship with the Government of India. The support, however, had only limited effect. Burmah secured an agreement that non-British oil companies should be excluded from Burmese oil concessions, but did not secure additional concessions itself. The Admiralty also supported Burmah in establishing a market-sharing agreement with Asiatic Petroleum, a joint Far Eastern marketing arm established by – then separate – Royal Dutch and Shell companies. The Government of India disliked this agreement as tending to raise prices but at that time, long before Offices of Fair Trading and the like, there was nothing it could do to prevent it, and so the Admiralty's support for the agreement was really irrelevant. In return for the dubious value of Admiralty support, Burmah constructed refinery and storage capacity for a substantial tonnage of fuel oil, which the Admiralty did not actually have to purchase. So although Burmah got its market-sharing agreement, it would have got this anyway and otherwise both the Admiralty and the Government of India emerged with more gains than losses.[32]

The reactions to APOC's negotiations over selling fuel oil to the Admiralty were similar in their diversity but very different in their result. By 1912 the Admiralty's future requirements for oil were set to increase sharply. And the question of another long-term supply contract was on the agenda. In the tortuous negotiations which followed Charles Greenway, APOC's managing director, was one major player. Greenway's apparently stuffy conservatism led to him becoming 'Old Spats and Monocle' in Upton Sinclair's *OIL!*. But he proved wily and determined. The other key figure was Winston Churchill, and it was Churchill's elevation to the Admiralty in 1911 which was the catalyst for the eventual agreement.[33]

Persian oil was familiar to the British government. During the negotiations over the D'Arcy concession the Foreign Office (FO) had given D'Arcy low-key support. The FO saw moderate British influence, in what was then a fragile and poor country surrounded by colonial powers, as the best policy. Excessive and overt attempts to wield influence would arouse the ire of Russia, Persia's northern neighbour. This was anathema to the post-Boer War mindset which wished to avoid in Persia 'any addition to our political or territorial responsibilities'.[34] In 1912 the FO's general principle was the same but the results were rather different. Relations with Russia were now friendlier, while APOC had become an established presence in Persia. It was changes to the existing state of affairs which might now involve instability. Changes would be even more deleterious, in the FO's view, if they involved a foreign company gaining control of APOC's oil. The 'foreign company' which seemed to present such a threat was the Shell group, which was of course more Dutch than British. And the reason the FO feared it was not just because of Dutch influence, but because Greenway had spent a great deal of time telling the British government of the threat which Shell posed.[35]

After the 1907 Royal Dutch/Shell merger, Shell had quickly become a European equivalent to Standard Oil in the demonology of those hostile to powerful oil companies. These comprised a surprisingly large grouping. There was a widespread belief – not entirely unjustified – that British companies in a range of industries were forming 'trusts' (the word in this context was imported from the USA) – that is making agreements or combining with the intention of raising prices. There were newspapers and car enthusiasts who were concerned about the price of petrol. They were a vociferous group even though only a small minority of the population owned cars. And there was a predictable sub-current of Edwardian anti-Semitism, allied with jingoism, which found Marcus Samuel an easy target. Unfortunately Samuel himself did not help. He frequently protested his patriotism and there is no doubt that this was entirely genuine. But he also became increasingly self-important, pompous and verbose, qualities which rubbed politicians and civil servants up the wrong way.[36]

Basil Henriques' biography of Samuel was partly devoted to exposing the fancied injustices to Samuel, and Shell, stemming from the hostility to him (Henriques was married to Samuel's granddaughter). In reality, Shell suffered much less from governmental slights than Henriques made out. Greenway's campaign to persuade the government that the alternative to its financial support for APOC would be Shell's hegemony influenced the Foreign Office but did not convince everyone. The India Office was extremely cynical. It had experience of Shell's 'foreignness' being raised before, also by Greenway when he represented Burmah Oil over their concession, at a time when Shell and Royal Dutch were jointly involved in Asiatic Petroleum. Burmah had then gone on to establish its own market-sharing agreement with Asiatic. So the Government of India was not inclined to help APOC out of its financial plight, and gave the company no support in its attempts to sell fuel oil for use on Indian railways.[37]

Fortunately for APOC, it had support not just from the Foreign Office – which was not actually in the market for oil – but also from the department which was, the Admiralty. This was not because the Admiralty had any particular animus against Shell. It bought some of its fuel oil, and by 1914 Churchill's relations with Deterding were good. But in 1913, as the oil price rose and supplies became tight, the fruits of Churchill's policy of pushing ahead strongly with oil-firing were about to ripen in the form of five fast oil-fired battleships. A long-term contract for oil, which Shell refused to offer, seemed essential, as Burmah's capacity was too small and too remote to meet future needs.[38]

Churchill provided, again, the final impetus to the British government share-holding in APOC. Churchill had earlier played an important role, as President of the Board of Trade, in some of the interventionist measures of the Liberal government, for instance in establishing labour exchanges and trade boards – bodies which set minimum wages in various industries which lacked strong trade unions. But although giving some precedent for intervention these and other Liberal measures were very different from taking a majority share in a private company, albeit at the company's request. Almost certainly here Churchill's own immense self-conviction, and his ability to convince others – even the aloof Asquith was fascinated by him – played an important part. More concretely, Churchill was able to argue that to support APOC was to support *laissez-faire*, since it would prevent a Shell/Standard of New Jersey duopoly in the British market.[39] Thus in his final speech to Parliament justifying the Act necessary to make the investment in APOC, Churchill once again used the 'Shell menace' as a major argument for the government shareholding. In reality, the Admiralty was relaxed about Shell and Churchill liked Deterding. But the 'oil trust' argument was too popular with MPs and the public for Churchill to miss.[40]

OIL WORLDWIDE

In 1915 Hermann More and Andrew Mearns, partners in an insurance broking firm, brought 200 shares in the Ural Caspian Oil Corporation. Hermann More, my grandfather, personifies the cosmopolitan nature of British capitalism in the era before the First World War. He had emigrated from Germany in the late nineteenth century and set up an insurance brokerage in London. Subsequently he became a British citizen and in 1909 changed his original surname. His and Mearns' purchase of Ural Caspian shares illustrates this cosmopolitanism. British capital played a substantial part, not only in imperial oil development, but also in the development of oil in other far-flung parts of the world. Its role was not surprising. By 1914 the value of British capital overseas, whether in the Empire or elsewhere, was around four billion pounds; equivalent, very roughly, to around 200 billion pounds, or 400 billion dollars, today.[41] China's much vaunted foreign reserves were around $1,700 billion in March 2008. But Britain's population in the 1900s was around 40 million; China's today is 1.3 billion.

Some of Britain's extraordinary wealth, the product of a hundred years of world leadership in trade and in key industries, was likely to flow into oil. There is no precise figure for how much, since the nominal capital of oil companies quoted on stock markets was not always called up, while some of their investment was in tankers or distribution in Britain. One estimate is that, on the eve of the First World War, around 40 million pounds' worth of British overseas investment was in oil. Of this perhaps one-third was in Russia.[42] The history of this investment is not in itself remarkable. British firms did not pioneer the large-scale extraction of Russian oil – this was done by the Nobels and the Rothschilds. The firms were not particularly well-directed, the smaller British oil companies indeed being notorious for their inefficiency. And by around 1912 much of the region's production – including a holding in the Ural Caspian Corporation – was controlled by the Shell group. On the other hand, British companies opened up new and therefore riskier oil regions: Ural Caspian, for example, worked the remote Emba field to the north of the Caspian Sea. Now its share certificate, worthless except for its collector's value (not much as it is in poor condition) languishes in my desk.[43]

British companies also produced oil in other South American countries besides Mexico, the continent having long been a destination for British capital. The main operator was set up by a British trading house, Balfour Williamson. Such trading houses played a large part in the early oil industry, for instance acting as managing agents for APOC and Burmah. The Samuel brothers had themselves started as a trading house while another oil company in Burma, the Indo-Burma Petroleum Company, was run and owned by Steel Brothers, another trader. Balfour Williamson's company, in Peru, had the delightful name of Lobitos. In the inter-war years it also established a small Ecuadorian oilfield. Lobitos built a British refinery and was, it seems, an efficient little company. Fittingly, it was eventually taken over by Burmah, in 1962. Outside Peru and Ecuador, however, British exploration in South America came up against US hostility and political pressure. The target, predictably, was Pearson whose attempts to explore in

Colombia were stymied. Nearer to home, Royal Dutch/Shell had substantial interests in Romania, established by Royal Dutch before the merger.[44]

As in Mexico, the British government kept out of British companies' adventures and misadventures in other South American countries and in Russia, even though US diplomacy had no hesitation in opposing British expansion in South America. Indirectly, the government did get involved in the affairs of companies which tried to exploit oil in the Empire. As in Burma, this involvement did not take the form of uncritically supporting the companies, but rather involved balancing various considerations, such as economic development in colonial territories and the Admiralty's periodic obsession with British-controlled sources of supply. Thus when the development of Trinidad's oil was under consideration in 1904, the Colonial Office and the Admiralty established a joint committee. The government was also well aware of issues which would later exercise other governments dealing with oil companies, such as ensuring that companies actually worked their concessions. As was almost inevitable in imperial oil development at this time, the major players in Trinidad when interest hotted up in 1910 included Burmah, APOC and Shell. Burmah and APOC's hypocrisy over Shell's 'foreignness' and alleged monopolistic tendencies was exposed by the fact that all three had a share in the company most interested in Trinidad's oil. Schooled by Burmah and APOC's own propaganda, the Colonial Office and Admiralty were at first hostile to Shell involvement. But since it seemed that Trinidad's oil industry would not be developed without Shell's financial backing, the Colonial Office came to accept Shell on the basis that development was better than no development. Similarly the Admiralty, however much it wanted a British owned source of oil in Burma and Persia, would rather have some oil from Trinidad than none at all and also came round to accepting Shell. Pragmatism prevailed.[45]

It prevailed too in the prolonged negotiations over oil concessions in Mesopotamia – modern-day Iraq – then part of the Ottoman Empire whose core was Turkey. D'Arcy had become interested in the possibilities of Mesopotamian oil early on, but the negotiations were fruitless. In 1912 the pace became more rapid. A new consortium, the Turkish Petroleum Company (TPC) was established, linking Shell, the British-owned National Bank of Turkey and the Deutsche Bank. For no very good reason APOC saw this as a threat to its position in Persia, and Greenway predictably used it as part of his drum-beating about the 'Shell menace'. As with Persia, the Foreign Office seems to have been more influenced by this than were other government departments. But again, pragmatism and a desire to avoid rocking the diplomatic boat prevailed. The Foreign Office accepted German involvement, thus reducing economic rivalry in the area. The National Bank of Turkey dropped out and a new division of the TPC was agreed in March 1914 giving APOC a 47.5 per cent share, with the rest divided between Shell, Deutsche Bank, and a fixer and go-between, Calouste Gulbenkian, who became the legendary 'Mr Five Percent' – his share. As elsewhere, the British government put wider diplomatic consideration before support for 'national champions' while APOC came to terms with Shell when it suited it to do so.[46]

Since war broke out and oil was not yet discovered, the carefully contrived arrangements about Iraq soon broke down. As new claimants emerged, the tortuous search for agreement over the oil of that unhappy country was to resume even before the war was over.

OIL IN THE FIRST WORLD WAR

In February 1918 a small force of British troops toiled up a hill in north-western Persia. They were pushing their Model T Fords, for the road was too steep to drive. It was part of a route which was many centuries old: 'the road from Persia to Babylon, the road trodden by the Medes and the Persians'. And at the top of the cliff which it was ascending, 'on the rocky bare hillside of the Persian mountains, sat a youngster from the kindly Hampshire downs'.[47] He was a soldier of the Hampshire regiment, and the route he was guarding was being taken by one of those exotic expeditions the First World War could surprisingly produce, associated as it is with mud, blood and trench-warfare. It was led by General Dunsterville, a boyhood friend of Rudyard Kipling and the 'Stalky' of Kipling's stories, and it is Dunsterville himself who describes the scene in his book *The Adventures of Dunsterforce*. Dunsterforce had been formed to thwart the threat posed by the Turks and the Germans to the Caucasus, as the Russian armies melted away after the Bolshevik revolution. It had set off from Mesopotamia, modern-day Iraq, and was aiming for the Caspian Sea via northern Persia. In the minds of the British there were many possible repercussions of the Germano-Turkish threat. Northern Persia would be disturbed and rebellious tribes might attack Tehran and overthrow the Persian government, with obvious implications for APOC's oilfield to the south. Further north, Turkey and Germany might occupy the 'enormously valuable' oilfields of Baku and obtain the other foodstuffs and raw materials of the area.[48] This did indeed occur, although not until September 1918, much too late in the war for them to be of any use. In the meantime Dunsterville had brought a brigade of troops into Baku via the Caspian Sea, and tried to organize a defence there before being forced to retreat. In the course of his travels he had bartered some of his Model T's for petrol with the Bolsheviks, and allied himself with the Social Revolutionaries who held Baku.[49]

The east had lured the Germans since the beginning of the war. As with the Western Allies, they liked the idea of shortcuts which avoided the Western Front, while success in the east had the added advantage that it might undermine Russia. Depriving the Allies of oil or getting it themselves was a possible bonus, although not the main attraction. The British had reacted early on to the threat, sending an Indian division to Bahrain in October before Turkey entered the war.[50] Subsequently the Turks attacked in the Caucasus, but were unsuccessful. And in early 1915, with the help of German military advisers, they mounted raids from Mesopotamia, then part of the Ottoman Empire, on the pipeline to Abadan. By now the British had pushed their forces up to Basra and Abadan itself and the raids, although they did some damage, were of no long-term significance. Later in 1915 German intrigues in Persia were stymied by Russian military pressure from the north, while the British gradually, and after setbacks, occupied Mesopotamia.[51] It was not until the Russian collapse that the threats in the east reasserted themselves.

The early failure of these Germano-Turkish initiatives in Persia, and the later adventures of Dunsterforce, seem to illustrate Lord Curzon's oft-quoted remark, in a speech to the Inter-Allied Petroleum Council just after the war had ended: the Allies had 'floated to victory upon a wave of oil'.[52] In this analysis it was the Allies' access to oil supplies, and the Germans' isolation from the centres of oil production, which turned the balance.

The Allies undoubtedly had a vast superiority in oil supplies. The British naval blockade prevented Germany and Austria obtaining oil from the Americas, while after their failures in 1914–15 Middle Eastern and Russian oil was also inaccessible to the Central Powers, who were therefore cut off from 95 per cent of world production.[53] But most countries used very little oil in 1914. Trains, barges and ships, all fuelled by coal, were the means of transport for bulk and long distance goods. In Europe, heating, industrial power, gas production and electricity generation were usually dependent on coal, of which Germany was the second largest European producer. Shortage of oil therefore posed no immediate threat to German civilian life and industrial production. But oil had become vital for the lubrication of machinery and for a few specialized military purposes, those for which the internal combustion engine was the only appropriate prime mover: aircraft, submarines, lorries and later in the war tanks.

While Germany did not have much oil, it had access to a certain amount. Galicia in Poland, then ruled by Austria, produced substantial quantities. It was overrun by Russia early on, but regained in 1915. A more important producer was Romania. Romania was neutral until 1916 which meant that, at least in theory, it forbade the export of petrol and fuel oil to the Central Powers as these might be used for military purposes, whilst allowing kerosene and gas oil exports. Certainly there were sharp cutbacks in production and the Central Powers could not depend on Romanian oil. In 1916 Romania entered the war on the Allied side, an ill-advised move since the Germans quickly occupied most of the country, capturing large stocks of oil. Most of the oil installations, however, were destroyed by the Allies. By the end of the war the Germans had restored about 75 per cent of production in Wallachia, the main oil-producing area. Once they had got production going again, therefore, the Central Powers had access to steadily increasing quantities of oil.[54]

Limited although German civilian use of oil was, shortages did affect it. In winter rural districts, lit by kerosene, had to stay in darkness while poor quality lubricants caused locomotives to freeze up.[55] However, the Central Powers' military operations do not seem to have been seriously affected. In the air, the Allies gradually got the upper hand but this seems more to do with overall industrial superiority and a technical lead in aircraft design. Nevertheless the German air force managed to virtually double its size – and its petrol allocation – between mid-1917 and early 1918. It had enough petrol to mount bombing raids on Britain, and subsequently on allied supply depots in France, in 1918.[56] Tanks were a quite unimportant factor in military operations. A mass tank attack by the British – only the second in the war – marked the start of the Battle of Amiens in August 1918. The next day two-thirds of these tanks had broken down or become casualties. German slowness in the adoption of tanks seems to have been due not to problems in obtaining fuel but to a certain conservatism in the high command – a belief, often justified, that technological fixes did not win battles. In the case of road transport, the German military had seen opportunities even before the war and had subsidized the civilian purchase of lorries. By 1913, 3,700 were available, half of which were usually occupied as beer delivery trucks.[57] Not surprisingly most of them broke down when pressed into military service. The Allies subsequently took the lead in the use of road transport, although German usage seems to have been held back as much by shortages of rubber as of oil. And again, military conservatism played a part; even in the Second World War German generals remained wedded to horse transport except for armoured formations. Anyway, for most of the First World War motorized road transport was still peripheral to both sides. Once the front lines were fixed, from late 1914, rail resumed its dominance in supply, with the regular railways supplemented on both sides by extensive light railways running almost up to the trenches.

The final important military use of oil was for diesel engines in submarines. Again, shortage of oil does not seem to have affected the German submarine offensive – which was, of course, ultimately unsuccessful. Indeed, its contribution to bringing America into the war suggests that Germany might have been better off without submarines. Naval warfare brings us to oil-firing for steam powered vessels, the cause of Britain's concern over oil supplies in the pre-war years. Its continuing supply was certainly vital to the wartime Royal Navy, which because of oil's advantages was rapidly converting its vessels to burn it. But although oil conferred benefits it was not critical to fighting efficiency in the short distances involved in North Sea naval warfare. The German High Seas Fleet stayed in port for most of the war not because it was coal-fired but because it dare not risk suffering a major defeat at the hands of Britain's numerically superior Grand Fleet.

One other military use for oil was in the production of toluene, the basis of trinitrotoluene (TNT), the main explosive in World War One. Toluene could be produced from oil and much has been made of Shell's secret dismantling of its Dutch toluene plant and its re-erection in Britain – Holland, being neutral, would not sell arms or explosives to either side. Shell's plant seems to have produced a large proportion of British toluene. But oil was not the only source for the stuff. The Germans produced it from coal and seem to have experienced no significant problems in supply. Both sides mixed TNT with ammonium nitrate but German shells actually contained a higher proportion of TNT than the British, which may have made them more effective.[58]

The oil crisis for Germany came right at the end of the war, and it came from an unexpected direction. From 1915 the Allies had been engaged in what seemed for a long time a hopeless sideshow, an attack on Bulgaria – an ally of the Central Powers – via Greece. This rapidly became bogged down. But in the late summer of 1918, as the Germans withdrew troops from Bulgaria to shore up the Western Front, active warfare restarted and Bulgaria quickly collapsed. The Allies now had a route to Romania. The German high command estimated that, if Romanian oil was denied them, they would have to cease air and mechanized land warfare within two months.[59] It seems likely that this was one factor in scaring the high command into its demands for an armistice. But there were many others. Germany had already experienced food and other material shortages, while it was being steadily forced back on the battlefields. Historians still differ as to whether it was the shortages and the consequent problems on the home front, or military defeat, which should be given primacy in accounting for the German collapse. But all agree that the German army was in severe straits by the autumn of 1918. Oil was only a small factor in its immediate problems. Impending shortages of oil no doubt seriously worried the Germans, but by that time they had many other worries. Ultimately, indeed, the worries about Romanian oil had been caused by the Central Powers' own military weakness, which caused them to lose Bulgaria and doubt their ability to defend Wallachia.[60]

Oil was not yet critical to most aspects of warfare given the ruling technologies. And it is doubtful even if the war accelerated its subsequent peacetime use in Britain to any great extent. The development of motorized road transport was possibly advanced a little by the availability of cheap army lorries after the war, but it is hard to see this as of long-term significance. Lorry engines still used petrol, with consequent penalties in fuel consumption. The most important development, diesels light enough to be used in lorries, did not come about until the 1930s. The war did, however, have an effect on the shape of the British oil industry.

Shell remained pre-eminent among British, or partly British, companies. This was in spite of a determined and unscrupulous attempt by Greenway of APOC to undermine it. Depicting Shell as 'unBritish', Greenway's favourite tactic, had particular resonance in wartime. His most egregious action was an attempt to break APOC's marketing agreement with Shell, now thought to be unnecessary, by getting APOC's production companies – legally separate entities – to sell their oil to a new company. APOC itself would therefore apparently be deprived of its crude and unable to sell it on to Shell.[61] This piece of crookery was too blatant to gain government approval. But Shell was at first vulnerable to attack over its part Dutch ownership and over the actions of various subsidiary companies, such as its Romanian subsidiary which was constrained to sell oil products to Germany. Eyre Crowe, a senior civil servant in the Foreign Office, described Robert Waley Cohen, one of Shell's top men, as a 'slippery and dangerous person', and this was typical of much comment in the privacy of internal government memoranda.[62]

In the end, however, Shell became perceived by the government and the public in a more favourable light. Marcus Samuel was super-patriotic while Henri Deterding was also strongly pro-Allied. His main residence had been in England since 1902 when Asiatic Petroleum, the first joint venture between Royal Dutch and Shell, was established. It was actions, however, rather than Samuel's words or Deterding's place of residence which did most to change attitudes. Shell's well-developed facilities made it essential in supplying the armed services' oil requirements and it became the main supplier to both the British Expeditionary Force and the Royal Flying Corps, the antecedent of the RAF. Shell was not slow to use these facts in its advertisements, although their self-promotion was mitigated by the plaintive phrase, perhaps produced by Marcus Samuel, that 'Quality tells more than calumny'.[63] Pro-British it may have been, but the Shell group also made huge profits during the war – so much so that, conscious of public opinion, it tried to hide their extent by accounting strategies such as accelerating depreciation. In fairness, however, the money was not made so much from directly supplying the Allied governments as from the high oil prices caused by the war, the profits mainly being made in the group's American and Far East operations.[64]

In spite of the failure of some of Greenway's machinations, APOC gained even more from the war than Shell. In 1914 APOC was still loss-making; by 1918 it was making substantial profits. Ironically, this was achieved even though most of its fuel oil and other products were not used for ships serving in British waters, as it was more economical in tanker tonnage to use American oil. But there was plenty of military and naval demand nearer to Persia, in particular because of the transport needs of the British Expeditionary Force in Mesopotamia. Equally important for the future, APOC had acquired its own marketing company and tanker fleet, through the purchase of the British Petroleum Company (BP) and various associates. Before the war, BP had actually been owned by a German company, the Europaische Petroleum Union of Bremen. It distributed Shell products and had the largest share of the British market after Anglo-American, Standard Oil's British subsidiary. After the outbreak of war the Public Trustee took control of German assets and APOC then lobbied to buy BP. In this case its argument that other outcomes – for instance a takeover by Standard Oil or Shell – would further reduce competition in the British market was obviously reasonable. It acquired BP in 1917, and Shell then set up its own marketing operation.[65]

The BP takeover had been preceded by a plethora of other schemes, mostly inspired by Greenway, to create a large British oil company involving APOC. Mexican Eagle, for instance, was one fancied participant in such a merger. Burmah was another, especially as that company was itself now leaning towards Shell.[66] The schemes foundered on various rocks and by the end of the war the government, having come to view Shell in a more friendly light, was less inclined to listen to APOC's propaganda. However, the issue of 'national' control of Britain's oil supplies remained on the agenda. One reason for this was a nasty scare over oil in 1917. The direct cause was the German submarine campaign and the resulting increase in tanker sinkings, but indirectly it was related to the inadequate controls on consumption and the lack of coordination in supply matters. The problems were gradually sorted out but they ensured, as Curzon's phrase shows, that oil remained prominent in the post-war government's thinking.

2

The World of Oil 1918–39

GOVERNMENTS AND OIL COMPANIES: UNFINISHED BUSINESS

In 1922 a tragic death brought to an end a political dynasty. The death was of Lewis (nicknamed Loulou), Viscount Harcourt, the son of William Harcourt who had been one of the contenders for the Liberal leadership after Gladstone's resignation in the 1890s. The tragedy lay in its circumstances. There were suggestions that Harcourt committed suicide as his alleged habit of exposing himself to children threatened to become public. His death was also symbolic in the world of oil. He had been chairman of the grandly named Petroleum Imperial Policy Committee, known as the Harcourt Committee, set up towards the end of the war to establish what the government's oil policy actually was. But by 1922 the fruits of the committee's labours had failed to ripen and instead withered away. There were various reasons for this. Notwithstanding Curzon's pronouncements about oil's wartime importance, British government policy towards it remained a shifting sand. As before the war, there were different departmental views whilst politicians were influenced by the general climate of opinion, which was itself subject to change.[1]

Nevertheless for a time after the war, which had seen a huge increase in government intervention in many areas of life, there was still a widespread belief in the potential benefits of such intervention. For instance, various programmes were started to find alternatives to petroleum, one possibility being alcohol produced from vegetable matter – a forerunner of today's biofuels. To that end two acres of Jerusalem artichokes were planted in Dorset. A more important initiative was a prolonged effort to achieve a 'national' oil company such as Greenway of APOC had mooted during the war. However, with the wartime *rapprochement* between the government and Shell, it was the latter company which was now at the centre of the government's thoughts. The main agency was the Harcourt Committee, and in January 1919 Harcourt and Deterding initialled an agreement by which British interests would acquire majority control over Royal Dutch/Shell, while the group's operating companies would become predominantly British registered and have government nominees on their boards. Shell would therefore become a 'national' company and would be the centrepiece of the government's policy.[2]

However, the Harcourt-Deterding agreement was never ratified and finally faded away. Shell had had its own motives for the agreement. With oil apparently now as much a matter of geopolitics as a commercial affair, it had hoped to enlist the British government's support in various theatres of operation, particularly Romania, Russia and the Middle East. But the government's contradictory policy towards the third region, discussed later, eventually deterred it. The scheme for greater government influence was then replaced by another – for less. In this, there would be a gigantic three-way merger between Shell, Burmah and APOC. It would still produce a national company, because British interests would predominate, but the government would sell its interest in APOC.[3] The rapid change in the government's attitude, both towards its involvement in general and towards APOC in particular, came about for two reasons. Firstly because APOC, once the star, was now seen as badly managed and in urgent need of a shake-up. Secondly because of a wider disenchantment with government intervention. The majority of MPs in the Coalition government which ruled from 1918–22 were Conservative, and after a while the government's munificence with public money began to gall on them. This chimed in with the inclinations of the Treasury. In spite of economies, the government's financial commitments were far greater than before the war, while the Treasury was beginning to reassert its traditional role as keeper of the nation's purse-strings. APOC's continued expansion was a concern because it might lead the company to call for further state subventions. So getting rid of the state's shareholding via the merger proposal was seen as a blessing. At the same time, the dream of a national company would still be realized. The issue sputtered on until the Labour government of 1924 when the amalgamation proposals were finally put to rest. The government therefore remained the majority shareholder in APOC.

This conclusion has been seen as an early assertion of Labour's belief in nationalization but Geoffrey Jones argues that it was not. The government directors had rarely interfered with APOC's running and continued to refrain from so doing. The decision to drop the merger was essentially a reassertion of the *status quo* and came about through pressure from the Admiralty. Even though they had drawn little oil from Persia during the war, in peacetime conditions they could do so and the contract with APOC seemed very good value for money. In the absence of a strong push from anyone else, their desire to keep APOC independent overrode other factors. Within the government, departmental politics had once more become the arena in which issues were decided, and any notion of a unified oil policy went by the board.[4]

Marcus Samuel had retired and to the hard-headed realists who now dominated Shell the idea of a 'national' oil company had always been subservient to the benefits of reducing costs and increasing profit margins. Initially the 'national' company had seemed good for Shell but they had come to believe that other forms of cooperation could replace a formal merger. The British ones among them were not unpatriotic, and Deterding was pro-British, but the idea that a national oil company would actually benefit Britain in any tangible way had never been their way of thinking about it. A national company could not guarantee the supply of oil so long as that was imported. The only guarantee in those circumstances was seapower. Robert Waley Cohen's comment of 1923 sums up Shell's attitude. 'The whole question of control was very largely nonsense. It is a matter of sentiment, but if by transferring control to the Hottentots we could increase our security and our dividends I don't believe any of us would hesitate for long.'[5]

The government also had to take decisions about its course of action in the international world of oil. Before the war it had already come up against the American belief that European powers should not interfere in Latin America (see Chapter 1, 'Entrepreneurs in oil'). But the Foreign Office had constantly downplayed diplomatic resistance to the United States. Ultimately wider diplomatic considerations – basically keeping on good terms with the USA – were more important than the affairs of oil companies. After the war the perceived importance of oil initially led the government to concern itself much more with British oil interests overseas and Britain in this period has been credited with 'recognising the need to evolve a coherent oil policy and attempting to operate one'.[6] It is true that, for a time during and after the war, the government showed some consistency in following Harcourt's precept of 1918 that 'it is absolutely vital to the British Empire to get a firm hold of all possible sources of petroleum supply . . .'.[7] Purchasing the APOC shareholding in 1914 could be seen as the first step towards this end, and the negotiations with Shell as part of it. But, as Geoffrey Jones has argued, the fact is that even in those few years policy was hardly coherent.[8] And as the 1920s wore on and the perceived need to mollify the United States became paramount, Harcourt's stated aim bore less and less resemblance the one that was actually followed.

American interest in foreign oil was underpinned by a number of factors. The long-standing belief that Latin America was in the US sphere of influence was one. But more important was a fear – short-lived but intense while it lasted – in the United States that its oil was running out. Looking around the world, it saw a large proportion of potential oil supplies under the surface of the British Empire. And the Empire limited foreign companies' access in various ways, for instance by 'British control' clauses applicable to leases on Crown lands. On the other hand, the US itself allowed foreign-owned companies – notably Shell – to exploit its own oil, although it had powers to deny access to government lands if it felt that reciprocity was not forthcoming.[9] It was not surprising, therefore, that American oilmen and diplomats started to look further afield than the Americas for oil supplies. American initiatives reached their peak soon after the war when they negotiated their way into the Turkish Petroleum Company; but even after the US had recovered from its fear of imminent oil depletion, and indeed was suffering from over-production, they put strong pressure on Britain to allow American firms into the British controlled areas of the Middle East. These initiatives are discussed in the next section. The British took the view that, morally, the Americans did not have much of a claim to the rest of the world's oil given that they were far and away the largest producers. But good relations with the US ultimately took priority and Britain consistently gave way.[10]

GOVERNMENTS AND OIL COMPANIES: THE MIDDLE EAST

Today the term 'Middle East' is almost inseparable from oil. The juxtaposition is apt, for while the region is one of the cradles of civilization, the commonly used name for it dates back only to 1902 and was little used until the First World War. It was popularized in Britain in 1916 when Lloyd George, always on the look out for some escape route from the stalemate on the Western Front, turned his attention to renewing attempts to knock the Ottoman Empire out of the war. The 'Middle East', almost coterminous with the Ottoman Empire with the exception of Turkey itself, became a term which could embody 'a revived nationalised landscape between East and West, that was to be free of Oriental despotism and [which] would achieve redemption under Allied protection'. But, as a radical turned imperialist, Lloyd George was not just concerned with nationalism but perceived the area as vital for another Empire – the British. These different aims were, of course, impossible to bring into harmony and attempts to realize them were to bedevil the region in the future as well as complicating oil policy at the time.[11]

At the end of the war, however, hardly any oil had been discovered in the Middle East or was even suspected, and therefore in most parts of the region there was no reason to consider it at all. In Persia, of course, oil had been discovered, but Persia was not then a significant political actor in the region. Within Persia itself, nationalism was stirring but in the years immediately after the war APOC and British influence seemed well established. And in Mesopotamia, shortly to become Iraq, the existence of oil was suspected and will be discussed below. But elsewhere, and to a large extent in Iraq too, what influenced government thinking was a whole nexus of factors. Safeguarding the Suez Canal, the main route to India, was a major concern as it had been for many years. Trying to honour some of the numerous and incompatible promises and agreements Britain had made to and with Arabs, Jews and the French during the war was another. More altruistically, honouring the fact that Iraq was a League of Nations mandate and not a site for the exercise of British privilege was a third.[12]

Mesopotamia had been part of the Ottoman Empire and therefore had been in the concession area of the pre-war Turkish Petroleum Company (TPC) mentioned in Chapter 1. Greenway, who had muscled APOC into the TPC consortium before the war, predictably tried to use the 'Shell menace' to take it over during the conflict but, as with his other wartime attacks on Shell, overreached himself and was rebuffed by the government.[13] After the war, all concession arrangements were thrown into the melting pot. The TPC (as its name remained until 1929) focused on renegotiating a concession with Iraq, which had been separated from Turkey after the war and made a League of Nations mandate. The mandated power, in this case Britain, had only limited rights and was expected to develop the country to a position where it could become independent. It was also expected to maintain an 'Open Door' policy – in other words not to favour its own nationals or companies.

Negotiations involving the TPC had a number of threads. First, there was Shell's role. If the Harcourt-Deterding agreement was brought to fruition, Shell would obtain dominance of the TPC and government support in restarting the concession negotiations. From the government's point of view, in the immediate flush of victory it considered that it could make arrangements about the concession more or less as it pleased. The only non-British interest it initially considered was the French. The Sykes-Picot agreement of 1916, one of the contradictory agreements which bedevilled the post-war Middle East, had assigned post-war spheres of influence to Britain and France. France's included Mosul, in the north of Mesopotamia and the area thought most likely to yield oil. So after the war, promises were made to cut the French in on the TPC, the French in return waiving their political claims in the area. However, the habit of assuming that the victors could simply divide the spoils was the subject of a warning by Balfour, the Foreign Secretary, to his colleagues in September 1919. Balfour accepted that the Open Door policy had to be taken seriously. The warning only had limited effect but shows that the internationalism of the League of Nations was beginning to have some impact.[14]

Policies were further confused because Lloyd George tended to negotiate independently of the Foreign Office, leading in 1919–20 to a saga of Franco-British agreements, cancellations and renegotiations. These were further complicated by Lloyd George's decision in early 1920 to give the British state the rights to Iraqi oil, if it existed. This occurred at a time when there had been a brief recrudescence of anti-oil trust sentiment in Britain. Lloyd George was therefore favouring domestic radicalism – hostility to trusts – over the internationalism of the League of Nations – the Open Door. However, this was the high-water mark of the post-war Coalition government's desire to intervene in almost everything. Anglo-French accord was finally reached in the San Remo agreement of April 1920, which gave British and French interests primacy in the planned exploitation of oil in Iraq and put the issue of state or private control to one side. While this shows that a colonial mentality, rather than a full acceptance of the spirit of the mandate, was still at work, there was provision in the agreement for an Iraqi shareholding in the TPC.[15]

So far, therefore, some threads had proved to be permanent and others had unravelled. Involvement by the British state was soon forgotten, and the TPC remained a multinational consortium, with Shell, APOC and French interests represented. There was, however, some acceptance of the mandated power's duty to its mandate. From Shell's point of view, the British government's constant reversals of policy had helped to wean it off the idea of becoming a 'national' company in which the government participated, and had therefore helped to end the Harcourt-Deterding agreement. Now another thread was inserted. As noted in the previous section, the Americans had become interested in oil outside the Americas, and this led to American demands to be included in the TPC. They could, of course, use the Open Door principle to underpin their demand. Effectively this was agreed by the consortium in 1923, although it was only in 1928 that a split of 23.75 per cent to each of the four main participants (the French, several American companies in a mini-consortium of their own, APOC and Shell) and the remaining 5 per cent to Calouste Gulbenkian was finally settled.[16]

The Iraqi government, of course, lost out because it agreed a concession with the TPC, in 1925, without getting a shareholding. But although this suggests a degree of international ruthlessness at odds with the mandate principle, the Iraqis had effectively had autonomy in the negotiations and little British government pressure was put on them. To Colonial Office demands for pressure, the Foreign

Office countered that, 'if the Irak [sic] Government refuses to fall in with our views, I do not see how we can force them to grant a concession to the TPC'. The Iraqis probably foresaw some political advantages from settling when they did and to that extent Britain's ultimate control of Iraq was a factor. But, apart from the shareholding issue, the agreement otherwise was quite favourable to the host country by the standards of the time.[17]

Oil had still not been found at the time the concession was granted. On October 15th 1927 the Baba Gurgur No 1 well near Kirkuk, in the north, was discovered. In productive oilfields the oil is often under pressure, and this was the case here. The well was a 'gusher', shooting oil 50 feet into the air and producing almost 100,000 barrels a day which drenched the surrounding countryside before the well was capped. The field was then developed and linked to the Mediterranean by two pipelines, one running across Syria and Lebanon and the other across Jordan (then Transjordan) and Palestine. All were mandates carved out of the Ottoman Empire, the first two French, the second two British. The national interests at work are obvious. Iraq became a significant producer, with an output of five million tons in 1938, compared to Persia's ten million.[18]

The process of expanding Persian production to this level had not been without hiccups. From 1906 the Shah was head of a nominally constitutional government, but the central authorities remained weak and local leaders strong. It was only by keeping on good terms with the latter that APOC had been able to carry out its earlier explorations. Furthermore the payment of royalties calculated on a share of the profits was fraught with difficulties. Did these, for example, include profits made by the company outside Persia? An agreement which was intended to clarify such issues was made in 1920 but was repudiated by the Persian government in 1928.[19]

Before that happened Persia had been set on an entirely new course. Riza Khan, a colonel, emerged as the effective ruler in 1921, although it was only in 1925 that the old dynasty was overthrown and he became Shah, founding the Pahlavi dynasty. With his accession to the throne, the country became known as Iran. Riza Shah, as he became, was energetic and autocratic, and determined to strengthen the central government's powers and develop the country. To do this he needed money and the oil royalties were an obvious potential source. After the repudiation of the 1920 agreement with APOC a series of negotiations over revising the terms of the concession took place. Settlement was constantly delayed by Iranian second thoughts, and meanwhile crude oil prices fell as the world depression took hold from 1929. In the 1920s falling prices had been compensated for by rising sales. But from 1929 sales were also falling and the result was dramatically reduced profits, and royalties, when the Shah expected increases. In November 1932 his patience snapped. Calling for the file on oil negotiations, he had it flung on a stove and cancelled the D'Arcy concession.[20]

After years of delays, settlement was surprisingly swift. The British government was determined to be firm, and immediately appealed to the League of Nations on the grounds that the cancellation was illegal, the concession having been for 60 years. Edward Benes, the Czechoslovakian Foreign Secretary, was bought in by the League to mediate. He made the sensible suggestion that proceedings before the League would be suspended until May and in the meantime negotiations should be resumed. This concentrated minds and by April 1933 a new agreement had been reached. At the critical meeting, the Shah himself presided. He 'gave a little homily to his ministers, who, he said, were down on the ground and could not see very far beyond their noses, whilst he was placed on a pinnacle and could see the great world around him . . .'. Since the Shah appeared from his role in these negotiations to be quite favourably inclined towards APOC, it is possible that the earlier failure to settle occurred because his ministers were too scared to bring before him a settlement which they wrongly thought he would not accept. On the other hand, he might have been frightened by the British government's firm stance.[21]

The new agreement was based on a per ton royalty rate, as was common elsewhere, and an Iranian share of APOC's dividends. For a time the new arrangements combined with economic recovery and rising production to boost royalties. But in 1938, with depression temporarily returning, royalties fell and further friction threatened. The Shah was mollified by the promise of export credits from Britain, but the Iranian expectation of ever-increasing revenue was clearly still a potential problem for the company. In 1935 one further change, of great symbolic importance to Iran, occurred. APOC renamed itself the Anglo-Iranian Oil Corporation (AIOC).

When the negotiations over the final allocation of shares in the TPC were being concluded in 1928, the story goes, Gulbenkian sat down with a map of the Middle East and drew a red line around the old boundaries of the Ottoman Empire. The line encircled most of the Middle East as we know it today, with a few exceptions such as Persia and Kuwait; the latter had long been independent although a British protectorate. Within this area the members of the TPC would not compete against each other in concession negotiations. This was the famous Red Line Agreement. Sadly Gulbenkian's story is romanticized, and the details were prosaically decided between the British and French governments.[22]

At about the same time oil companies began to be interested in other Middle Eastern countries. Interest was fostered by an itinerant New Zealand born mining engineer, Frank Holmes, who had been touting the possibilities of oil in the region since the early 1920s. Holmes was a 'rover in the world of oil' in one sceptical British official's opinion.[23] As with the early days of the oil industry in America, there were a number of such characters in the inter-war Middle East. Since companies outside the TPC – including a number of American ones – were not included in the Red Line Agreement, the TPC still faced competition to exploit these possibilities. Standard Oil of California (Socal), one such non-TPC company, secured concessions in Bahrain and Saudi Arabia. Saudi Arabia had emerged from the ruins of the Ottoman Empire as an independent kingdom. Bahrain, never in the Empire, was a British protectorate. The TPC, which became the Iraq Petroleum Company (IPC) in 1929, was not actually very interested in either of the two countries. Its view was formed by APOC's chief geologist who, in one of the bigger misjudgements in history, had written off Arabia as an oil region. Nonetheless the British government hoped to retain exploitation in British hands and at first resisted Socal's bid in Bahrain. It quickly gave way, contenting itself with the figleaf of Socal registering its interest through a Canadian subsidiary.[24]

Even when oil was struck in Bahrain in 1932 the IPC remained sceptical about Saudi Arabia, but like a dog in a manger was prepared to enter the bidding for a concession there in order to discourage others. The Saudi King, Ibn Saud, was desperate for cash, because the depression had cut the number of pilgrims to Mecca, at that time the country's main source of foreign currency. A deal with Socal was brokered by another rover in the world of oil, Harry St John Philby. Philby, known as Jack and best remembered as the father of the Soviet agent, Kim, had been in the Indian Civil Service (ICS) where he learnt Arabic, since the Government of India took responsibility for British affairs in the Persian Gulf. He developed a strong affinity for the Arab world and Arab life, as did other middle-class Englishmen in that period such as T. E. Lawrence. Disliking British policy in the Middle East, Philby resigned from the ICS in 1925 and set up a trading company in Saudi Arabia, where he converted to Islam. He enjoyed twisting his compatriots' tails, so helping to set up Socal's concession and do down the IPC was a satisfying exercise. As in Bahrain, oil was struck before the Second World War but production at first remained limited. This was partly because Socal lacked distribution arrangements in the eastern hemisphere until a tie-up with Texas Oil in 1936 produced a new consortium, Caltex.[25]

APOC took some interest in Kuwait, also under British protection, which was outside the Red Line area. Holmes had also been interested in oil here and persuaded Gulf Oil, another American company (named after the Gulf of Mexico not the Persian Gulf) to bid for a concession. But as with Bahrain the British government wanted to enforce a British nationality clause in Kuwait, and this time its defence was more vigorous. Gulf seemed to be excluded. Meanwhile APOC decided there was no oil there and, as a result of the government's attitude, was confident that no one was going to be able to exploit the country even if oil was found. In 1932 it was about to drop its interest when Britain bowed to US government pressure and dropped the nationality requirement. APOC, true to its policy of spoiling the party for everyone else if possible, renewed its interest. With two competitors, the Shaikh of Kuwait prepared to bid up the price. Gulf and APOC therefore merged their interests in another consortium and secured the concession. APOC was spectacularly wrong again. Oil was struck in Kuwait in 1938 although development was suspended during the war.[26]

The IPC consortium model had therefore become common in the Middle East. The IPC itself in the 1930s negotiated concessions in other small coastal states on the Gulf. In 1939 they discovered oil in Qatar, although again development was suspended during the war.

In spite of the steady increase in oil exploration in the Middle East, the British government remained broadly neutral in its attitude towards British oil companies and their concessions, and concession-hunting, in the area. Certain key interests were asserted, but in a low-key way. In Iraq, Lloyd George's initial enthusiasm was cooled by time, diplomacy and the growing constraints on his government's initial activism. From the early 1920s Britain became anxious not to be seen to interfere in the concession negotiations, although in the 1930s it did secure one branch of the Iraq-Mediterranean pipeline for British-controlled territory. And in 1932 complete independence was granted to Iraq, albeit with a treaty giving the British military bases in the country. By contrast Egypt, which in many ways had a better claim to independence, remained firmly under British suzerainty. The Suez Canal was far more important to Britain than retaining control of an oilfield. In Iran Britain did hold firm over contract renegotiations – but within the context of the League of Nations, not by exercising gunboat diplomacy. In other instances it left British or partly-British firms and consortia to fend for themselves, giving minimal support in Bahrain and Kuwait before retreating in the face of American pressure.[27]

MAGNATES AND CAUDILLOS

The first page of Eric Ambler's marvellous 1937 thriller, *Uncommon Danger*, introduces the reader to an oil magnate. The magnate is Joseph Balterghen, the chairman of Pan-Eurasian Petroleum, and over the next few pages he is shown planning to suborn Romanian politicians in order to obtain the revision of an oil concession in Pan-Eurasian's favour. As the book unfolds, it becomes clear that Balterghen is prepared to employ agents who will use any methods, including murder. Their efforts are thwarted, however, by the alliance of a journalist, Kenton, and two Russian agents, Andreas Zaleshoff and his beautiful sister Tamara.[28]

Ambler's novel was a classic representation of the Popular Front view of international capitalism, itself derived from pre-1914 radicalism seasoned with a strong dash of pro-Sovietism. As Kenton reflects:

> It was the power of Business, not the deliberations of statesmen, that shaped the destinies of nations. The Foreign Ministries of the great powers might make the actual declarations of their Government's policies; but it was the Big Business men, the bankers and their dependents, the arms manufacturers, the oil companies, the big industrialists, who determined what those policies should be.[29]

Balterghen himself seems to contain elements of both Gulbenkian and Deterding. He is Armenian by birth, like Gulbenkian. His sexual appetites are not detailed but, if they had replicated Gulbenkian's, they might have been unsuitable for a 1930s novel; Gulbenkian always had several mistresses on the go, one of whom had to be under 18 'on medical advice'. Like Deterding, however, Balterghen is a professional manager not just a Gulbenkian-like fixer and like Shell, Pan-Eurasian has interests in Venezuela, Mexico and the Middle East as well as Romania. Balterghen's politics, it can be inferred, would also have been close to Deterding's. Deterding had been strongly pro-British in the First World War but subsequently he became increasingly right-wing. In 1936 he married his German secretary and retired to Germany where he consorted with the Nazis.[30] However dubious some of the personalities involved, did that make the oil companies themselves the corrupt, manipulative entities depicted by Ambler, and if it did, how much power did they really have?

As Chapter 1 and the previous section of this chapter showed, the British government was usually fairly resistant to oil company special pleading. When pressure was successfully applied, most notably over the pre-1914 government shareholding in APOC, it was because it fitted in with a strongly held departmental point of view. And even here the added ingredient of Churchill's persuasiveness was important. As with most of Churchill's obsessions, there can be no doubt that he genuinely held the view he put forward – at least at that point in time. But among British politicians, it was Churchill who came closest to making an unsavoury deal with an oil company. When out of office and of Parliament in 1923, Churchill was approached by Waley Cohen of Shell to push the mooted merger of that company with APOC and Burmah (see earlier section 'Government and oil companies: Unfinished business'). By this stage of the merger talks the deal included the sale of the government's share in APOC. For a suggested fee of £5,000 Churchill would be lobbying against the government holding shares in the company; a state of affairs for which, ten years before, he had argued so strongly. Churchill was quite prepared to do it, and approached Stanley Baldwin, then Prime Minister. As soon as Baldwin called an election in November 1923, however, Churchill scented a return to Parliament and possible office and dropped his oil company brief. So he could be accused of greed and inconsistency, but not of attempting to further the scheme for profit when he was in office.[31] Baldwin himself viewed the approach quite favourably but as the man who after the war had anonymously given one-fifth of his own fortune to the government to reduce the National Debt, he was hardly a likely candidate for dishonesty. His motive was probably to continue reducing the National Debt, since the government's APOC shareholding was now worth £20 million. In the event, of course, the Admiralty's continued support for retaining the shareholding carried the day.

When they were dealing with each other, oil companies certainly liked making anti-competitive arrangements, or conspiring against the public as Adam Smith would have put it. The most famous of these was the 'As-Is' agreement of 1928. In the late summer of that year Henri Deterding rented Achnacarry Castle, a nineteenth-century 'Scottish baronial'-style mansion and the centre of a sporting estate in the Highlands. Here he entertained, among others, Walter Teagle, the head of Standard Oil of New Jersey (Jersey Standard), and Sir John Cadman, who had replaced Greenway as the head of APOC. Jersey Standard, now Exxon but best known in Britain through its trade name Esso, was the largest of the old Standard Oil companies and inherited its business outside the United States. The house party's purpose was anything but sporting. It was to extend a number of existing market-sharing agreements by setting up a global one.[32]

Market-sharing had various rationales, not all about profit – although it was very important. There was a growing belief among many thinkers in the 1920s that excessive competition in any field of commerce was a bad thing. This, of course, was a contrast to the pre-war dislike of 'trusts' as unwholesome monopolies. The new ideas had several sources. One was the war, when restricting private competition had achieved economies in many activities. Another was the post-war fall in prices, which was almost continuous after a brief boom had ended in late 1920. Price falls at first seemed good, as they came after a period of sharp inflation. But as they continued, and in Britain were also accompanied by depression in major industries such as coal and heavy engineering, they began to seem malign. Price falls appeared to threaten economic stability, by discouraging investment and making it harder for companies to pay interest on loans. A general belief grew, therefore, that large organizations had advantages. On the one hand they could rationalize and thus reduce waste and lower costs. On the other, they would prevent the price falls caused by excessive competition. These views were not entirely compatible but most people have never been too concerned about holding views they want to just because those views are contradictory.[33]

In Britain, one result of the consequent shift in perspective was government support for the mooted oil company mergers of the early 1920s. After these foundered, the government as a shareholder in APOC took a permissive attitude to the subsequent market-sharing agreements.[34] The change in governmental attitudes was such that in the 1930s the British government actively aided the restriction of competition, by bringing in tariffs and legislating for minimum price agreements in, for instance, coal and agriculture.

From the oil companies' point of view, market-sharing took place within a context of falling prices. Crude oil in the US, $3.00 per barrel at its peak in 1920, was below $1.50 by 1928.[35] By minimizing competition, market-sharing should stabilize prices. Burmah and Shell had already, in 1928, amalgamated their distribution arrangements in India into Burmah-Shell. The new joint company took its crude in the first instance from Burmah, and then equally from Shell and APOC. As a *quid pro quo*, the latter would not enter the Indian market on its own account. Then early in 1928 APOC and Shell amalgamated their distribution interests in southern and eastern Africa up to and including Egypt, along with the countries bordering the eastern Mediterranean. This was known as the 'Consolidated' area.[36] Both Deterding of Shell and Cadman of APOC have claims to be the begetters of As-Is itself. Deterding had long been an enthusiast for such agreements and knew Walter Teagle well. But the agreement actually seems to have been drafted within APOC, in August 1928. The gathering at Achnacarry set the imprimatur on it through mutual conviviality, although it is sometimes referred to as the Achnacarry Agreement.[37] As-Is had one simple basis: each of the subscribing companies was to accept its existing market share. There followed a number of provisions designed to limit new investment by sharing each other's facilities – which of course would give the subscribing companies a cost advantage. Finally, the agreement enshrined the existing pricing mechanism – the price at any port of origin would be the American Gulf Coast price.[38]

For some years As-Is represented an aspiration rather than a solid achievement. Since the US was still the world's biggest producer, the success of As-Is outside that country rested on controlling its exports in order to minimize competition. But agreement on that seemed likely to violate US anti-trust laws. By 1930 three further factors were at work to undermine As-Is. World depression was reducing oil demand; US supply was increased by further big discoveries, notably the East Texas field in 1930; and the Russians and Romanians were aggressively pursuing market share. The result was a further collapse in prices. By 1931 the average barrel of crude in the US was selling for little more than 60 cents.[39]

The companies had more immediate success with limited agreements in individual areas. Where they had reasonable control over distribution, they had some chance of making such agreements effective. The UK was one such area, and Shell and APOC merged their UK marketing and distribution in 1932. Jersey Standard refused to join – another indication of the limitations of As-Is – and cheap Russian oil was another dangerous competitor. But as demand picked up in the 1930s and Russian oil exports declined, the Shell/APOC joint venture was quite successful, from the companies' point of view, in maintaining prices. Within production areas Venezuela, where Shell and Jersey Standard had strong positions, was also an As-Is success, the companies agreeing on output limitations. Further afield product price falls were limited in Asiatic markets, with beneficial effects on Shell's profits in 1932–3. This was, however, one area where cartel agreements had been established earlier. From 1934 As-Is became more effective globally. There were regular inter-company conferences and oil prices remained remarkably stable in the immediate pre-war years. But this was in the context of generally improving market conditions and in 1938, with Teagle's retirement, Jersey Standard's policy changed. It gave notice of withdrawal from As-Is. But in the event, the Second World War supervened and changed the situation entirely.[40]

One of As-Is's problems was Russia. A major producing area for Shell before the First World War, its oil subsequently created problems rather than opportunities for Western companies. As a result of the Soviet triumph, Shell and other Western oil companies lost their Russian investments. When the Soviets re-established their oil industry, they re-entered Western markets as price cutters. An importing company, Russian Oil Products (ROP) was established in Britain in 1924 and quickly built up a substantial business. Ironically the main British suppliers, including Shell and APOC, actually brought ROP into a local agreement on prices and quotas in 1929. Russian oil still exerted downward pressure on European prices, however, until rising demand in Russia curtailed exports during the 1930s.[41]

Russia tweaked the oil companies' tails. In Latin America, the companies had more opportunities for exploration and profit but governments were still capable of biting back. In spite of the instability which had bedevilled Mexico from 1911, Weetman Pearson's Mexican Eagle (*El Aguila*) remained a large and profitable producer (see Chapter 1). In 1919 Pearson, who had become Viscount Cowdray, sold a large proportion of his shares to Shell, and a Shell group company became the manager of the Mexican Eagle properties. Shell's absorption of Cowdray's

British distribution company produced Shell-Mex.[42] Mexican Eagle was not one of Deterding's best investments, because in 1922 the famous Potrero No. 4 and other wells in the field were invaded by salt water. Nevertheless, Mexico continued to produce substantial amounts of oil. Some political stability had returned, while there was a stand-off over a 1917 law which had reasserted government control over subsoil rights, hitherto in private hands. But the oil resources had become a focus for nationalism and, as production in Mexico's relatively high-cost fields declined, the government increasingly pressed the companies in various ways. In 1938 their properties were expropriated. Ironically, whereas British 'colonial' attitudes were often the target of national feeling, in Mexico the main target was the USA. But Shell, as the largest producer, suffered equally. It finally received compensation in 1947.[43]

Other, smaller Latin American states proved almost as problematical. The US interest in the region was strengthened by post-war fears over oil shortages and it put pressure on both the Costa Rican and the Guatemalan governments to oppose British concessions there.[44] However, South American governments were often resistant to US pressure; instead indigenous nationalism, as in Mexico, limited oil company penetration. APOC was trying to diversify away from the Middle East and made some moves in Colombia and Argentina. But it made little progress in the first because of laws preventing the involvement of foreign governments in economic exploitation – laws which dated back to the early days of independence when the danger was perceived as Spain, not Britain. Here, and for the same reason elsewhere in Latin America, the government shareholding was a liability to APOC. In Argentina, oil concessions were essentially a political pawn. APOC's small concession was under constant legal threat and government drilling took place close to APOC's wells, thus degrading the reservoir.[45]

It was Venezuela that proved to be the oil companies' bonanza. Venezuela, a backward agricultural country before the war, was a classic example of the Latin American pattern of rule by caudillos – strong leaders, often unelected. From 1908, its caudillo was Vicente Gomez, whose government and attitudes were something of a rerun of Diaz's in Mexico. Gomez conferred political stability but at a price. He and his family obtained concessions and resold them at a profit to the companies. Sensing that they operated within a political arena which, while ostensibly stable, could explode, oil companies built their refineries on the Dutch offshore islands of Aruba and Curacao. Oil was not discovered in any quantity until 1922, although Shell had been exploring around Lake Maracaibo from 1914. It was deeply inhospitable country. The 'Mosquitoes were the worst and largest of any place I ever saw' wrote a geologist, and Shell had to protect its tractor drivers with thick cloth to keep out local tribespeople's arrows. But

Shell had the indomitable George Reynolds, who had found oil for APOC in almost as bad, if different, conditions in 1907. In 1922 an explosion took place, but it was not political. Barroso No. 2 well blew out and gushed at the rate of 100,000 barrels per day – another Potrero de Llanos. From practically nothing in 1922, Venezuelan production rose to 10 per cent of the world total by 1930, a large share of which was Shell's.[46]

Venezuela illustrates a number of things: the competing influences on oil companies, the limits of their powers and the difficulty of locating precisely who was responsible for corrupt practices. Although British diplomats were prepared to intercede forcefully in support of existing Shell concessions when these were disputed in 1920–1, as elsewhere there were limits to such support. With American companies upping the pressure to obtain their own concessions, the Foreign Office urged Shell not to stand in their way: 'In view of the power of the dollar, British oil interests in Venezuela will do well to compromise with their American *confreres*.'[47] And while Gomez's economically liberal regime generally encouraged oil companies, that too was within certain limits. Subsequent to Shell's pre-First World War acquisition of concessions, a more competitive post-war regime pushed up the price oil companies had to pay. As a result Venezuela received a slightly higher price per barrel than Middle East countries during the whole period 1913–47, and thus received a higher percentage of the companies' total receipts (26 per cent as against 19 per cent). The higher average suggests that the companies as a whole by no means had *carte blanche*. Shell, however, paid about one quarter less than the other, mainly American, companies. But this favourable treatment does not imply that British diplomatic intercessions somehow had irresistible force. Rather, by preserving the position of the strongest non-American oil company, the Venezuelan government preserved a competitive concession regime which helped the country to gain its relatively favourable percentage of receipts.[48]

Where there was outright corruption, it was most marked within government circles. Gomez and others connected with him and his family obtained concessions on favourable terms for resale to the companies. But few government officials were involved in oil-related corrupt practices, showing that there were limits to how far these could be taken – although whether the limits were self-imposed by the companies or the result of honesty among officials is not clear. Brian McBeth, however, has unearthed two examples of British companies – not in the Shell group – resorting to bribery, in one case a minister and in the other Gomez directly.[49]

There were smaller British interests in the Americas, most notably Trinidad where Trinidad Leaseholds maintained a fair-sized output on its own account and also had joint interests with Shell and APOC. In the whole world of oil, though, Trinidad was a small producer at about two million tons a year in the 1930s – about 10 per cent of Venezuela's output. On the other side of the world, Burmah Oil still produced steadily, although in very different circumstances from the free-flowing wells of the Middle East and Venezuela. In 1933 its 3,077 wells produced just 4.8 barrels per day each, on average. But the Burmah-Shell agreement helped it make steady profits in spite of its high-cost production.[50]

Less far from Britain, but almost as exotic, was Romania, the scene of Balterghen's fictional manipulations. There were two big foreign operators by the inter-war period, Shell through a subsidiary called Astra Română, and Jersey Standard through Româno-Americană. Romania was something of a bed of thorns for both of them. The dominant party until the late 1930s was the Liberals, who in the topsy-turvy world of Romanian politics were xenophobic, protectionist nationalists. The Liberals passed various mining laws which were intended to favour 'national' – that is Romanian – owned companies over 'foreign capital' ones, as well as complementary legislation such as a law restricting the proportion of foreign staff. There was a brief respite in the pressure on foreign companies during the National Peasant Party government which came to power in 1928. The National Peasant victory owed nothing to the oil companies, but was due to the unpopularity of the Liberals who fell out among themselves and lost office, thus failing to manipulate the elections in their usual manner. For most of the period, however, the foreign-owned oil companies were on the defensive against government pressure. If they did try to suborn Romanian politicians, they were remarkably bad at it. Since they were technically more competent than the Romanian companies, one result of restricting their activities was a steady decline in production from 1936.[51]

In 1947 the Peasant Party politicians were arraigned in a Communist show trial, and their 1929 Mining Law – which actually had made only very modest adjustments in favour of the foreign-owned oil companies – was used against them. Their aim, it was alleged, had been to 'turn Romania into a semi-colony of international trusts'.[52] It was an irony that Communist skulduggery, the rhetoric of dishonest nationalistic politicians, and Popular Front fantasy all tarred the oil companies with the same brush.

In spite of Eric Ambler's exaggerations, however (pardonable as he told such a good story), the oil companies did not exactly have clean hands. The final section of the chapter attempts to assess their overall record.

MAKING MONEY, MAKING FRIENDS, MAKING ENEMIES

Much of the criticism aimed at oil companies, from the days of Standard Oil to the present, has occurred because they made a lot of money. Furthermore they often made it by producing oil in countries which remained poor. But just how much money did they make and how much remained with the producing countries? APOC is the clearest example because all its oil, with the exception of its share of Iraqi output, came from Iran and therefore most of its profit ultimately came from there too. Making some assumptions as detailed in note 53, the rate of return which all of APOC's investors received on their capital over the whole period 1922–38 was just under 12 per cent.[53] This is good, considering it encompassed the years of the depression. But although it is good, it is not stupendous. Judging simply by the dividend on their ordinary shares, Shell and Burmah consistently did better than APOC. As note 53 suggests, dividends by themselves are not a precise indicator of profitability. But it is likely that Shell and Burmah made a higher return than APOC, because more of their capital investment was made in the pre-war years when prices were lower. Even so, their dividends indicate that profit levels fell significantly in the inter-war years. Shell's, 35 per cent in the pre-war years, fluctuated around 25 per cent in the 1920s before falling as low as 7.5 per cent in the early 1930s. APOC followed a similar trajectory at a lower level. Burmah did better, maintaining high dividends in the 1920s and cutting less in the early 1930s. It benefited from the Burmah-Shell agreement which allowed it to maintain prices and output levels in the Indian subcontinent.[54] American firms suffered even more in the depression. Frederick Godber, a Shell director, found on a visit to the United States in 1931 that oilmen were 'very pessimistic' and 'almost panicky'. In fact over the period 1929–36, spanning the depression, a sample of 28 US oil companies actually did worse than a large sample of industrial companies. In their worst year, 1931, the oil companies collectively lost money, whilst the industrial companies, on average, just kept their heads above water.[55]

Were profits made at the expense of the producing countries? About £70 million was returned to APOC's investors either directly or indirectly between 1922 and 1938. In the same years, Iran received about £40 million in royalties and tax, implying a company/government profit split of 64/36.[56] This would, of course, have been less good for the Iranians had they not insisted on renegotiating the concession. On the other hand, it includes APOC's global profits on refining and distribution and on Iraqi oil – although it could be argued that APOC's worldwide earning power ultimately stemmed from Iranian oil and the profits APOC had made from it, so it is only fair to take account of its other earnings. This

64/36 profit split cannot be directly compared with the 50/50 split established in the 1950s, which in practice left a smaller share to the companies. To that extent, it suggests that in the inter-war years APOC did exploit Iran. But low inter-war oil prices, and hence relatively low profits, mean that the profit split by itself does not tell us much. Rates of return may be a better indication of the fairness of the overall distribution, and as noted above APOC's return was good but not outstanding.

The extreme example of apparent exploitation was Mexico. Mexican Eagle's peak dividend year was 1920 when it paid 60 per cent. Up until then, while expenditure would have been incurred in Mexico on wages and materials, hardly any royalties would have been paid although a fair amount of money would have flowed to Mexican ministers, landowners and rebels via bribes, legitimate payments and levies. But from 1924–34, the company's experience was very different: it estimated that the government had received fourteen times more revenue than paid to shareholders. Even if this is taken with a pinch of salt it illustrates, again, that oil was not always a high-profit business.[57]

And the oil companies could, of course, point to the risks they had taken and continued to take. In financial theory, which in this case accords pretty well with common sense, returns should increase with risk. To put it simply, we're content with 5 per cent when we stick money in a bank deposit but hope to make a lot more when we put a tenner on an outsider in the Grand National – if we win, that is. Exploration, in the early days, involved huge risks and also huge expenditure by the standards of the day. It was more akin to the Grand National than a bank deposit. Pre-1914 Mexico, Iran and Russia have already been discussed in Chapter 1. Other areas were the same: '... successful participation in Peruvian oil was ... fraught with problems. The early history of Lobitos showed how much capital, tenacity, patience and luck it needed.' And even though Peru eventually came good, if in a relatively small way, other areas of exploration did not. The inter-war history of APOC is littered with unsuccessful ventures: Australia, Croatia, North Borneo and Newfoundland among others.[58]

The chequered inter-war profit experience of oil companies, whether British or American, throws into relief the limitations of cartelization in the period. As-Is had come into existence in 1928 because oil prices had already fallen substantially, with the upsurge in Venezuelan production a large contributory factor.[59] Then the depression, a series of big US finds, its 'rule of capture' which stimulated independents' production, and Russian oil all conspired to keep prices down. With some control over US production from 1933 and a decline in Russian exports it became possible for the big companies to make something of As-Is: prices recovered somewhat and from 1934 fluctuated between 1 dollar and

$1.20 per barrel.[60] These, however, were well below 1920s levels. Cartelization, therefore, was only really effective when there were some real constraints on the numerous suppliers who were normally outside the cartel. The big companies could exert more control over product prices, at least in Europe, and this is discussed in Chapter 3.

Accusations of high profit levels undoubtedly have something in them, however, and throughout the period, but particularly early on, there is no doubt that profits flowed away from the oil producing countries. But developing countries were not necessarily naïve or hopelessly corrupted victims of oil company exploitation even if they received only a limited proportion of the profits. In Mexico oil company investment in the Diaz era was viewed, with relatively open eyes, as necessary for the country's modernization. The same was true of Venezuela and, at times, of Romania, while in Iran Riza Shah also had modernization plans based on oil revenues. Oil development had some beneficial side effects apart from the revenue which flowed to governments. In Mexico kerosene prices came down because *El Aguila* broke the previous monopoly, and in Iran and Iraq local prices were lower – although not much lower – than those charged elsewhere.[61] Oil exploitation necessitated substantial spending on infrastructure and gave rise to significant employment opportunities. In Venezuela oil workers' wages were relatively high, although labour conditions were often poor and the workers quickly became militant. Oil workers in Mexico, in the early period at least, were also relatively well paid and were not militant. The volume of employment in what is sometimes seen as a capital-intensive industry was potentially large. In Iran, APOC employed 27,000 local workers by 1930. The total then fell before rising to 46,000 in 1938. Again, APOC's wage rates were good by local standards and it also put substantial sums into housing, schools and hospitals – all strictly speaking an Iranian responsibility. And its proportion of local managers rose, although not as quickly as the Iranian government wished, to about 15 per cent of the total in 1938.[62]

Indigenization of more senior staff was a vexed issue to other producing governments as well, such as Romania. Slowness in promoting local managers highlights another and perhaps more fundamental criticism of oil companies: that they actually hampered indigenous development, for instance by appropriating opportunities which should have gone to local capital. But of course, the latter would not usually have done anything. For the most part it simply did not exist on a big enough scale: Lobitos in Peru, a minnow in the global stream of oil, was still larger than any other company in the country. And local 'entrepreneurs' were often more interested in what economists call 'rent-seeking' behaviour – that is, appropriating a surplus which already exists or may come into existence through the actions of others, but doing nothing to actually produce it. This was the case in much of Latin America and in Iran. In Mexico local shareholdings in *El Aguila*, after Weetman Pearson had floated the company and made some shares available, were limited, most of the non-Pearson shares being owned by Western investors. His main motive seems to have been the opportunity to give directorships to prominent locals – a voluntary distribution of rents (given that directorships were largely honorific as Pearson still firmly ran the show) to buy peace and quiet.[63]

Pearson's actions were hardly corrupt, since acquiring influence in this way is almost a *sine qua non* of business and political interaction, however undesirable in an ideal world. But bribery was certainly a weapon oil companies were prepared to use, to gain concessions or ensure legal cases went their way. Venezuela has already been mentioned. In Mexico in the 1930s, the local manager of *El Aguila* recounted how in one court case they had bribed two of the five Supreme Court judges, thinking that was sufficient since they had been assured that a third was so honest that he was unbribeable. The court found against the company, however, and 'they discovered that the honest man had been given an extra large bribe by the other side'. In spite of this salutary tale, in 1934 a minister was demanding a bribe which was so high that the company thought it would be cheaper to let the case go to the Supreme Court again, and this time bribe a majority of the judges.[64] As this suggests, the use – no doubt the companies would have said necessity – of bribery was related to the existence of cultures in which it was endemic. Unfortunately, this was the case in much of Latin America. But, as the manager's story also suggests, bribery was often not very effective. If it had been, Western oil companies would have paid even lower taxes and got their way more often. It was not very effective because (apart from the possibility of counter-bribery) political pressures could not be ignored even in countries with a culture of corruption.

These political pressures cut both ways. On the one hand, as noted above, a number of governments positively encouraged foreign investment. On the other hand, there was nationalism, which was growing in strength throughout the period and tended the other way. Furthermore, even when governments were economically liberal, there was often a desire to avoid one developed country gaining undue influence, and thus local governments would grant favours elsewhere. In Latin America, this tended to mean that the British – and in the case of Shell, the Dutch – were favoured. In the Middle East, it tended to mean that American companies were. Thus the rulers of Saudi Arabia, Kuwait and Qatar showed a distinct enthusiasm for American concessionaires. However, in the end consortium arrangements became dominant throughout the Middle East until after the Second World War. This meant in Kuwait and Qatar, as earlier in Iraq, joint exploitation involving American and British firms. Given the propensity of oil companies to form joint ventures, the lack of these in South America needs to be explained. One salient point here may be the early rivalry between Pearson and Shell, on the one hand, and Jersey Standard on the other, which established a continuing pattern. After the First World War the Mexican political situation was too delicate for a reorganization of interests. In Venezuela Shell's early position of advantage gave it no incentive to allow others in. Correspondingly, the perceived advantages of the country as a producer made Jersey Standard and Gulf, another American company, desperate to gain concessions.

What is clear is that one of the left's favourite stories, mentioned in Eric Ambler's novel with which the previous section began, is a myth. In the words of Andreas Zaleshoff, Ambler's Russian agent and one of his good guys, the overthrow of governments so that the new one would revise concessions in a company's favour was '... an old game. The big oil interests played it in Mexico for years. That's why there used to be so many revolutions.' The revolutions in Mexico have been the subject of many similar allegations, by no means all from the left – before the First World War the Americans accused Pearson of inciting revolution. As scholarly studies of the subject have made clear, there is no evidence for the allegations and plenty against. The oil companies' interests were in stability, not violent change.[65]

In these political cross-currents, what is also notable is the weakness of Western governments. In the view of another of Ambler's heroes, Kenton – a view which has been echoed by plenty of writers of more serious books – governments were the tools of big business. We might therefore expect them to represent it vigorously. On the face of it, the British government's usual tendency to retreat in the face of US pressure suggests that the US was willing to exert influence, even if Britain was not. But in fact America itself, after its early assaults against British influence in the aftermath of the First World War, and sporadically thereafter in the Middle East, did not consistently press oil company claims with any persistence. And by the time of the Mexican expropriation of 1938 Roosevelt was far too concerned about maintaining 'hemispheric solidarity' in the face of the growing Nazi threat to want to rock the boat by excessive protest – while his administration was not particularly keen on big business either.[66] Britain itself could be resistant to US pressure, its vigorous defence of Shell concessions in Venezuela after the First World War being the best example. But, as noted earlier, Britain was pushing at a half-open door here because Venezuela wanted foreign capital and it wanted it from non-American sources to preserve competition. In other circumstances, as in Romania on various occasions and after the Mexican expropriation, the Foreign Office protested and the USA was supportive or neutral – but in neither case was anything achieved.[67] As in the pre-war period, there were usually far too many other things at stake for the government to go out on a limb for oil company profits. In addition, by the inter-war period it was acutely aware of its military weakness. So recipients of diplomatic protests knew that there was not much Britain could do except threaten the future displeasure of the City of London – something of a sanction to governments which might need to raise money, but one with diminishing force. Once the brief period of post-war activism had calmed down, there was also growing concern in the Foreign Office that League of Nations' principles should be honoured. After the early 1920s, the one area where government firmness scored a major success was the renegotiation of the Iranian concession in the early 1930s. Major national interests were involved and there were no other parties likely to interfere. But the government was still careful to act with propriety by appealing to the League. In other cases involving APOC it was much less forceful with, as in previous oil disputes, different departments taking different views. Its failure to act vigorously drew bitter complaints from the APOC chairman in 1934.[68]

So oil companies, and Western governments, were often much more restrained in dealing with oil producing countries that the latter's later propaganda, or Popular Front views, might suggest. On the other hand, European and American companies treated peoples of other races and cultures in ways which, while predicable given the ideas and customs of the period, were clearly not welcome to the recipients. A relatively benign example of this was APOC. On the positive side, it invested substantial sums in welfare facilities. This may have been because the company was aware of the sensitive nature of its position as the sole operator of a gigantic and profitable concession, but nonetheless it was a fact. However, this was not matched by much engagement on a personal level with the Iranians. In 1930 Edward Elkington, APOC's general manager in Iran, observed that the 'average Britisher' had a 'peculiar disinclination to meet on a pleasant social basis with foreigners'. This was probably not just a product of racism. It may also have been caused by reserved British manners and, quite possibly, the inability of Iranians along with practically every other nation in the world at that time to take much interest in football (not then a world sport), let alone cricket.[69] But whatever the reasons it was an attitude which caused resentment. Americans do not seem to have been any better. Oil companies in Venezuela behaved badly irrespective of nationality. The volume of complaints against them, taken seriously by the authorities even though Venezuela was a country which was positive about Western investment, makes this irrefutable. Untreated pollution, dubiously legal or at least insensitive land seizures and poor living conditions for workers were all frequent issues.[70] In Mexico at the same time, George Philip thinks that the companies' attitudes did much to bring nationalization on themselves. In *El Aguila*'s case, the problem was not so much the local management but Shell, the part owners and managers. Deterding's shift to the right politically seems to have strengthened a natural high-handedness and led to an insensitive and non-conciliatory response to Mexican demands. This points up the skill with which Pearson, almost 30 years earlier, worked. Apart from floating *El Aguila* so that, at least nominally, it was a Mexican company, he and his wife lived for part of each year in Mexico City and played an active part in its social life.[71]

However reprehensible the companies' behaviour sometimes was, as economic actors they successfully built on the foundations laid before the First World War. British or part-British companies were active in many parts of the world. Royal Dutch/Shell was a giant, in the same league as Jersey Standard. Venezuelan production made up for the loss of its Russian and Mexican fields, while the group still had Royal Dutch's original Sumatran fields, Shell Transport and Trading's early discoveries in Borneo, its share of IPC production, Romania and substantial production in the USA. In the latter, Shell had grown rapidly in the 1920s on the back of discoveries in California and elsewhere. Its distribution arm in the US pioneered standardized filling stations and had a nationwide presence, whereas most US companies, after Standard Oil's break-up, were more localized. Also in the United States, Pearson interests had developed Amerada which became a successful production company, although the Pearson share in it was disposed of after World War Two. The wide spread of British trading companies and the extent of British capital export also meant there were a number of locally successful smaller British companies, such as Burmah, Lobitos in Peru and Phoenix in Romania which produced about 10 per cent of the country's oil. In European markets, Shell vied with Jersey Standard for leadership. Finally, APOC had made considerable progress but only had about half Shell's market share in Europe and did not have a presence in the USA. It was still primarily a crude producer and fuel oil supplier.[72]

3

Kerosene Lamps and Petrol Pumps: The British People and Oil 1900–39

USING OIL

'She wants Easy Starting' ran a BP advertisement of 1923 (she being an attractive girl, portrayed turning a starting handle on a car) 'and she gets it – she always runs on BP'.[1] As the advert implies, use of the car had already spread beyond work-related purposes, or the very rich, to the well-off middle classes who might use it for leisure. But while the spread of cars, and other internal-combustion engined vehicles, in the period was one key to increasing oil use, there were other important sources of increasing demand for oil.

The only significant use which was declining was that of the kerosene lamp, whose spread in the later nineteenth century had sparked the original oil boom. As gas and then electric lighting grew in popularity, the kerosene or paraffin lamp market shrank. Kerosene itself was also used in stoves, more common in pre-central heating days than now, and in types of internal combustion engine which powered tractors and other agricultural machinery, and fishing boats.[2] And kerosene for lamps was still in the inter-war years a big part of the oil companies' business in Africa and Asia. It was one rationale for the market-sharing agreements in those regions which preceded As-Is.

Oil was used as a fuel to raise steam as early as it was used for lighting. Where coal was expensive because of transport costs and oil was relatively cheap, it was an obvious substitute. Its advantages for the Royal Navy were discussed in Chapter 1 and as old coal-burning warships were scrapped its use became ubiquitous. For merchant shipping such bunker oil, as it was called, also had clear benefits over coal. It was cleaner, much easier to take on board, and produced around twice the amount of heat per kilo. However, it had a drawback. Even though fuel oil was usually a residual after distillation of the lighter fractions such as petrol, kerosene and so on, it was often more expensive than coal – not just per ton, but in terms of heat produced. The growth of cracking (see 'Scientists and practical men') meant that a higher proportion of the more valuable distillates, notably petrol, could be produced from a given amount of crude, so limiting the production of residual oil and pushing up its price. And with most refining still done near to the source of crude, fuel oil for use in Britain had to be expensively shipped in. Around half came this way in the late 1920s, the other half being the residue from crude refined in Britain. So fuel oil was not usually competitive with home-produced coal, which was still among the cheapest in the world.[3]

To a large extent this must account for the relative slowness with which British shipowners converted from coal to oil, although their tardiness has been lambasted by historians as indicating sloth and backwardness.[4] There were certainly shipping routes, notably to the Middle and Far East via the Suez Canal, and to Central America, where oil firing, at least on the homeward voyage, was likely to be economically rational because bunker oil could be bought cheaply in those areas. As a result some ships had dual firing, that is they could use coal or oil, depending on whether they were outbound or inbound.[5] Passenger liners, too, were likely to benefit from oil. Being faster, they needed much more power so the reduced weight of oil in relation to power produced was a major advantage. But the freighter trading between Britain and the continent, where British coal was available cheaply at ports, or to North America where cheap coal was also available, was not necessarily going to benefit from oil. When British shipowners did shift, they frequently preferred to switch to diesel rather than 'oil under the boilers'. Diesel engines used much less fuel, although their capital cost was higher. Where oil was relatively expensive because of transport costs, it was rational to use diesel propulsion which minimized its use. By 1939 the diesel-engined proportion of the British merchant fleet was, at just over 25 per cent, slightly higher than the world proportion. The oil companies themselves, whose modern fleets belie the notion that British shipping was universally backward, had many diesel ships. In 1931, 60 per cent of APOC's fleet was turbine or diesel, and 40 per cent of Shell's, as against only 25 per cent of Jersey Standard's. And their fleets were big. Shell in the 1920s owned 10 per cent of the world's tanker tonnage.[6]

Outside the world of shipping, oil firing made some progress in a few industrial applications where precise control of temperature was particularly important, with oil's cleanliness also being an advantage. A 1930 source lists bakeries, other food producing industries and glass and china. There were a variety of uses for other fractions of refined oil; as with fuel oil, most of the growth came after the First World War. Gas oil produced a high-quality gas used to enrich water-gas, which was produced by passing steam through heated coke, the residual by-product of the manufacture of coal gas – itself the normal type of gas in those pre-North Sea days. A less important oil usage, which utilized various grades of distillates, was for central heating systems. Domestic ones were still very scarce, and they and the more common institutional and commercial ones would as likely or not run on coal. Christopher Brunner, a strong advocate of oil, thought that 'Britain still counts her installations in hundreds where America counts in thousands'.[7]

Much more important was oil for lubrication. This was one of the earliest uses for mineral oil which, being cheaper, superseded the animal or vegetable oils which had previously been used. Apart from lubricating oil for industrial and agricultural machinery, railways and ship's engines, markets which expanded only slowly, there was a rapid growth in lubricating oil for motor vehicle engines, which needed far more, relative to their fuel use, than today.[8] Another vehicle related use was oil for bitumen. Certain crudes, especially the Central American ones, produced as a residue a much more viscous product than fuel oil, namely bitumen. Bitumen was in direct competition with coal-derived tar, and it is the latter which gives its name to the ubiquitous road-surfacing material popularly known as tarmac, even though nowadays that is formed from bitumen. Around 1930 tar was still the predominant material for 'tarmacking' roads, no doubt because it was cheaper, but the figures Brunner gives suggest that bitumen was making rapid inroads into the market, as for others such as waterproofing.[9]

It was newly tarmacked roads, of course, that carried the increasing number of motor vehicles which constituted the main source of increasing demand for oil, in the form of petrol or gasoline. The key was the development of the internal combustion engine, relying on an explosion inside the cylinder to provide power. The original form of this, dating back to the 1860s, was the gas engine – meaning then, of course, coal gas. But the gas engine was effectively immobile. From the 1870s through to the 1890s the petrol, or Otto-cycle, the hot-bulb engine and the diesel were all invented, and internal combustion engines could now use types of fuel which were easily portable. In the first a piston compresses a mixture of air and petrol, which is ignited to cause the explosion; in the diesel the piston compresses air alone, thus heating it enough to ignite the oil introduced into the cylinder at the top of the compression cycle. Diesels are more fuel efficient, but in their original form were slower running and thus needed to be much larger to achieve an equivalent power. Hot-bulb engines, often called semi-diesels, were a British invention. The compression and ignition are carried out in a separate chamber – the bulb – outside the cylinder. They can use virtually any liquid fuel. Fuel for diesels is usually more specialized but is a much less volatile fraction of the constituent crude than petrol – in fact the early diesels ran on a mixture of gas oil and residual fuel oil.[10]

Hot-bulb engines were popular up to the inter-war years, powering agricultural machinery, small fishing boats, trawlers and many stationary applications. But they were very heavy in relation to power produced and operated in only a narrow speed band, both of these limiting their use.[11] Until the late 1920s diesels were mainly used for ships, in which as has been mentioned they made steady progress. They were too heavy for either cars or commercial vehicles, which depended on the petrol engine. The development of the car, in 1900 only a puny infant, is too well known to need much discussion here. It required, of course, rapid change in all aspects of the vehicle including the engine. By 1910 Henry Ford was already developing the American mass production car industry. Britain, lacking a large market of consumers with a relatively high disposable income, was slower but by the early 1920s William Morris and Herbert Austin were building up their mass production empires. Their success helped to bring prices down so sales kept increasing. There were 53,000 private cars and 24,000 goods vehicles in 1910; about ten times as many of each in 1925; and almost two million and half a million respectively by 1938.[12]

Although as the 'Easy Starting' advertisement implies there was a growing middle-class leisure market, cars were most important for occupations which needed mobility such as doctors and commercial travellers, better known nowadays as reps. Cars were also part of the process which saw 'ribbon development' – the spread of middle-class housing along the roads radiating out from towns. However, this sort of development, leading in larger towns to the development of extensive suburbs, was even more the consequence of the motorbus. Buses had converted from horse to petrol before the First World War, and the inter-war years saw them at the peak of their importance, as they increasingly superseded trams.

The growth in motoring was helped by incremental change in engine design and petrol formulation. Harry Ricardo, who probably did more than anyone else to advance engine design in the inter-war years, estimated that power output for a given size of petrol engine doubled in the period. Equally important, by the late 1920s design changes meant that diesels could achieve much higher speeds and thus had a better power–weight ratio. Such high-speed diesels were suitable for commercial vehicles. Brunner dated the first diesel lorry on the road in England, a Mercedes Benz, to 1928. Tom Rolt, who was to become a well-known writer on industrial history, helped to test one of the first British-made diesel lorries in 1929. It was manufactured by Kerr Stuart, hitherto a steam locomotive maker (they also made some of the earliest diesel locomotives). The great weight of these early lorries – diesels still being heavier than petrol engines – meant that, in the days before power assistance, drivers developed mighty biceps and calf muscles to cope with the steering, brakes and clutch. Sadly Kerr Stuart went bankrupt in 1930 but the road-going diesel was here to stay. By 1939 most lorries and buses manufactured in Britain were diesel. At ten miles to the gallon, compared with six for the equivalent petrol vehicles, and with fuel which was then much cheaper than petrol, the diesel helped to adjust the economics of transport in favour of road over rail.[13]

SELLING OIL

When cycling along the Wye valley towards Tintern Abbey, an indignant reader wrote to *The Times* in the early 1920s, his anticipation of its sacred beauty was 'profanely broken in upon by a horrible yellow advertisement of [*sic*] petrol . . . quite close to the spot which Wordsworth's poetry had doubly hallowed'. The reader's anger was sparked by one of the weapons – in this case an iron roadside sign – in the war which the oil companies were then waging for market share. BP, APOC's marketing arm, had alone erected 12,500.[14]

In the early 1900s the then small petrol market had been dominated by Anglo-American, the British arm of Standard Oil, and later of its successor Jersey Standard, with its brand 'Pratts'.[15] Shell then aggressively won market share. After the war, it was BP's turn to be the aggressor. The result by the mid-1920s was market shares of around 30 per cent each for Shell and Anglo-American, and just over 20 per cent for BP. The big companies' collective share was subsequently eroded a bit, fluctuating between 70 per cent and 76 per cent throughout the 1930s.[16] Shell's share includes its sales, mainly to goods vehicle and bus operators, of 'Mex', its commercial-grade petrol, the name originating with Shell's 1919 takeover of Weetman Pearson's Anglo-Mexican. Smaller operators included Power, British owned but using Russian oil, and National Benzole which sold a mixture incorporating benzole or benzol, a coal by-product. Benzole mixtures were popular in hilly areas because of their anti-knock properties. Cleveland and Dominion were both small subsidiaries of American oil companies. More important in terms of its competitive input was Russian Oil Products (ROP), which chose the quirky trade name of Zip.[17]

The big companies had two strategies to enforce their grip on the market. One was building their brands. This was partly, of course, through advertising, both in the press and through roadside signs and the like. Anglo-American rebranded Pratts as Esso in 1935 and simultaneously mounted a big press campaign to reinforce the new name.[18] But branding also involved attempts to distinguish products as offering advantages which lesser brands could not. By the inter-war period petrol was sold in two main grades, 'No. 1' and 'No. 3'. No. 1 had a higher octane rating. Most commercial vehicles, which until the early 1930s were predominantly petrol-engined, used No. 3. Branding was less evident here but by 1930 there was a growing tendency towards it: Shell's 'Mex' was a good example. As pumps were established the companies could add to the mystique of their brands by putting seals on the tanks, initially for No. 1 and then increasingly with No. 3. This also had the practical advantage that underhand garage owners could not fill the tanks with cheaper fuel from rival companies. But the big companies went further by developing up-market brands, notionally more suitable for high-powered cars and motor-cycles, such as 'Shell Racing Spirit' and 'BP Plus'. Sales of these grades were small and one suspects they were developed as much to highlight the brands as for any other purpose.[19]

Apart from branding, big companies suppressed rivalry in a more practical way by attempting to dominate distribution through their control of petrol pumps. Until just after the First World War retail sales were usually in two-gallon cans and wholesale by the barrel. Anglo-American, and then Shell, established their position through their willingness to invest in numerous rail-served depots which distributed locally – initially kerosene, and then petrol too – by horse and cart. Petrol pumps were developed in North America by the Bowser Company, and by 1920 Anglo-American had introduced them in Britain. Their subsequent adoption was rapid since they offered big advantages to everyone. Distribution costs could be radically cut by pumping from a road tanker directly into a tank underneath the petrol pump. By 1925 Anglo-American and BP each controlled about 6,000 pumps, and Shell-Mex over 4,000. The disproportion between BP's large number of pumps and smaller market share no doubt partly reflects its eagerness to expand in the early 1920s, which led it to place its pumps particularly vigorously. Unlike Shell and Anglo-American, which had large markets in the US and Europe, Britain was initially BP's main market for petrol, since the African and Middle Eastern markets in which it had a presence were hardly large petrol buyers. But BP's qualitatively poorer position – since a lower throughput per pump would mean extra expenses per gallon sold – may also reflect poor commercial judgement on its part in the siting of pumps. If this was the case, it would not be the last time that BP showed itself less good at marketing than Shell or Jersey Standard. Significantly, its market share continued to slide and was only 14 per cent in 1930.[20]

The pattern in which new entrants temporarily fought for market share, followed by a period of stability, was well established. In the 1900s Shell had been the upstart, initially mainly in the kerosene market. By the mid-1900s European-wide agreements among the major players had stabilized prices, and it was at this time that British Petroleum, which at the time acted as Shell's marketing arm, was formed. There was a later price war in 1910 between Shell and Anglo-American.[21] When that calmed down the resultant increase was followed by a litany of complaints from consumers, including taxi drivers, about high prices. High prices again just after the war led to another spate of complaints about 'the petrol ring'.[22] The problem, however, was not just price-fixing but the post-war boom which pushed up all prices. APOC had now purchased BP (see Chapter 1, 'Oil in the First World War') and its aggressive drive for market share, combined with the decline in world oil prices, drove petrol prices down again. BP having established its place in the market, relative stability returned in the mid-1920s. Typically oligopolistic market conditions obtained, in which price-fixing kept up profits while branding was a relatively cheap way of deterring smaller interlopers.

By the 1920s the focus of price-fixing was the petrol market. Kerosene was still the subject of an agreement among the major companies, but price-fixing was less firmly maintained than with petrol, partly because it was difficult to police the myriad of small retailers who sold kerosene. Other products such as lubricating oil were less susceptible to branding and more liable to price competition from small importers.[23] Petrol was key to the oil companies for two reasons. It was an increasingly important part of their business: from a third of the oil market in 1921 it rose to 55 per cent of a much larger market in 1938.[24] Secondly it was relatively easy to police as apart from the dominance of the 'Combine' companies, as the big three became called, another set of actors were also concerned with enforcement – the retailers. They banded together in two bodies: the Motor Trade Association enforced resale price maintenance on their members, although they relied on the Combine not selling to those who broke the rules. The Motor Agents Association tried to restrict new entrants to the trade.[25] The retail dealers also prevented the oil companies setting up the 'solus' system of dealers tied to one company, with which we are familiar today and which was common on the Continent. Instead garages had pumps belonging to different companies. The companies usually sold them to dealers on hire purchase, so the initial expense of large-scale pump purchase was a barrier to new entrants in the wholesale market. At £100 a time – multiply by 40 or 50 for contemporary values – pumps were not cheap. However, it was possible for a company to finance a dealer who would buy out the original supplier and switch to the one now providing the finance, and thus it was possible for a new entrant to buy their way in slowly.[26]

The Combine's agreements on prices became formalized in 1926 when they agreed quotas. Establishing market shares in this way obviously helped to solidify price-fixing by reducing the temptation to surreptitiously undercut in order to increase sales.[27] They also introduced a rebate to all dealers who refused to sell non-Combine products. Whether or not the rebate was a factor, most of the non-Combine companies came into the agreement in 1928. In Britain, therefore, As-Is did no more than set the seal on a pre-existing arrangement. The Combine's cohesion was further cemented when in 1932 Shell-Mex and BP amalgamated their British and Irish distribution. Ostensibly this was to reduce distribution costs, which of course it did, but it obviously made effective competition yet more difficult.[28]

Competition did not go away entirely, though. The chief agent in the late 1920s was ROP, which aimed to sell at one (old) penny per gallon less than the Combine. Its purpose was, quite blatantly, to acquire foreign currency by disposing of Soviet oil. ROP actually lost money, which gives some credence to claims that price-fixing only took place to achieve a fair profit. ROP's financial problems, however, might have resulted not so much from its cut prices but its further role as a provider of employment to members of the Communist party. In 1929, 33 per cent of its employees were members, while in 1930 OGPU instructed the Soviet consul to purge 'outside elements' in ROP. ROP's market share peaked in 1931 and then fell rapidly as Russia scaled back oil exports, needing the oil for its own industrialization.[29] There were also some very small independent petrol distributors who mainly bought from brokers who imported into the wharves at Thames Haven. Brunner, who worked for Shell, complained bitterly in his 1930 book about these 'Pirates' who failed to give a national service. Insofar as the Combine company profits were low in the early 1930s while, as he points out, the wages and working conditions they offered were relatively good, he had a point. But of course he was really lamenting the inability of price-fixers to maintain complete control. Another brief price war occurred in 1931–2 when Standard of Indiana tried to win market share for its Cleveland brand, but this was bought out by Anglo-American in 1932.[30] After this stability seems to have returned to the British market. Shell-Mex and BP strengthened it still further when they bought the angelic twins, Dominion and Power, in 1934. The only company in the 1930s to rapidly increase market share was Regent, owned by Trinidad Leaseholds, but it was relatively small.[31]

The Combine companies' increasing cosiness from 1926 meant that they could wind down expensive and controversial forms of advertising. The Tintern cyclist was not the only one to object to roadside advertising, and the oil companies agreed in 1923 to remove their signs on country roads, but signs plastered all over garages remained. Patrick Abercrombie, a founder of the Council for the Preservation of Rural England, complained about 'tin petrol advertisements which do not scruple at the vilest degradation of the national flag' – he meant

BP signs carrying the Union Jack. BP's tradition of flying the flag, literally or metaphorically, was obviously an ingrained tendency since it had used this tactic in its pre-war and wartime disputes with Shell. It was, of course, hypocritical since its oil was no more British than was Shell's or Anglo-American's. Once again, by 1927 the companies were instructing garage owners to remove their signs. But by now petrol pumps were also becoming a target. Since retailers might have several from different companies, each painted in violent colours, forecourts presented a lurid sight. As a result, in 1927 BP decided to paint its pumps the familiar green.[32] (The company colours of green and yellow had actually been devised earlier by J. E. Taylor and Edmond Paix of the Paris office, 'one spring day after a lunch in the country'.)[33] In other cases, because of press campaigns following Abercrombie's lead, dealers painted all their pumps in one colour. According to Brunner the difficulty of maintaining a distinctive colour scheme led to the companies adopting distinctive glass globes for their pumps – the globe, in which the petrol could be seen as it flowed on its way to a car's tank, being an integral part of early pump design. BP's Scottish shale oil operation, which sold under the Scotch brand, apparently had a thistle-shaped globe.[34]

The oil companies used their abandonment of garish advertising to claim an affinity to nature and beauty, but of course it was also a cost-reducing pay off resulting from the decline in competition. Oil companies as 'green' was also a theme of the highly thought-of Shell advertisements and publicity material of the 1930s – the posters of rural Britain by well-known artists such as John Nash, and the Shell County Guides which were started by John Betjeman in 1934. BP, on the other hand, seems to have retained its fondness for portraying attractive females in ambiguous advertisements. A 1938 magazine advertisement shows a sophisticated woman sitting in a high-powered car with two well-dressed men standing by it. One remarks to the other, 'She'll never say "No" on "BP" Ethyl!'.[35]

WORKING IN OIL

Both the left and the right of the political spectrum have often portrayed capitalism as a ruthless Darwinian struggle for survival in the jungle of competition, this process being bad or good depending on one's point of view. In reality, British capitalism for much of the twentieth century has been more like a peaceful paddock in which large herbivores (the companies) have grazed their patches, not making trouble so long as rivals kept off. Established oil companies, with a combination of sole or joint concessions and cartelization, were in a particularly good position to utilize this gentlemanly system to make substantial profits, and as has been seen they usually did so apart from a difficult period in the early 1930s. High profits meant that some of the surplus could accrue to the workforce and there were a number of factors, within oil companies and other big employers, which strengthened this tendency. Good conditions of service would reduce employee turnover which had obvious practical advantages. In a less definable way, such conditions might increase 'team spirit'. There was also a growing conception that, quite simply, reputable companies treated employees well. Whatever factors were at work, the period up to 1939 saw a proliferation of benefits: company sports grounds and social clubs went alongside more substantial benefits such as pensions.[36]

Shell's benefits were particularly lavish, as befitted a company which had built up much of its business before the war when prices were lower. Shell Transport and Trading, the British arm, had accumulated a provident fund of £25 million to pay pensions and other benefits – around one billion pounds in today's money. During the depression it paid out £10 million of this to redundant employees at a time when there was no statutory redundancy pay. It had already, in 1921, established a sports and social club, the Lensbury Club, at Teddington, with 'pleasant terraces, sports courts and pitches . . . bars, dining rooms and overnight accommodation.[37] Another form of conspicuous consumption was the impressive head office. Each of the big two companies headquartered in Britain felt the need for one. The Lutyens designed Britannic House, in Finsbury Circus, was built for APOC in the mid-1920s, crossing Vanbrugh-style monumentalism with a French Renaissance roof. The enormous Shell-Mex House, built on the Embankment for Shell's marketing arm in the early 1930s, was by contrast an example of modernism.

For APOC this relative indulgence towards staff extended to their work, at least for those in Britannic House. APOC had never been able to get its administration right. The whole operation in Persia was notoriously inefficient in the early days, with a layer of incompetent management in London superimposed on top. Cadman, the managing director and later chairman after Greenway, reformed things quite effectively in the 1920s. But slackness crept back. By 1947 a further efficiency drive involving management consultants led to an hilarious report on one department at head office. The clerical staff spent their time from arrival at 9.15 until 10.00 'titivating' and then relaxed for coffee until 10.30. Some work was then carried out until 11.45 when the first lunchers' departures signalled a general relaxation until 2.15 when the last lunchers returned. An hour of work was followed by an hour for tea and relaxation until a final brief spurt accompanied the arrival of the afternoon mail.[38]

Expatriate staff posed different problems. Plenty of young middle-class male Britons had been accustomed to go abroad, to serve in the Indian army or colonial civil service, or to work in British trading, railway and mining companies overseas. So recruiting staff for overseas service was not a novel problem. But oil companies in some overseas countries might work on a large scale, and this particularly applied to APOC whose long pipelines, huge Abadan refinery and need to provide infrastructural services meant that it required a large supervisory staff in Iran. It has been suggested that in such large expatriate communities the creators felt the need to shore up the community's sense of 'oneness', achieving this partly by a proliferation of clubs, dress codes, charity work and so forth. This, in turn, was part of a felt need to 'create' Empire. In order to achieve this fully, it was important that the communities should include women – preferably married – as well as men.[39]

The development of APOC's expatriate community exhibits some of these tendencies. Persia, or Iran as it became, was not of course in the Empire but it was generally thought to lie within Britain's sphere of influence, while APOC's directors were imperially minded. On the other hand, as indicated earlier (see Chapter 2, 'Making money, making friends, making enemies'), APOC was becoming increasingly concerned in the 1930s about maintaining good relations with Iran, one ingredient of which was treating Iranians with respect and promoting them to managerial positions.[40] So the management did not want to promote 'Empire' too aggressively. In the early days before 1914, it had stated firmly that employees 'must not consider the question of marriage during the earlier stages of the Company's work . . .', no doubt both for practical reasons, conditions in Persia still being primitive, and because it was thought wives might be a distraction. As Abadan developed and the number of expatriate workers grew, other practical problems arose which tended in the other direction: 'visiting the "dentist"' in Basra, the standard remedy for unmarried men, was becoming too common and the company attitude towards marriage changed. As a manager said in 1924 'there is very great difficulty in keeping good men; the real trouble arises out of the scarcity of women'. More wives on site would alleviate the need for 'dental treatment'.[41]

To achieve this, APOC made conditions as comfortable as possible, meaning the employment of numerous servants. Part of this reflected customary expectations at a time when middle-class families in Britain still routinely employed servants. But of course attempts to solve one problem led to others, at least as perceived by senior management. The expense of servants worried the company which saw it as driving up staff salary expectations. As this expense was thought to be partly caused by staff competitiveness in entertaining each other, one solution was to encourage wives to cook. This had the added advantage that it discouraged them from 'messing at the Restaurant' where they were 'a damned nuisance outside their normal surroundings'.[42] So the conventional attitude of the period to female work, which restricted most women to typing or, for managerial wives, no paid work at all, meant that APOC's management, having got wives out to Iran, then bemoaned the fact that they had too little to do.

In practice, of course, wives often had plenty to do even if it was not paid work. Many oil company personnel were on the sales side and duties for senior managers included socializing. Thus Shell's 'up-country' manager in inter-war China, based in Shanghai, had an indoor staff of seven which his wife would have to supervise, while most evenings there were social functions involving them both. Moving home with its accompanying disruption was another necessity – as indeed it has remained ever since for expatriates. The average stay for Shell personnel was three years, and one wife remembered four homes in two years. Moves within Shell's far-flung empire might involve long sea voyages.[43]

Benefits such as those outlined earlier were, in the oil companies' British operations, largely for staff rather than manual workers. This was partly because manual employment, although substantial in total, was scattered. Much of it was in numerous small depots, which had a couple of storekeepers and a few drivers. Because refining in Britain was on a small scale, employment in refineries before the Second World War was limited. Employment in the production side of the petroleum industry actually fell between the 1920s and the 1930s, because of the run-down of the Scottish shale industry, and was only just over 4,000 in 1935.[44]

SCIENTISTS AND PRACTICAL MEN

In its early days the oil industry was dependent mainly on practical knowledge and rule of thumb. By the 1920s, however, the big oil companies were becoming leaders in the application of science to industrial problems. The all-important first step, the discovery of oil, illustrates this trajectory. The early discoveries were made simply by following up obvious clues. Thus Burmah Oil drilled where there was a long established local industry: the Burmese had dug wells by hand, into which the oil seeped and was raised by rope and bucket. In Persia George Reynolds, APOC's invaluable first supervisor and a self-taught geologist, found the rocks at Masjid I-Suleiman, where the company was to make its find, 'saturated with oil'. As time went by it was realized that oil was likely to be trapped in sedimentary rocks under impermeable anticlines – dome-like structures of rock – and companies took on professional geologists. One classic anticline, visible on the surface, was Signal Hill in California. In 1921 the Hill was in the process of being developed for housing as a suburb of Long Beach when Shell, whose geologists had led it there, struck oil. Acre for acre Signal Hill became the most productive oil field in the world, although its small area meant its total yield was not on a Middle Eastern scale.[45]

Oil-trapping anticlines, however, might be underneath other rocks and completely hidden from view – as was often the case in the Middle East. And since, by definition, completely impermeable rock does not allow seepages, these might not be evident or might appear miles from the actual reservoir. So improved understanding and technologies became vital for major discoveries. Various techniques were developed in the 1920s for mapping underground rock structures, leading to the science of geophysics. One American oilman at the time thought that Shell was ahead of American companies scientifically, and APOC seems also to have been reasonably well advanced. (Not surprisingly given their scientific prowess, the Germans pioneered some of the techniques during and just after the First World War. But their scope for using them was limited.)[46]

APOC also became expert in maximizing the oil producing capacity of a field. Such effective conservation – the word then had this relatively narrow connotation – was desired by all big oil companies, and was strengthened by the periodic scares about the imminent depletion of world oil reserves. However, in the United States where most oil was still produced conservation was a Holy Grail, sought for but never reached. By the American 'rule of capture', anyone owning surface land had the right to any sub-surface oil they could find, wherever that came from. Thus oil discoveries in the United States were usually accompanied by the frantic purchase, sub-division and resale of the overlying territory, followed by over-drilling which frequently led to the premature reduction of gas pressure and other deleterious consequences which lessened the field's capacity to produce. Signal Hill, for instance, had 270 wells by 1923 on a few hundred acres. Shell, the biggest operator, had 78 in order to maximize its own 'capture' of oil. Because of lobbying by independent oil drillers who preferred a free-for-all, it was not until the 1930s that the USA introduced some measures of control. Middle Eastern fields, by contrast, were developed by one company or consortium – and APOC was the first. From the early 1920s on, it consciously developed its fields – Masjid I-Suleiman and later others – as one unit, a technique known as unitization. In 1928 an American geologist thought that the Masjid field was 'probably the most efficiently developed oil pool in the world'.[47]

In spite of the big companies' use of best practice techniques, however, science had its limits and sometimes the practical man still won. It was Frank Holmes, the 'rover in the world of oil' – a mining engineer but one whose expertise was in gold and tin, not oil – who was convinced that the western littoral of the Persian Gulf would yield oil, and it was APOC's and Shell's trained geologists who were sceptical.

The geologists' task was to identify where oil was most likely to be found, but proving it was there, and subsequently exploiting it, depended on drilling. The old percussion method of drilling was gradually superseded by rotary drilling. This was not new – it seems to have been first used to drill for oil around 1900 – but adoption was slow both in the United States and elsewhere. For APOC, the problems were partly expertise and training, and partly that in a high-pressure field such as Masjid I-Suleiman rotary drilling posed more risk of blow-outs. From the early 1920s APOC started training British staff – the company history refers cryptically to the 'growing social problems' of American drillers and less cryptically to their cost. Rotary drilling, meanwhile, became safer because of the use of mud. This seems anything but scientific but in fact oilwell mud quickly became a specialized product and the subject of research, for instance in Shell's US laboratory in California. The mud was continuously pumped down the drill-pipe and back up through the borehole, lubricating the drill bit and lifting out rock cuttings. In high-pressure reservoirs, heavy mud minimized the risk of blow-outs.[48] By 1930 rotary drilling was well established in Persia. A wartime episode suggests, however, that Anglo-Iranian, as APOC had become, may have suffered from its lack of experience of drilling production wells outside the Middle East. When its British field at Eakring was expanded during the war American drillers, and equipment, were brought in. The American rigs were lighter and could therefore be shifted more quickly to a new location, while the crews worked much faster due to simplified procedures. AIOC's deep drilling in Persia accustomed it to heavy duty equipment, and with that may have gone some hidebound practices. It seems likely that, if Shell had developed the Eakring field, it would have known better how to do it. Shell's worldwide experience gave it more exposure to different types of good practice and the company had organized itself from early on to disseminate such practices widely.[49]

Early oil refineries were as primitive as early exploration and drilling techniques. Refining was simply by distillation (see Chapter 1) and refineries were very small scale. Even when refinery technique developed and became more scientific, most refining was carried out close to the oilfields. Tankers were still the size of normal cargo ships, rather than the giants they became in the 1950s and beyond, and could unload at ports rather than needing offshore moorings. So most oil was imported as 'product' – kerosene, petrol and so on – rather than in crude form, and refineries in Britain remained small throughout this period. As demand developed, however, the base-load refineries near the oilfields became much larger and were also transformed technically. In 1913 thermal cracking had been developed by Standard of Indiana, one of Standard Oil's successor companies, and this was to prove the way ahead. By heating the feedstock to extreme temperatures and pressures, its molecular structure could be altered and much higher quantities of the desired products, in particular petrol, could be produced.[50]

The development of Abadan illustrates the changes. By the early 1920s it was a large but disastrous piece of engineering, described by a manager in 1923 as a 'crippled plant'. Rushed initial construction, bad management and the expediencies necessary during the war when it was a base for British troops were all responsible. Through the 1920s it was extensively modernized, although the first thermal cracking units were only ordered in 1929, APOC having experimented with them at its small Welsh refinery at Llandarcy from 1926.[51] Their relatively late adoption may owe itself to APOC's strength in fuel oil production and relatively smaller need, compared to American companies, for petrol. By the 1930s Abadan was modern and efficient as well as being the largest refinery in the world. Shell, as befitted its worldwide scale, had a number of large refineries, for instance in Borneo, Curacao where it refined Venezuelan oil, and the USA. Like APOC, its refineries in the UK were relatively small; they included Stanlow and Shellhaven, both of which expanded hugely after 1945.

The increasing complexity of oil exploration and refining meant that large oil companies needed to spend more on research. But their size and profitability were also factors. At a time when many British firms lagged in their use of scientific research, Shell and APOC could afford large research budgets. Early on Shell was concerned about 'knock', the premature detonation of fuel in the cylinder. (Many readers will be unfamiliar with knock, or 'pinking' as it was sometimes called, but it was once very common with low octane-rating petrol. It manifested itself as a high-pitched ringing sound, reducing power and resulting in carbon deposits in the cylinder head. I remember a mid-1960s continental holiday with a friend when our Standard Eight's already low power output was further reduced by poor petrol in Yugoslavia, which led to constant pinking.) Harry Ricardo had cooperated with Shell during the war on the problem and subsequently received a large research contract from them which helped in the establishment of his research consultancy – still a leading firm in the field. Shell also had its own large laboratories in California and ones in Holland and London, and from 1928 the company expanded its research effort into chemicals. It also developed liquefied petroleum gas (LPG) and in 1931 added the world's first LPG carrier to its tanker fleet.[52] APOC was more focused on research into oil extraction and refining. It had set up its first laboratory in Sunbury-on-Thames in 1917, where a mansion and 2.5 acres were purchased for £950, and a major extension was made in 1921. Both companies continued research into octane ratings. Even in the mid-1930s aviation spirit only rated 87 octane – well below today's standard rating for petrol for cars. Both Shell and APOC were leaders in the field, Shell being the first to synthesize iso-octane, an essential component of high octane aviation spirit. It and APOC (by then AIOC) developed the alkylation method for its manufacture virtually simultaneously in 1936. Other big oil companies were also working in the field and in 1939 the Alkylation Agreement pooled their research efforts. The process was to become important in the Second World War.[53]

BRITAIN'S OWN OIL

Britain's own oil production actually started back in the mid-nineteenth century and fittingly enough, given the later harvest of the North Sea, Scotland was the main location of this earlier industry which extracted oil from oil shale. Oil shale contains kerogen, and one variety of this substance is a precursor of oil, formed of similar source material but less 'cooked' and not liquefied. The shale was mined like coal and heated in retorts to extract the oil, which was then refined in the ordinary way. It was a labour and energy intensive undertaking. The industry reached a fair size in the Almond valley to the west of Edinburgh, and had outliers in other parts of Scotland and at Kimmeridge, in Dorset. With improved technology, it managed to compete against imported oil into the twentieth century, but by 1913 it only had 14 per cent of the – still small – British oil market. After the First World War APOC took over the Scottish industry. The government seems to have leaned on it to do so, although the details from published sources are unclear. By the mid-1920s the industry was uneconomic. Duty on imported petrol and diesel (see below) gave it a reprieve by effectively raising the price of product in Britain. It staggered on, making a small contribution to Britain's oil supply, until 1962 when the abolition of the import duty led to its closure.[54]

Even before the war, with shale oil becoming increasingly marginal economically, some people began to wonder whether Britain might possess its own oil fields. The potential attractions of making a discovery were heightened by wartime patriotism and high wartime prices. Not surprisingly, it was Weetman Pearson who was the first to explore in a serious way. There were no discoveries, although he continued to be hopeful, until in 1918 the government in its wartime interventionist mode made a grant of one million pounds, an enormous sum. Oil was found at Hardstoft in Derbyshire in May 1919, but by then the war was over. No more discoveries were made, and the grant was exhausted by 1922.[55]

In the same year the government, its interventionist urges spent, declared itself unwilling to legislate on the question of petroleum rights. With oil prices falling, this deterred further exploration as operators had to deal with numerous private landlords over royalties. However, in 1934 the Petroleum Production Act, which vested petroleum rights in the Crown and prohibited drilling without government licence, was passed. The Act was sensible, as it encouraged exploration but prevented wildcat drilling as occurred in America.[56]

Exploration was also encouraged by the duty on imported petrol which had been instituted in 1928, the earlier duty levied before the war having lapsed in 1920. The new rate was 4d a gallon, a substantial proportion of the pump price of around one shilling and sixpence after tax. It was raised to 6d and then 8d in 1931 to help alleviate the government's financial difficulties during the depression. A final pre-war increase in 1938 took the duty to 9d. Diesel fuel for road vehicles had been brought into the net in 1935, presumably because of the rapid increase in diesel lorries and buses. Since these were customs rather than excise duties, petrol and diesel produced from indigenous oil were not liable to them.[57] Extensive exploration took place from the mid-1930s, mainly by Anglo-Iranian (AIOC), as APOC had become, and also by Jersey Standard through its British subsidiary Anglo-American and Gulf, another American company. AIOC's exploration company, both here and in other parts of the world, was called after the company's progenitor, William D'Arcy. An attractive story has Sir John Cadman, AIOC's chairman, being persuaded to explore for oil in Britain by a scramble over the outcropping bituminous sands at Lulworth Cove in Dorset, near to the Kimmeridge oil shale. Attempting to rise from a rock on which he was sitting, he found his trousers stuck to the softened bitumen. In fact, Cadman seems to have been persuaded of Britain's exploration potential earlier and it was partly down to his lobbying that the 1934 Act was passed. The company took over the Hardstoft well and produced oil from it in August 1938, then started production at a very small field at Formby in Lancashire and at a field near Eakring in Nottinghamshire in 1939. It seems, therefore, that Hardstoft was both the first discovery and the first producing oilfield.[58] The Isle of Purbeck in Dorset, where Cadman lost his trousers, was to become the site of Britain's biggest onshore field but it was not discovered until much later. Pre-war exploration extended to Scotland but with no significant results. Anglo-American operated one very small field and D'Arcy Exploration made a small gas discovery, both in Midlothian.[59]

The duty on imported petrol also encouraged managers at Imperial Chemical Industries (ICI), then the leading British chemical firm, to invest in one of the great hopes of inter-war scientific research – oil from coal. The leading process was hydrogenation, which produced a high-grade petrol. It became a practical proposition in the late 1920s and it was then that ICI became seriously interested. A 'Hydrogenation Cartel' as it was usually termed was formed in 1931 between IG Farben, the German chemical combine, Jersey Standard, and ICI. APOC wisely steered clear of the project and Shell only had a peripheral interest. ICI used an existing ammonia plant – another great hope which had turned out less than successfully – at their Billingham complex on Teesside as a basis for their hydrogenation plant. It started production in 1936 and was producing 150,000 tons of petrol a year by 1938.[60]

It was not, however, really a success. Lignite or brown coal, common in Germany but not in Britain, was more suitable than bituminous coal so the plant ended up using creosote, a coal by-product, as its feedstock. Even with the help of the duty, which raised the price of imported petrol and therefore enabled ICI to sell its product at a higher price, the firm made a negligible return on its investment of four million pounds. The government, meanwhile, decided that national security was not best served by building further oil from coal plants. Investigating the alternative domestic sources of fuel from the national security angle had been the main remit of the Falmouth Committee of 1937. It concluded that shale oil was never going to be of more than marginal importance, while oil from coal was far too expensive. In wartime, cost *per se* did not matter so much. But the process was expensive because it consumed a vast quantity of resources, and it made even less sense to use these in wartime when there were many alternative uses. The committee estimated that a Billingham sized plant cost the same as building tankers which could carry twelve times the amount of fuel to Britain annually as Billingham's production. The plants would also, of course, be vulnerable to bombing.[61]

One final source of indigenous liquid fuel was a coal by-product, benzole or benzol. Benzole was distinct from the petrol produced by hydrogenation, but it could be used as a 'motor spirit', to use contemporary terminology, although as such it was not very satisfactory. It was, however, useful as a petrol additive and was particularly prized for its anti-knock qualities (see 'Scientists and practical men' above). Benzole was a by-product of coke manufacture, coke itself being produced for iron and steel making and as a by-product of carbonizing coal to produce gas. In the latter case, the coke was valuable as a feedstock for supplementary gas production and therefore little benzole was produced, but the iron and steel industry was not interested in producing more gas and so benzole was worth exploiting in its own right. The industry's main companies had combined to finance a petrol manufacturer and retailer, National Benzole, which used APOC's petrol and added benzole. Some other petrol companies also sold a benzole mixture. National Benzole had a steady business throughout the inter-war period, with its market share for petrol rising from around 6 per cent in the late 1920s to 10 per cent in the late 1930s. However, like the various types of indigenous oil, benzole was useful but essentially marginal to the overall supply situation.[62]

PREPARING FOR WAR

Since before 1914 British policy towards oil had been concerned with national defence, the investment in APOC being the prime example of this. After the war, however, it becomes difficult to separate out considerations of national defence from more general foreign policy imperatives. Following the chaotic but brief Lloyd George period of activism (see Chapter 2, 'Governments and oil companies: unfinished business'), various imperatives came to the fore. They interacted with more specific oil-related questions to produce oil policy.

One imperative discussed in Chapter 2 was the exercising of influence, through political control or informally, in the Middle East. From the 1870s the main aim had been to safeguard the Suez Canal, and this remained a major commitment. Maintaining a degree of British influence in the Persian Gulf area, on the western flank of the Indian Empire and the site of APOC's activities, was another concern. But Britain did not attempt to cling on to political control of Iraq, the largest League of Nations mandate and the region's second biggest oil producer. An important reason for this was that Britain took the League seriously. No one wanted another world war, and to many the League was the best means of preventing that eventuality. In 1926 a Foreign Office memorandum – secret, so it was not manipulated for public consumption – put the League's Covenant first among Britain's commitments.[63] Maintaining influence in the Middle East was, therefore, not an absolute but subject to other policy considerations.

In both the Middle East and elsewhere, one other imperative was to remain on good terms with the USA. This was not because Britain saw that country as a potential ally. Following the USA's rapid post-war slide into isolationism, military alliance with it seemed unlikely. Rather, it was thought, the US needed to be conciliated because of its economic power, its political dominance in the Americas and its considerable influence in the Pacific and Asia. Britain, still possessing a worldwide Empire, had no means to guard that Empire against every conceivable threat. Keeping on good terms with a country which had the potential to project its power worldwide, and had a navy equal to Britain's own, was common sense. As was shown in Chapter 2, Britain consistently conciliated the US when oil was a potential subject for dispute. One subject for potential dispute was the British policy of discouraging foreign exploitation of oil, in the Empire and in Britain itself. The latter prohibition was lifted by the Petroleum Act of 1934 (see 'Britain's own oil') while in 1938 Britain formally lifted the policy throughout the Empire – although in practice American companies were already active in Kuwait and Bahrain.

These were the underlying foreign policy concerns which, in the inter-war period, helped to shape policy towards oil – such as it was, for it would be wrong to see oil as looming particularly large in the government's mind for most of the time. From the early 1930s, however, specific threats started to appear. They demanded concrete plans, both for oil and for many other aspects of foreign policy and national defence. In 1931 Japan invaded Manchuria and this provided the first warning that 1920s assumptions that war was obsolete were over-optimistic. Fairly soon the threat of a rearming and militantly nationalistic Germany came to be seen – rightly – as the most critical one. But the Japanese threat had not gone away and by the late 1930s Italy, too, was a potential menace, with implications for the tanker route to Britain from the Persian Gulf via the Suez Canal and the Mediterranean.

Britain's main oil planning agency for the eventuality of war was the Oil Board, established in 1925 as a sub-committee of the Committee of Imperial Defence. Until the late 1930s shortage of funding held back the realization of the Board's plans, but subsequently they had a more realistic chance of fulfilment as the government released more money. In the light of the threats outlined above, there were numerous possible scenarios. The Board's planning focused partly on identifying potential sources of supply, and partly on practical problems of tankerage, storage and so on. It also considered the implications of new technology such as oil from coal.[64]

The only areas of supply which could be deemed completely reliable politically were those in the Empire. But Empire production was relatively small. Initially it mainly comprised production in Burma and Trinidad (Canada was then a very small producer), although Bahrain, where the American consortium Caltex was the concessionaire, was by 1939 making a growing contribution. Bahrain was only under indirect political control but was effectively dependent on Britain. However, the planners also put heavy reliance on Iran and, increasingly, Iraq as its oil production built up. The concessionaires were British or included substantial British interests, while the governments were neutral and, perhaps more important, were weak and hence susceptible to pressure. So they could be regarded as fairly reliable suppliers. Iraq's output, which because of the need to build pipelines had only come on stream in 1934, was increasing rapidly in the late 1930s. Some was destined for France, but a large proportion was effectively under British control. Furthermore, from the British point of view Iraq had the advantage over Iran that one section of the Iraqi pipeline ended at Haifa, on the Mediterranean. Haifa was in Palestine, then a British mandate, and the location obviated the need for the long voyage from the Persian Gulf through Suez. Important though Middle Eastern oil was, however, with Iran contributing around 20 per cent of Britain's supply in the late 1930s, by far the biggest contributor was Venezuela with 40 per cent. Much of this was refined in the Dutch West Indies but was Venezuelan in origin. Shell produced a large proportion of Venezuelan output and by the 1930s the British government's earlier concerns over Shell's political reliability had been more or less forgotten.[65]

One important conclusion to which the Oil Board came in 1937 was mentioned in 'Britain's own oil' – the Falmouth committee's recommendation that oil from coal was not a sensible policy for Britain to follow on any scale. The recommendation was unquestionably correct but, since it confirmed that Britain would be heavily dependent on imported oil, it threw into relief the fact that tankers would be needed to shift these imports. Calculations here were complicated by one other important development. In 1935 the USA had passed a Neutrality Act. This was not instigated by Franklin Roosevelt, the President, but resulted from the isolationism of much of Congress. The Act forbade the export of US munitions to belligerents in time of war. It became reasonably clear that oil was not covered by the Act, but doubts remained. They were not assuaged when the Act was modified in 1937. It now seemed clear that items like oil could be sold, but only on a 'cash and carry' basis – that is not on credit.[66] The Oil Board cautiously assumed, even so, that US oil might not be available at all. The worst case scenario, then, was the denial of US oil and the closure of the Mediterranean because Italy was hostile, resulting in Persian Gulf oil having to be hauled round the Cape. Even on these assumptions, the Board estimated that there would be almost enough tankers available to meet British wartime requirements. Large tanker fleets were owned by European countries which were likely to remain friendly neutrals, notably Norway, and a number of tankers could be used which were currently laid up idle. To make up the small gap foreseen, the government agreed to buy second-hand tankers, but not much was achieved before war broke out. Almost as important as tankers was storage in Britain. Here good progress was made in purchasing oil stocks – the Navy, for example, stocked around six months worth of estimated wartime consumption by the late 1930s. But the siting and protection of oil tanks against air attacks was less satisfactory. From 1936 the government constructed substantial facilities in the west of the country, considered then to be much less vulnerable to air attack. And the Navy's new tanks were very well protected, although others were less so. But the oil companies themselves, while reluctantly agreeing to build new capacity, constructed most of it where it suited them – in the east, notably the Thames estuary.[67]

So by 1939 the Oil Board had achieved a fair amount, both in planning and in concrete achievements, although there were still gaps. Provision of greater facilities for aviation fuel manufacture was also under way. Both this and the value of the other work which had been done will be discussed in the next chapter. How far was Britain's wider foreign policy effective in terms of its impact on wartime oil supply?

Brian McBeth has argued that Britain had a policy of encouraging Middle Eastern oil development but that this was less than successful and, as a result, Britain was over-dependent on Venezuelan oil on the eve of the Second World War. But this argument over-exaggerates the importance attached to Middle Eastern oil. It was only immediately after the First World War that it was seen as the salvation of Britain's oil supply problems. Subsequent to that, although some hope was placed on Empire oil development, more was put on simple diversity of supply. McBeth suggests that the oil companies' restrictive arrangements, in the Red Line Agreement and As-Is, reduced Middle Eastern production but the critical element here was simply the slow economic growth of the inter-war period. If the market had grown faster, so would have oil production.[68] As for Venezuelan output, so far from it being a problem for British security, it was a huge bonus because it diversified supply. And Venezuela was nearer to Britain than either of the two Gulfs – the Mexican or the Persian.

It was also hoped to encourage diversity of supply by conciliating the US and US oil companies. The Neutrality legislation suggests that this was a failure. But just after the war started, Roosevelt persuaded Congress to lift many of the Neutrality Act's restrictions.[69] And early in 1941 the United States ensured Britain a virtually limitless supply of oil, as well as munitions, through Lend-Lease. In retrospect, it would hardly have been sensible for Britain to have antagonized the United States in the inter-war period by insisting on keeping American companies out of the Middle East. For during the war American oil was even more critical than Middle Eastern oil to the Allied war effort.

4

Britain, Oil and the Second World War

THE EARLY YEARS

On 29 July 1940 Flight-Lieutenant Bill Keighley was piloting a Bristol Blenheim, a medium bomber and one of four engaged on a daylight raid over Germany. His target was oil – in this case refineries at Hamburg. But as so often, with no cloud to protect the vulnerable Blenheim, Keighley decided to divert the attack to his secondary target, an airfield. And as also happened all too frequently, he was shot down, although fortunately he survived to spend five years as a prisoner of war. The hopelessness of these early air attacks was summed up by a photographic intelligence report on the Mannheim Rhenona Oil Works in June 1940: 'no evidence of damage is visible'.[1]

An even more hopeless venture in the same year had been a lunatic attempt to take barges up the Danube and sink them in a narrow stretch called the Iron Gates, thus blocking the river which was a major route for oil from Romania to Germany. Security being 'appallingly bad', the expedition was discovered by the Romanians, who fortunately did not make too much of it as they wanted to avoid German interference.[2]

Yet in spite of such failures, pressure on Germany's oil supplies was one of the main elements of Allied strategy until the end of 1940. Initially the primary instrument was blockade, although increasingly bombing and other military action was used. At first strategy was formed jointly by the British and French; after the fall of France it was predominantly British. As the example above shows, the instruments for carrying out the strategy were defective. But the strategy itself was not altogether stupid. There were cogent reasons for thinking that Germany would be vulnerable to pressure on key areas of her economy, particularly oil supplies.

These reasons were simple. Germany had very little oil itself and, as not much was likely to get through by sea because of blockade, access to only a small proportion of world supplies. We saw in Chapter 1 how, in the First World War, Germany's lack of oil probably only had a limited effect on her war effort. But there were good reasons for assuming that the situation was now different. While coal was still the main source of industrial power in Germany, oil was much more critical than it had been to waging war. Air forces, adjuncts to the other armed services in the First World War, were now as important. German's navy was oil-fuelled, whereas in 1914, apart from diesel-engined submarines, it still used coal. And most important, petroleum was now integral to land warfare. German infantry divisions still relied substantially on horse transport. But tanks, of limited importance even in 1918, were now recognized as vital. To keep up with them substantial portions of the infantry, artillery and supply services also needed to be mechanized.

Oil was not the only commodity of which the Germans were short, but in the minds of Allied planners it was a key one. In 1940 Germany and Austria produced around one and a half million tons of crude oil themselves, and three and a half millions of synthetic oil, made from coal.[3] Whereas Britain had decided in the 1930s not to invest heavily in oil from coal production (see Chapter 3, 'Britain's own oil'), Germany had done. The process could produce aviation spirit, thus ensuring Germany a reasonable supply. As for imports, the only source of which Germany could be reasonably sure was Romania, which produced over five million tons in 1940. Some had to satisfy demand in Romania itself and some went to other countries, Germany receiving about three million tons a year.[4] In 1940 these totals together came to eight million tons or less, but on 24 August 1939 the Nazi-Soviet Pact had been signed, ensuring Germany supplies of, among other things, Soviet oil. In fact imports were not huge, amounting to one million tons by the time of the German invasion, but they were a useful addition. Furthermore Germany captured significant stocks after the fall of France.

In spite of these additions, oil was still a scarce commodity in Germany relative to Britain as suggested by Britain's much higher consumption – over eleven million tons in 1940.[5] Of course Britain needed more for shipping but, nonetheless, the comparison is stark. It was statistics such as these which made Allied planners so sanguine about the effects of blockade. But they were, of course, too optimistic. In spite of the conquest of France, military fuel use was relatively limited compared to later stages of the war and so Germany could operate with surprisingly low levels of consumption. Even the bomber offensive against Britain was small scale compared to the later British effort. Finally, Germany was prepared to operate with far smaller stocks than Britain. In 1941 German stocks were around two million tons. The British regarded seven million tons as dangerously low.[6]

In the early months of 1940 the Allies had become more pessimistic in their estimation of the effects of the oil blockade and as a result had started to think of ways of accelerating its action. The Iron Gates scheme shows how reckless they could be, but it was on a small scale compared with the plan that was mooted. This was a madcap scheme to bomb the Caucasian oil fields, and thus block Russian supplies to Germany – risking, of course, war with Russia. Fortunately Neville Chamberlain, then Prime Minister, was opposed and it came to nothing.[7]

Such plans were overtaken by the fall of France in June 1940. However disastrous this was militarily, it did not immediately change the basic diagnosis of Germany's economic vulnerability and the policy of targeting oil through blockade and bombing continued.[8] In retrospect, it is clear that the policy was supported in Britain partly because it was a psychological necessity to believe that there was some way in which the war could be won. Britain was almost completely on the defensive, besieged from the air and by submarine and threatened by Italian forces in the Mediterranean and North Africa. With the fall of France, successful land action against Germany was almost inconceivable. Air attack seemed to offer almost the only possibility of ultimate victory. And since it was the only positive way in which the war could be carried to Germany, Churchill's natural aggression led him to support it. As Bill Keighley's experience showed, however, the reality of bombing at that time could not have been further from the hopes resting on it. And night attacks, although they suffered a lower loss rate, were even more inaccurate.

But as autumn gave way to winter in 1940, the oil plan gradually faded from centrality. There were a variety of reasons. Success in North Africa against Italian forces raised hopes that this might become a significant theatre of war and eventually a route to eliminating Italy from the war. Churchill started to favour the area bombing of German cities as retaliation for the Blitz on Britain. And psychological necessity again came into play, encouraging a belief that German morale would not stand the level of bombing which Britain had experienced.[9] So morale rather than the economy became the prime target. This helped to rationalize the continuation of bombing when it was realized in 1941 how hopelessly inaccurate night bombing was. These new beliefs and realities combined with other developments of even greater significance, such as Hitler's invasion of Russia and American entry to the war, to push Germany's lack of oil on to the back burner in terms of Allied planning.

BRITAIN'S OIL SUPPLIES

It was not only Germany which had a potential oil shortage in the summer and autumn of 1940. With the fall of France, Britain and the Empire countries were fighting almost alone and their problems were multiplied by the closure of the Mediterranean as Italy entered the war in June 1940. Closure reacted on oil supplies by increasing the tanker haul from Abadan in Iran, the location of AIOC's huge refinery, from 6,600 miles to 11,200 as ships now had to take the long route round the Cape of Good Hope. Then Fawley and Southampton, which had handled 10 per cent of pre-war oil imports, were closed to shipping because of the danger of air attack. With the further closure from September of east coast ports from the Thames to the Humber, another large proportion of oil unloading facilities was out of use. The strategic situation was dire. The military situation was dire. And the oil supply situation seemed equally dire.[10]

In fact it was not so bad as it seemed. The fall of France actually increased the availability of tankers. France itself no longer had to be supplied, while Dutch, Belgian and most importantly Norwegian tankers continued to ply their trade from Britain or neutral countries. To that extent, as with the military and naval forces and personnel which some continental countries supplied, the Empire was not alone. Tanker tonnage available to Britain rose from around six million deadweight tons to around seven million during the summer of 1940. Of course losses and the inefficiencies due to convoy, let alone the additional distances travelled, conspired to keep the situation difficult. By December 1940 liftings from Abadan to Britain had to be cut and most tankers directed to the much shorter Atlantic run in order to keep up supplies, in spite of the adverse effect on dollar expenditure – and dollars, for Britain, were a precious commodity. But the dollar position was soon to ease. Although Franklin Roosevelt's Lend-Lease Bill was not passed until March 1941 and Lend-Lease oil did not reach Britain until July, it soon became clear that dollars would no longer be a problem. After a brief pick up in Iranian loadings for Britain early in 1941, they ceased for the duration of the war in May of that year. Abadan was still important to the war effort, but not because it supplied Britain directly.[11]

More of a concern in the second half of 1940 than the availability of tankers were the problems in British ports. Closure of most of the Channel and east coast ports pushed the task of unloading onto west coast ports in the Mersey, Clyde and Bristol Channel. Since not just tankers but virtually all shipping was being diverted to them, the potential for congestion was obvious. Pre-war planners had not overlooked the possibility of being forced back on west coast ports, since it was always assumed that the east coast was vulnerable to bombing. But they had underestimated or simply miscalculated capacity under wartime conditions. By October 1940 west coast ports were handling no more oil than in a normal pre-war month, and other ports virtually none. Total petroleum offtake was one half the pre-war level and the situation looked serious. Fortunately, however, the problems either sorted themselves out or were sorted out. East coast ports were being used again from November as German daylight bombing ceased. Incremental improvements to procedures speeded the rate of discharge and by the summer of 1941 west coast port offtake had virtually doubled from the dark days of October.[12]

The rapidity of the improvement owed a lot to the efficiency of the organization set up to control Britain's oil supplies – the Petroleum Board. Within a week of the war starting the Board had been established in Shell-Mex House on the Embankment. Here pre-war planners got it right, since these moves had been worked out in advance. From then on all petroleum supplies with the exception of the navy's oil were within the oil 'pool', distribution and allocation all being controlled by the Board.[13] It was the Board which sorted out the port problems at the end of 1940. And whereas there were serious difficulties in distributing coal and other goods in the winter of 1940–1, the Board's arrangements ensured that there were no major problems with the distribution of oil. The existing road tanker fleet worked double shifts thus enabling, for example, the West Riding of Yorkshire to be supplied from Merseyside by road. The fleet of oil barges on the river Severn was augmented and helped to supply the West Midlands. The railways took much of the strain, and here too pre-war planning had been effective. Sidings and bulk oil discharge facilities had been established near London on railway lines from the west. These replaced the docks and wharves along the Thames which had previously received oil for London and the south-east. Rail tank cars ran straight to their destination in block trains, thus avoiding the time-consuming marshalling necessary in pre-war days when most tank cars would have been bound for small company depots. The new arrangements ensured that, by 1943, mileage per tank car rose about three times compared to pre-war.[14]

Amidst all the difficulties the greatest pre-war fear of all, bombing, proved a less serious problem than anticipated. Of course indirectly it had a major impact, as it was fear of bombing and particularly the threat it posed to shipping which necessitated the closure of east coast ports. But only about 5 per cent of storage tanks were actually destroyed by bombing, and many of these were in the east where less oil was now unloaded. This was in spite of the fact that the pre-war programme to build protected tanks was only partially complete with, as a result, the navy's oil tanks suffering heavily during the big raid on Plymouth in November 1940. But the Germans failed to concentrate their bombing on a few objectives – a mistake also committed by the British. This was one reason for the low losses. The other was simple: most high explosive bombs missed. Incendiaries often landed on the tanks, but they either did not penetrate them, or they failed to ignite the heavier grades of petroleum product. The chief danger, which the French had anticipated but the British had not, was of hot bomb splinters rupturing the tanks and igniting the escaping contents. The reaction was rapid once the danger was realized, and a programme of protecting tanks with splinterproof walls was rapidly put under way.[15]

While bombing had relatively little impact on oil supplies, by mid-1941 the accumulated tanker losses from submarine and other maritime attacks were becoming serious. Film buffs will remember the sinking of the *Africa Shell* by the surface raider *Graf Spee* in that classic war film *The Battle of the River Plate*. A less well known film, made in wartime to boost morale, was *San Demetrio London*. This was based on a real incident when the *San Demetrio*, an Eagle Oil tanker, was damaged by another surface raider in mid-Atlantic. It was abandoned but then reboarded by its crew to eventually reach Britain.[16] But unfortunately tankers did not usually survive attacks and losses were mounting. American tankers could not directly supply Britain, in spite of Lend-Lease, because Roosevelt did not want to provoke the lingering isolationist sentiment in the United States and was therefore reluctant to repeal US neutrality laws which forbade American ships from carrying goods to countries at war. But indirectly American tankers made a vital contribution by carrying oil from the Gulf of Mexico to east coast US ports in what was termed 'the Shuttle'. The journey from these ports to Britain was much shorter than from the Gulf so British tankers could make more voyages. A sharp fall in sinkings also improved the tanker situation. This was caused partly by better convoy protection but also by reading the German Navy's signals coded on the 'Enigma' machine, thus enabling convoys to avoid submarine concentrations.[17]

Once again, however, the improvement was temporary. At the end of 1941 the Allies again lost the ability to decode much of the Enigma traffic, while America's entry to the war enabled the U-boats to prey on US east cost shipping which, for a long time, was virtually unprotected. With American tankers now forming an integral part of the Allied tanker fleet, American losses were almost as critical to Britain as losses of its own tankers. Later in 1942 US escort vessels were diverted to protect its coastal convoys, but this reduced the number of Atlantic convoys. Even so, the strength and flexibility of the American economy meant that the impact on Britain's oil supplies was relatively limited. In spite of its own losses, America actually loaned tankers to Britain. It managed to do this through a combination of petrol rationing in the eastern states, reducing coastal tanker traffic further by using the newly built 'Plantation' pipeline from the Gulf to North Carolina and increasing rail supply. And US resources were such that additional tankers were found to carry the major additional fuel requirements necessitated by the 'Torch' landings in North Africa in November 1942.[18]

As the war went on, American economic strength meant that by 1943 the problem was not survival but meeting the ever-increasing demands for fuel, particularly aviation spirit for the bombing offensive and later fuel for the Allied forces invading the Continent. New and larger tankers meant that increasing numbers of fast 'Greyhound' convoys could be run across the Atlantic. And two pipelines were built from Texas to the north-eastern United States – the 'Big Inch' and the 'Little Big Inch', freeing other tankers for transatlantic work. As a by-product of military success, the reopening of the Mediterranean in May 1943 allowed the Western Mediterranean theatre to be supplied by Iraqi oil refined at Haifa. It also, of course, cut the oil needed for ships' bunkers as the long haul round the Cape was no longer necessary.[19] As a result of all these developments, by the last year of the war Allied oil consumption in Britain and northern Europe was over twice British consumption in 1940–1, and practically all of this was supplied from the Americas. The impending escalation in Pacific petroleum usage, as the war grew ever nearer to Japan and further from the United States, was by early 1945 posing problems as to tanker allocation between the two theatres. But they were the problems of success, and victory in Europe, in May 1945, solved them.[20]

Although the Americas supplied most of Britain's oil from 1941 onwards, there was some indigenous production, both of petroleum and of substitutes. British oilfields, particularly Eakring in Nottinghamshire which had been fortuitously discovered not long before the war, contributed around 100,000 tons of oil a year on average between 1942 and 1944, American drillers having been brought in to increase production. The oil, which when refined was particularly valuable for lubricating purposes, made a useful contribution. But even in the peak production year of 1943 it amounted to just 1 per cent of Britain's total usage. ICI's hydrogenation plant contributed about the same, and Scotland's shale oil a bit more. The biggest contribution came from two old stalwarts: benzole and creosote. The latter was a coal by-product which was little used as a fuel before the war but was now pressed into service. It was further stretched by mixing it with pitch, also derived from coal, the result replacing oil in industrial furnaces. But the total contribution of all these indigenous products amounted to less than 10 per cent of liquid fuel consumption in Britain.[21]

As military use increased, there was a continued squeeze on civilian consumption. Petrol both for private and for commercial vehicle use was subject to rationing from the start. The basic ration allowed for 1,800 miles per year, and there were supplements for specific purposes. It seems surprising that any fuel for non-essential motoring was allowed. But pleasure motoring was still, by modern standards, quite limited and many users were businessmen whose cars, if not essential, were important adjuncts to their work. Furthermore, after the ration was instituted private motoring actually used quite small amounts of fuel. The basic ration accounted for less than 4 per cent of total petroleum consumption in 1940, goods vehicles using far more. Nevertheless, it could be argued that a chance to abolish the basic private motoring ration was missed in 1940 at a time of national crisis. Abolition of non-essential private motoring would then have made it possible to clamp down on unnecessary goods vehicle usage. The 1942 tanker crisis was the signal for the abolition of both the basic commercial vehicle ration – which incidentally was the main source of black market fuel – and the basic car users' ration.[22]

In spite of the clamp-down on civilian vehicle use, more petroleum was used in Britain during the war than before it. The main drivers of increased consumption were fuel for the navy and aviation fuel. It was not the fighters of the Battle of Britain which were the main users of this, vital though they were in 1940. Aviation spirit consumption, 113,000 tons in 1938, rose only to 404,000 tons in 1940. It was the bombers of the RAF and, increasingly, the USAAF which demanded fuel. A Lancaster bomber needed 6 tons of petrol to get to Berlin, and with raids of 500 aircraft or more commonplace by 1943, it is easy to see how aviation fuel requirements mounted. In 1944 UK consumption was over 4.7 million tons.[23]

The provision of so much fuel raised complex technical problems. Aviation engines had developed rapidly in the 1930s and the octane ratings needed for aviation spirit increased as compression ratios rose. Tetraethyl lead was the standard octane-enhancing additive, but there were technical difficulties in using it in more than small quantities in the base petrol produced in Britain. Before the war, therefore, the Air Ministry made extensive arrangements to produce iso-octane, another additive which could be used more freely, by the hydrogenation process. Fortunately a simpler process for iso-octane production, alkylation, became commercialized at the outbreak of war. It was developed almost simultaneously by AIOC and Shell, although most of the aviation spirit eventually produced was refined in the United States. Production there was also assisted by a new aromatic, cumene, developed by Shell's American laboratories. In spite of American dominance in production, Abadan made a valuable contribution to the Middle Eastern and, later in the war, Far Eastern and Russian supply of aviation spirit. In the final year of the war it produced almost a million tons, although this was little more than 5 per cent of US production. A further technical development late in the war was '150' grade fuel, produced in small quantities to give additional performance to, for instance, the aircraft which intercepted V1 flying bombs.[24]

To distribute the growing quantities of aviation spirit a series of pipelines were built. The first in 1941 ran from Avonmouth on the Bristol Channel to Walton-on-Thames outside London, with an intermediate storage facility at Aldermaston in Berkshire. The network was steadily extended until by 1943 there was a line from Avonmouth to Shell's port and refinery at Stanlow on the Mersey, another from Stanlow to Misterton in north Nottinghamshire and, completing a full circuit, one from Misterton via Sandy in Bedfordshire to Aldermaston. The circuit linked major docks and a refinery with the main USAAF consumption areas, airfields in the east Midlands. Then in 1943–4 a further system was constructed linking Shellhaven, a port and refinery on the Thames Estuary, with the East Anglian airfields and with Sandy. The new line reflected the reduced threat of German air attack which enabled shipping to return to the Thames Estuary. An important branch off the old line led from Aldermaston to the Solent in order to provide fuel to the invading forces in Normandy. There was, in addition, a Scottish network linking various Clyde ports to Grangemouth and the Firth of Forth.[25]

At its southern end the pipeline system was eventually to link up with an ambitious attempt to supply the Allied troops when they landed in Normandy. The project was originally called the 'Pipeline Underwater Transport of Oil' (PLUTO), which was transmuted at some stage to the more romantic 'Pipeline under the Ocean'.[26] The plan was to lay a number of small diameter pipelines made of flexible pipe which could be unwound like a cable, one route running from the Isle of Wight to the Cherbourg Peninsula and the other, for the later stage of the operation, from Dungeness to Boulogne. Unfortunately the lines were an almost complete waste of resources. They pumped very little oil until early 1945, and in total supplied about 7 per cent of the 5.2 million tons delivered to the Allies in north-western Europe by the end of the war.[27] But PLUTO's relative failure does not really account for the oil supply problems which helped in September 1944 to halt the Allies' great advance from Normandy to Belgium. The problems were not caused by failure to bring oil into France, but failure to get it to the advancing troops. The Allies had virtually destroyed the railway system in northern France while their own supply lorries themselves needed ever-increasing amounts of fuel as the armies advanced. The Dungeness-Boulogne PLUTO, which might have been useful for the advance, was not completed until 27 October because of mine clearance off Boulogne. So even if it had worked well, which initially it didn't, it would not have alleviated the fuel shortage which struck the Allied armies in September. What could have made a difference was the port of Antwerp. It was captured, in good condition, on 5 September but it could not be used until the banks of the Scheldt were cleared of German troops, which did not occur until November. There are dark suspicions that Montgomery slowed the drive to clear the Scheldt in order to further his own plans for a direct thrust into Germany, although the whole episode smacks of cock-up rather than conspiracy.[28] Whatever the truth, Allied fuel shortages were undoubtedly a factor in slowing the advance. But those shortages were local scarcities in an abundant ocean of Allied petroleum.

THE MIDDLE EAST AND NORTH AFRICA

In the summer of 1942 Egypt was full of fears. Harriet Pringle, a character in Olivia Manning's novel *The Danger Tree*, expressed them: 'If the German panzers came down through Persia they'd meet up with Rommel and surround the British forces. 8th Army would be wiped out.' She goes on to ask, 'If Hitler got the Baku oil and the Middle Eastern oil, what would happen then?' Her alarm was not just idle speculation. Throughout the summer and early autumn of 1942 fears of such a move reached up to the level of the government and the Chiefs of Staff (COS). They summarize the paradox of North Africa and the Middle East during the war. To the British, the whole area was both one of opportunity, in which Italy might be defeated and the Mediterranean opened up, and one of threat in which the Allies' overall strategic position might be endangered and the Axis powers gain control of the oil of Iran and Iraq.[29]

The Middle East became a key area as soon as Italy entered the war in June 1940. At that stage relatively small British forces in Egypt and Palestine were threatened by much larger Italian forces on their western flank in Libya, and to the south in Ethiopia and Italian Somaliland, now Somalia. Syria, the Lebanon and much of the North African littoral beyond Libya were under the control of Vichy France, technically neutral but hardly friendly to Britain and potentially liable to German pressure. The other large Middle Eastern countries, Saudi Arabia and Iraq, were independent, although Britain had military bases in the latter. Just over Iraq's eastern border, in Iran, was Abadan, AIOC's great refinery. It processed most of Iran's pre-war production of 10 million tons of crude petroleum a year – about as much, allowing for refinery losses, as German's entire annual wartime consumption.[30] Iraq was also a significant producer, its fields owned by the Allied-dominated IPC, which exported its oil by pipelines through Syria and Palestine. The American consortium Caltex produced around one and a half million tons a year in Saudi Arabia and Bahrain, but recent discoveries in Kuwait and Qatar had not yet been exploited. Egypt itself was a small producer. In a strange irony, the existence of huge oil reserves beneath the Libyan deserts was undreamt of as the machines of war, thirsty for fuel, fought over them.

As early as August 1940 the COS committee which, in dialogue with Churchill and the Cabinet, decided strategy, voiced concern about Middle Eastern oil. And from the beginning the purpose of defending Egypt was, in part, to protect oil. Because the fighting in the Middle East and North Africa is so often written about in terms of the ebb and flow of desert warfare, or later on the 'Mediterranean strategy' of eliminating Italy from the war, the strategic importance of protecting oil is often missed by historians. Of course it was never the only object. Churchill, typically, argued for offensive action against the Italians.[31] This successfully took place in the winter of 1940–1 and from then on continued as an aspiration, although from early 1941 to late 1942 the success of Rommel in the desert meant that defence was often the main concern. In spring 1941 the seizure of power in Iraq by the anti-British Rashid Ali became another factor, because of Iraq's own oil production and because of its proximity to Iran. An invasion force was assembled and entered Iraq in May. Subsequently there was a similar operation in Syria. A final insurance against internal trouble in the oil producing regions took place on 25 August 1941 when Britain and Russia, now in the war, jointly occupied Iran. The Iranians bowed to *force majeure* and the three countries concluded a joint treaty.[32]

In May 1942 German and Italian forces launched their most threatening offensive so far, reaching El Alamein, well into Egypt. In June the Germans started their summer offensive in Russia, quickly advancing across the Ukraine and towards the Caucasus mountains. Even in March, before the attacks started, a pincer movement on the Middle East, with Rommel advancing from the west and the German armies in Russia coming down from the north through the Caucasus, had seemed all too possible to the British.[33] In the summer their fears appeared to become reality. Historians focus on how close Rommel came to occupying Cairo, and often fail to mention that, to the COS, this was not the biggest concern. That was oil, and Abadan. On 4 August Alan Brooke, the army Chief of Staff, wrote in his diary that the Middle East Commanders-in-Chief 'discussed the relative importance of Egypt as opposed to Abadan and all agreed that the latter's importance was paramount'.[34] A few days later Brooke, by now on the way to Moscow to attend the first meeting between Churchill and Stalin, saw for himself the danger from the north. Flying over the flat land between the Caucasus and the Caspian Sea he observed Russian defences against German attack: 'one half-completed anti-tank ditch, badly revetted and without any covering defences

. . . A working party of about a hundred men and two general-service horsed wagons . . . Beyond that nothing to be seen.'[35] A new Persia-Iraq command was set up under Henry Maitland Wilson – a general who specialized in dealing with awkward situations – to establish a defensive line in Iran. However, Churchill's reluctance to divert too many resources to Wilson's 10th Army was prescient. By November 1942, with the success of the Allies at Alamein and Stalingrad, fears of the 'pincer movement' already seemed past history.[36]

Abadan's importance did not lie in supplying Britain with oil, because it had ceased to do so in the spring of 1941 due to tanker shortages (see 'Britain's oil supplies'). Nevertheless it produced five and a half million tons of petroleum products in 1941, around two-thirds of the Middle East and Indian total. The products of Abadan and other local refineries were used to keep the economies of these areas and East Africa functioning, and they were used for shipping throughout the Indian Ocean. They also, of course, supplied the military effort in the Middle East. Then in 1942, with the Allies' fields in Burma and South-East Asia occupied by the Japanese, Abadan had to step up production further. Its products even reached Australia, and from 1943 aviation spirit went to Russia. In the final year of the war it helped to supply the US Navy in the Pacific, and in that year its output reached 13 million tons.[37]

In retrospect, the fears that Abadan and other fields and refineries would get caught in a pincer movement were exaggerated. Rommel was desperately short of fuel – something the British knew. What they did not know was the weakness of the German push towards the Caucasus, as many of Wehrmacht's best troops were sucked into Stalingrad. What they also did not realize is that Hitler had never been much interested in the Middle East and its oil, and therefore there never was a concerted German strategy of encirclement.

Before the war, and in its early stages, Germany had hardly any interest in the Middle East at all. So far as the Germans thought about it, they saw it as a venue for stirring up trouble for Britain, for instance by supporting nationalist movements. There was no real change when Italy entered the war, as Hitler accepted that Italy was the major Axis player in the Mediterranean and the Middle East. This was in line with his respect for Mussolini, which lasted a surprisingly long time in spite of the Italian dictator's ineptitude at waging war. A further complication for Hitler was his desire not to antagonize either Spain or Vichy France, both of which he saw as potential allies. The German military planners were largely of the same mind, and anyway by late 1940 were increasingly bound up with planning the invasion of Russia.[38] The German generals were not so obsessed as Hitler with the ideological and economic implications of war with Russia, but from a military point of view a land invasion was something they could understand and relate to. The complexities of warfare around the Mediterranean were much less familiar to them. The exception was Raeder, the head of the German navy. But even he saw the Mediterranean more in general strategic terms than as a gateway to oil supplies. The Germans' lack of interest in the area meant that they were slow to react to Rashid Ali's seizure of power in Iraq, allowing the British to gain the initiative. And Rommel and German forces were initially involved in North Africa to prop up Italy, not because Germany had any great plans there.[39]

Rommel himself, not surprisingly, was bullish about the possibilities. He constantly prodded his superiors for more resources and he was one German who did see the theatre as a basis for getting control of Middle Eastern oil. The high command disagreed and anyway the demands of the Russian front, as well as the increasing diversion of resources to anti-aircraft defence in Germany, left him on the periphery logistically as well as geographically. In the late summer of 1942, with Germany apparently triumphing both in Russia and North Africa, Middle Eastern oil briefly flashed across Hitler's mental horizon. Both in August and September he talked of occupying the Middle East and seizing British oil supplies.[40] As with the almost identical British fears, his dreams were soon to dissipate in the realities of German military defeat.

German lack of interest in Middle Eastern oil might, of course, have been realistic. Even if Britain had lost Egypt, the Germans would have been hundreds of inhospitable miles from most of the oilfields. By 1942 it seems unlikely that Rommel would have been strong enough to get much further than Cairo, especially as the Allies' resources were now far greater than they had been. Nevertheless the implications of a more determined German bid in North Africa in 1941, even it offended Italian susceptibilities, do form an interesting subject for speculation. Since it didn't happen, and since it would have required a complete change of German strategy for it to have done so, there is no point in wasting space on it here. Readers can speculate, or not, as they wish. Hitler's almost complete lack of interest in Middle Eastern possibilities is still curious. At the root of it, probably, is his obsession with Russia. To him it was Russia which would ultimately supply what Germany lacked, not just in oil but in many other commodities.

Since North Africa, the Middle East and the Mediterranean were secondary theatres for the Germans, many critics have concluded that they were something of a waste of effort for the British. But this German perception does not prove their lack of importance. How important they were in purely military terms is not our concern here. Instead the final focus of this section is on the implications of each side's oil situation for the fighting in North Africa and the Mediterranean, and conversely the implications of the fighting in these areas for Germany's overall oil situation.

The first is easily dealt with. It was shortage of fuel, as much as shortage of men and munitions, which held Rommel back, especially in the critical fighting in the late summer and autumn of 1942. The problem lay partly in the British ability by 1942 to sink tankers on a regular basis, based on their reading of the naval Enigma.[41] This constrained Rommel's planning. However, Martin van Crefeld has argued that tanker sinkings were not the main factor. It was rather that the Germans lacked the resources, particularly the vehicles, needed to truck the fuel hundreds of miles as they advanced into Egypt. The importance of fuel, or lack of it, in the actual fighting lends another dimension to estimating the value of the whole campaign to the Allies. As has often been pointed out, the British had to invest huge resources in bringing troops and munitions round the Cape to Egypt. But while the German and Italian supply lines for most things were much shorter than for the British, they were not for fuel. The British had almost unlimited supplies. Axis supplies were strictly limited and this was one reason for their defeat.[42]

Compared to the Germans, the Italian armies in North and East Africa were hopelessly under-mechanized. This helped to account for the defeats they suffered in the winter of 1940–1, but it also meant that they never required much oil. Their air force was always relatively small with correspondingly small petrol needs. The Italian navy was their big oil user. Before the war it had accumulated reserves of over one and a half million tons, compared with the German navy's half million tons.[43] But from then on fuel deliveries were far below consumption. The reason was simple – the Italians produced very little oil themselves. Once they were at war, their oil mainly consisted of the residue from Romania after Germany and the Romanians themselves had taken their pick, and doles from the Germans' other resources. Naval oil supply during 1940–1 was little over 250,000 tons, although another million was received in 1942–3, partly due to pressure from Raeder. Compare this with naval consumption of over 600,000 tons in the five and a half months of war to the end of 1940 alone.[44] From 1940–3 the frequent British naval operations in the Mediterranean, either offensive or in support of Malta convoys, forced the Italian navy to use oil if it was to react at all. There have been suspicions that the Italians concealed the amount of oil they actually had from the Germans in order to avoid putting to sea, but the Germans' own figures after they occupied Italy in September 1943 seem to put the lie to this. By then the Italian fleet had virtually no oil at all.[45]

The Italian navy was not very effective at the best of times, although it probably put up a better performance than the army or air force. But even allowing for its defects, the increasing fuel shortage must have been a significant brake on its performance. One cannot know whether this shortage was of critical importance in the Mediterranean war – whether, for example, a copious Italian oil supply would have so restricted the Royal Navy's actions as to make the resupply of Malta impossible. But clearly the Italians' parlous oil situation must have had some military significance.

So lack of fuel was, arguably, an important factor in the Axis defeat in the North African and Mediterranean theatre. Therefore even if the campaign had only limited strategic benefits for the Allies, it made quite good sense to fight it because their relative fuel position was so favourable. But was the campaign so peripheral for the Germans if their overall fuel situation is taken into account? The small size of the *Deutsche Afrika Korps* (*DAK*) was not reflected in its oil use because, unlike the Italian army or much of the German army in Russia, German forces in North Africa were highly mechanized. While there were never enough trucks, the *DAK* still used proportionately ten times more than the armies in Russia, although fewer in absolute terms.[46] There was also an air fleet, sizeable at times, based in North Africa, Greece and Sicily. It is impossible to say exactly what German consumption in the Mediterranean and North Africa was during the period of fighting. Most German fuel in North Africa was supplied through the Italian military, although not tank fuel as Italian petrol was not suitable for German tanks. Therefore Italian military consumption of 5.3 million tons will be taken as a proxy for all Axis consumption in this theatre, although the procedure must underestimate the grand total. However, around 3.5 million tons of the Italian total had originally been supplied by Germany. This supplemented Italy's own limited output, the drawing down of stockpiles, and Romanian imports. With around 9.5 million tons per year available to Germany during Italy's participation in the war, 3.5 million, or slightly over one million tons a year, does not seem much. But as the next section suggests, it may have been more important than it seems.[47]

The overall significance of the oil supplies of the Middle East and their relation to the fighting in the adjacent theatres can be summarized as follows. First, in spite of German lack of interest in Middle East oil, the British were constrained to defend it. If they had simply abandoned Egypt, it hardly seems likely that Hitler and Mussolini would have taken no notice of the oil fields lying beyond it to the east. So the British would have had to make a stand somewhere, in Palestine or further east still, and logistically these locations would have presented far more difficult problems for the British than staying in Egypt. Of course oil was not the only reason why Egypt was defended – apart from anything else Churchill's natural aggression made him reluctant to give up any position, once occupied. But had there been no other reason, defence of oil would have been a cogent factor. The Italian forces then proved so inept that success against them came about in spite of the British having very limited offensive plans. The Germans felt constrained to help the Italians and the real struggle then commenced. In a nutshell, the British had to fight in North Africa. It was not really a matter of choice, as it is often represented.

While the fighting was resource-hungry for the British, it was fuel-hungry for the Axis powers. So apart from the negative reason – it had to be defended – oil gave the British two positive reasons to fight in the theatre. Their local fuel superiority was one. Victory in North Africa would probably have occurred sooner or later due to the long-term build up of Allied resources. But oil superiority likely accelerated it. And, while the Axis suffered from a relative inferiority in fuel supplies, they were still forced to use a lot of oil. This had implications for Germany's ability to wage war elsewhere.

THE AXIS POWERS AND OIL

While the British were safeguarding oil in the Middle East, they were losing it in Burma. In March 1942 the Japanese advance was in full swing. As the British pulled out, they systematically destroyed the oilfields. Those in the denial team remembered two things above all: the overpowering heat; and the 'intense breathtaking silence when one stopped for a moment; the smoke pall seemed to absorb all noise'.[48]

The British efforts were successful. For the rest of the war Burmese production fell from around one million tons per annum to a tenth of that level. Denial attempts in the rest of the Asian oilfields occupied by Japan – mainly in Borneo and Sumatra – were less effective and in 1943, the peak year of production under Japanese occupation, around seven million tons were extracted. Given the relatively small size of the Japanese economy and the small needs of its unmechanized army this seemed more than ample. 'The mood of Japanese officials concerned with oil supplies in 1943 was euphoric.' Their euphoria owed itself in part to the fact that a perceived lack of oil had been a factor in Japan's decision for war. Like Germany, Japan lacked many raw materials. And like Germany, Japan was dominated politically by the extreme right. This saw the solution as the replacement of Western imperialism by Japan's own variety, which could then extract raw materials from other Asian countries.[49]

Japan's first initiative, in 1937, had been an attack on China. But this alarmed the USA, which in 1940 placed a partial embargo on oil exports to Japan. This was steadily tightened throughout 1941. With limited progress in China, Japan decided to solve its raw material problem by targeting the British, Dutch and

American colonial empires in the Pacific and Southeast Asia. America would be deterred from retaliation by the destruction of its fleet. But while pressure on Japanese oil supplies may have accelerated Japan's decision for war, it was not the underlying reason. This was the pervasiveness of a mindset which saw the Japanese as supermen, unfairly held back from realizing their superiority by the lack of raw materials and, because they were supermen, entitled to seize the raw materials rather than obtain them in the normal way by trading.[50]

The Japanese decision, of course, led in December 1941 to Pearl Harbor. But in spite of that initial victory and their rapid sweep through the Pacific and into the mainland of Southeast Asia, as well as their acquisition of substantial oil resources, Japan was soon in trouble. The navy had made practically no preparations for anti-submarine warfare, so American submarines aided by those of their Allies took an increasing toll of Japanese tankers. It became increasingly difficult to ship the fuel to their scattered bases or to the Japanese homeland itself. By 1944 their military and economic situation was hopeless, and in 1945, in the remaining months of the war, Japan imported no petroleum products at all.[51]

Although Japan's oil supply situation rapidly became disastrous, it was little more so than virtually every other indicator of the country's ability to make war. It is easy to forget that Japan's economy was then quite small. In 1944, the peak production year, it built 21,000 combat aircraft and 248 major naval vessels. In the same year America built 74,000 aircraft, many of them much larger than the Japanese ones, and over 2,200 major naval vessels. US national income was eight times greater than Japan's. Once the momentum of their early victories was lost, the Japanese could do little against an economy of this size once it had mobilized for war. Shortage of oil was just one of many reasons for their defeat.[52]

The Japan of the early 1940s was very different to Germany, which was an economic giant. But the giant had feet of clay. In the early and middle stages of the war, Germany did not produce nearly the volume of munitions as should have been possible with an economy of its size. In 1941 Britain, with a smaller economic base, produced almost 5,000 more combat aircraft than Germany and built a far greater tonnage of naval vessels.[53]

Historians have given different explanations for Germany's production weakness. The once popular idea that Hitler only geared up for a short war – a Blitzkrieg – is now at something of a discount. In fact, the Nazis considered that they were constructing an economy geared for total war. A more cogent explanation for their problems is that until 1941 German munitions production was hopelessly chaotic and badly run. This explanation is supported by the fact that production subsequently soared as Fritz Todt, Albert Speer and Erhard Milch (responsible for airforce procurement) imposed order on the chaos. Adam Tooze

has also highlighted the fact that, economic giant though it was, Germany suffered important capacity constraints. One major constraint was coal, at that time
the staple of industrial production, heating and rail transport. Initially Germany
produced enough for itself but, if Italy and the conquered countries of Europe,
which the Nazis planned to use as industrial auxiliaries, are included there was a
shortage. Before the war this had been made up by imports – from Britain. This
shortage, combined with German under-investment in rail transport, combined
to cause increasing problems of coal supply, both for other European countries
and in Germany itself. And coal shortages reacted throughout the economy and
from there into military production, with steel, synthetic oil and synthetic rubber
all depending on coal. By comparison oil was unimportant industrially. A post-
war British summary of the German oil position pointed out that there were no
references in the *Zentrale Planung* records to oil shortages hampering industrial
operations and added that, 'Those in the best position to know [including Speer]
are quite specific on this point.'[54]

Even if Hitler had had a lot more oil, therefore, it would not have made much
difference to the German economy's productive capacity. So if the Axis powers'
basic problem is seen as one of industrial production – that their economies were
too small, and too badly run, to compete with the vast resources of the Allies –
then the role of oil in the Second World War is obvious. Germany had a limited
but adequate amount, and therefore oil was not actually very important.

However, many historians would argue that industrial production does not
tell the whole story. Up to 1942 German victories depended on military skill
rather than a superior volume of weaponry. Could those victories have been
more complete and decisive – could Britain, or Russia, been knocked out of the
war before American munitions production became effective – if Germany had
had more oil?

It is difficult to argue this case prior to the invasion of Russia. It has been suggested that 100 octane petrol gave British fighters an important performance edge
in the Battle of Britain, and this may be so. But it would be stretching credibility
to argue that it conferred a critical advantage, because Fighter Command of the
Royal Air Force was superior to the German air force in several other ways. It had
a much better command and control structure, it had radar, and Britain built
more fighters overall. Of these the Spitfire was more or less equal to the standard
German fighter, the Messerschmitt BF 109. The slower Hurricanes were not, but
were more than adequate for attacking German bombers.[55] In other military
theatres in 1940–1 the Axis oil supply position was even less likely to have been
a critical factor. Italian defeats, for instance, were largely down to their own
ineptitude and lack of up-to-date weaponry.

So we come to Russia. Hitler himself, of course, justified his invasion partly by reference to Russia's oil wealth. But like the Japanese reasoning, this should not be taken at face value. Most countries in the world, then and now, do not have their own oil supplies. And most countries in the world, then and now, sell other products to obtain oil. Hitler, instead, decided that he had the right to seize oil and other raw materials rather than trade for them. The invasion of Russia was ultimately not about raw materials but about ideas of racial superiority and the presumed entitlements it gave.

When Russia was invaded in June 1941, fuel soon became an issue for the Germans. The Panzer divisions advanced rapidly but the German infantry remained, to a remarkable extent, dependent upon the horse and cart for supply. This had obvious implications for their progress in Russia's vast spaces. But lack of mobility was due as much to lack of vehicles as to shortage of fuel. It is tempting to conclude that, if it had had more oil, Germany would have solved its mobility problems by building more trucks. But here we return to the question of the country's overall industrial output. More trucks could only have come at the expense of some other vital component of war-making – tanks, or planes, or artillery pieces. In the 1942 summer offensive, with distances greater still, even the mechanized spearheads found their progress hampered by fuel shortages. But, although fuel stocks were lower than in 1941, the main reason for their lack of fuel was the difficulty of getting it to the front line and, here again, vehicle availability was a crucial factor.[56]

However, the Germans' Russian problems assume a different light if the fighting in North Africa and the Mediterranean is taken into account. Between mid-1940 and mid-1943 Germany supplied 3.5 million tons of petroleum to the theatre (see previous section). Total German petroleum availability in this period was almost 29 million tons. But much of this was dedicated to specific uses: lubricating oil and other non-military purposes, petrol for air warfare against Britain, diesel and fuel oil for the navy, and military training needs. So the 3.5 million tons was subtracted more or less directly from fuel available for the Russian front. North Africa also absorbed large numbers of trucks, thus exacerbating the problems in supplying fuel to the armies in Russia. As suggested above, these may have been more important than actual lack of petroleum. Extrapolating from this to predictions about 'might-have-beens' in Russia is a hazardous enterprise, and readers will be left to get on with it if they wish. But it is an interesting speculation.[57]

Once Germany started retreating in Russia and had pulled out of North Africa, fuel supply became less of a problem. Hitler had plenty of other things to worry about more. Then in the final year of the war oil took centre stage again and the

British decision to target it in 1940 (see 'The early years') was vindicated. But it needed the combined forces of the USAAF, protected by long-range fighters, and the RAF's Bomber Command, now with precision night-bombing capacity, to target it effectively. From May 1944 the Allied air forces kept up an unremitting attack on synthetic oil plants. Within four months production fell by 85 per cent, with aviation fuel output falling even faster. At the same time Romanian oil supplies were disrupted by mining the Danube, until they ceased when Russia occupied the country. Now shortages of fuel had a real effect. In 1944 German munitions production had reached record levels – but often the munitions could not be used. However, two points need to be made. In September 1944 another air offensive was launched, this time on the German transportation network. This rapidly brought about a collapse in industrial production. The two campaigns need to be taken together in assessing the overall impact of bombing in the later stages of the war. More important, no serious historian would argue that the war's outcome was uncertain without these campaigns. By 1944 Germany's defeat was inevitable, although petroleum shortages caused by Allied bombing may well have hastened it.[58]

So Germany's lack of oil was probably not a critical factor in the war, although there is one question mark over what might have happened if the fuel and vehicles used in North Africa had been available in Russia. Russia should also provide the final vignette. Germany had set aside substantial resources and a large 'Technical Oil Brigade' to exploit Russian oil and in August 1942 they occupied the Maikop oilfield. Russian denial had been extremely effective, however. Before German forces pulled out in January 1943, they produced just 1,000 tons of oil. That and 4,000 tons produced by a new field they had discovered was their entire petroleum haul from the Russian campaign.[59]

5

The World of Oil 1945–73

SEVEN SISTERS

'Le Sette Sorelle' – the Seven Sisters – was a well-known nickname for the big oil companies in the post-war years. It was famously applied to them by Enrico Mattei, of the Italian oil company AGIP, as a scornful reference to an Anglo-Saxon club from which he felt himself excluded. It was further popularized by Anthony Sampson's book of that name, first published in 1975. Sampson's book came out when the post-war oil system, which the companies epitomized, was coming to an end. And since that time the once-familiar phrase has passed into history.

Who were the sisters? The biggest was the American giant Standard of New Jersey (Jersey Standard), already frequently mentioned, known in Britain as Esso, a trade name it took in 1935. The rest of the American side of the family included two other successors of the original Standard Oil – Standard of California (Socal), otherwise known as Chevron, and Standard of New York (Socony), better known as Mobil. Finally there were Texas, which had partnered Socal in Saudi Arabia before the war, and Gulf, which partnered Anglo-Iranian in Kuwait. Then, of course, there were the two siblings from the other side of the Atlantic – Royal Dutch/Shell, and Anglo-Iranian itself, which in 1954 renamed itself British Petroleum and was usually known as BP.

Mattei's nickname was misleading, for a number of reasons. For instance, there were other large American companies such as Conoco and Standard of Indiana which were not included. The 'sisters' were labelled as such not so much because of size – although they were giants – but because they were yoked together in various consortia which produced and sold Middle Eastern oil. But even with this constraint the term is inaccurate because the French Compagnie Francaise des Petroles (CFP) participated in the Iraq consortium and that established in Iran in

1954. Furthermore, as time went by various large American 'independents' became Middle Eastern players – companies such as Armand Hammer's Occidental and J. Paul Getty's Tidewater. 'Seven Sisters', therefore, gives a factititous impression of a relatively small Anglo-American club, around which myths and legends could accrete – which was, perhaps, exactly what Mattei wanted.

Some of these myths and legends concerned profitability, and these had a substratum of truth. In the ten years or so after the war the companies made a lot of money. Their combined rates of return on foreign investments were above 20 per cent until 1957, and then fell to around 12 per cent. Rates of returns on all their investments were lower, however. One fundamental reason for these profits was the ever-increasing demand for oil. Between 1948 and 1972 world production increased from 8.7 million bpd to 53 million bpd. The growth in consumption will be examined in more detail in the next chapter, but the basic reasons for it are well known. The post-war Western world, plus Japan, experienced high and consistent economic growth, a sharp contrast to the depressed years of the 1930s. Prosperity enabled most Americans to consummate their collective love affair with the automobile, and many Europeans started one too. Oil also continued its push, which had begun before the war, into many of the markets previously dominated by coal. Ships and locomotives switched to oil. It became a common fuel for central heating and even made inroads into electricity generation. The chemical industry burgeoned on the back of oil as a feedstock. Although economic growth was one motor for demand increase, oil's increasing cheapness relative to coal was an important factor. Oil prices fluctuated, but between the late 1940s and 1970 the trend for Middle Eastern oil was downwards. Given the simultaneous decline in tanker rates, this meant that in an age of pervasive, if slow, inflation, the price of oil in real terms fell steadily.[1]

In the early post-war years the industry's profitability was underpinned by a series of events which sustained the oil price. In the early post-war years, the Middle East's huge reserves were still under-exploited while at the same time surging demand in the United States, liberated from petrol rationing, absorbed extra supply. Then the Korean war of 1950–3 coincided with the virtual removal of Iranian oil from the market, discussed in the next section. This was followed by the Suez crisis of 1956–7. From 1957, however, the continued discovery of huge new fields – 'elephants' in oilmen's jargon – in the Middle East and elsewhere meant that supply caught up with demand. By the early 1970s Middle Eastern output was around 40 per cent of world supply.[2]

Well before this, the split between producing states' royalties and company profits, very much in the companies' favour before the war, had been changed. The initial mover here, in the 1940s, had been a new democratic government in

Venezuela, and the 50/50 split it established was the norm for Middle Eastern oil by 1952.[3] Oil company profits, however, were barely affected. In the Middle East, at least, the cost of production was still far below the posted price, that is the price which companies quoted for their oil, so there was plenty of leeway to concede some additional share to the producers. Simultaneously the volume of production was increasing rapidly. Furthermore the royalties were accounted for as tax, which could then be offset against the companies' tax bill in their home country. US companies secured this concession first, and in a long-running saga of negotiations BP finally secured the same concession from the UK government. Shell did likewise, but it was less involved since much of its tax was paid in the Netherlands.[4]

It was the shift to an easier supply position from 1957 which reduced the companies' return on capital, because it led to discounting on the posted price of Middle Eastern oil. Since producer royalties were paid on the posted price, it was the companies' profits which bore the brunt of the discounts. By 1959, the extent of the shift led to the oil companies reducing the posted price in order to reduce discounts and thus increase their share of total revenues. (The actual selling price remained the same, at least for the time being, because discounts were reduced or eliminated; but with a lower posted price and a continuing 50/50 royalty/profit share, the producers received less revenue.) This reduction passed without much reaction because it reversed an increase made at the time of Suez, although in private producer representatives started to discuss the need to mount a common front. Then in 1960 Jersey Standard initiated a further cut. It was followed reluctantly by the other companies, which feared its political impact, and later partly reversed. But it galvanized the big oil producers and led to the formation of their own cartel, the Organization of the Petroleum Exporting Counties – OPEC. For the first decade of its existence, however, OPEC had little influence. Its momentous later history will be followed in a subsequent chapter.[5]

Each of the European sisters, Royal Dutch/Shell and BP, had distinctive features. Shell and Jersey Standard were in a league of their own in terms of size. In 1972 the latter, having changed its name to Exxon, ranked first in the world league of industrial firms if measured by assets, and Shell was second, although General Motors exceeded them if measured by sales. Shell had, however, grown a little more slowly than most of the big American oil companies since the war. It had other characteristics besides size. As befitted its Dutch-British parentage it was cosmopolitan, producing and marketing in a wider range of countries than any other company except Jersey Standard. Before the war, tensions between the Dutch and British sides had appeared in the top management when Deterding retired in the 1930s. They were now smoothed over. Shell's Committee of Managing

Directors (CMD) brought the two groups into constant contact and harmony was strengthened when John Loudon, son of one of Royal Dutch's early notables, became Chairman of the CMD between 1952. Loudon, who held the job until 1965, was far-seeing, tactful and, unlike Deterding, liberal in outlook. From as early as 1947 Shell had started to become genuinely international in its personnel policies. There were limits to this process – in 1970, 78 per cent of Shell's expatriates, who formed the core of its management and senior technical staff, were still British or Dutch. Nevertheless even this indicated that a marked change had taken place in the assumption of white superiority which all oil companies had tended to have before the war. In spite of its slow relative decline, Shell retained its strength in marketing and its reputation for producing 'premium' products. And unlike BP Shell was very strong in the United States. This helped to keep up its profits, since US prices were relatively high after import controls on oil were introduced in 1959. But high US prices also meant that American oil companies could use their profits to expand elsewhere, helping to account for the erosion of Shell's market share. Shell's weak point was its crude oil production. The epicentre lay in Venezuela, and it was said that Shell men had to shine there to get to the top. But it had lost its Romanian assets through expropriation after the war, just as it had lost its Russian assets after the First World War, and its Middle Eastern assets were quite small. In 1971 it had just 6 per cent of world oil reserves although it rivalled Jersey Standard in refinery output and product sales.[6]

By contrast, BP had very different characteristics. Although it had built up its European sales between the wars, it was still a long way behind Shell and Jersey Standard, as it was in its other big sales areas, Africa and the Far East. This weakness was partly historic, but for much of the period BP did not remedy the situation very effectively. Its management combined bureaucracy – also a Shell failing – with over-centralization, which Shell avoided. In 1956 BP's sales were greater than Socal's, then the baby of the sisters, but by 1970 Socal had overtaken it. And in a comparison with the other sisters in the early 1970s, BP rated itself bottom or second bottom in refining flexibility and profitability of product mix. But in contrast with Shell, BP was good at exploration. In 1971 it ranked with Jersey Standard in its proportion of world oil reserves, at 13 per cent each. BP's long history in Iran had accustomed its geologists to look for giant fields. Although they missed out in the 1930s on Saudi Arabia, in the long term they had accumulated a series of major finds: by 1970 BP had interests in the Middle East including Kuwait, in Nigeria, Libya, Trinidad and South America, but most importantly for the future in Alaska and the North Sea. At the beginning of the 1950s, however, BP's position was very different. It controlled an even larger proportion of the then known reserves, but a major proportion of these were in one country. And that country, Iran, was a political tinderbox where BP was very unpopular.[7]

THE MOMENT PASSES: IRAN

Britain's Moment in the Middle East is the title of a perceptive book by Elizabeth Monroe. The book's title encapsulates its subject – Britain's engagement with the Middle East in the first three-quarters of the twentieth century. The immediate post-war years saw that moment still at its peak. One of the first intimations of its passing was the fate of the Anglo-Iranian oil assets in Iran.

As shown in Chapter 2, oil was not usually a predominant factor in Britain's diplomatic or military calculations in the Middle East before the Second World War. Securing control of the Suez Canal came first. Beyond that there was a whole nexus of factors: supporting British oil companies, but also minimizing financial commitments, maintaining the principles of the League of Nations, and keeping on good terms with local rulers and with the other main international actors in the area, France and the United States. The war highlighted oil's strategic import-ance. But as in the First World War, much of the oil that fuelled Britain's armed forces came from the Americas, not from the Middle East, in spite of AIOC's production in Iran. So the war did not dramatically or immediately shift thinking about the significance of Middle East oil supply, which for some years after 1945 constituted quite a small proportion of the non-communist world's total.

But as the post-war world settled into communist and non-communist blocs, the Middle East assumed a new importance. To Britain, controlling it was still vital for strategic reasons. But with India newly independent, its significance was now as a stage on the route to Britain's Far Eastern and Australasian colonies and trading partners. At the same time the Middle East blocked the Soviet superpower, lurking on the northern borders of Iran and Turkey, from Egypt and East Africa. Another important factor in the equation was the need to minimize Britain's post-war demand for American goods and raw materials, all of which needed dollars which were now in short supply. Much of the Middle East, as well as Britain's colonial possessions in Africa, were part of the 'sterling area' in which international transactions were conducted in that currency. Sterling area reserves were held in London and were at that time inconvertible into dollars. For Britain they were a bank on which it could overdraw in times of need, while the sterling area countries had an incentive to use their reserves on British goods.

So the Middle East was important to Britain, but for many reasons besides oil. And, leaving aside Britain's exit from Palestine in 1947, the first major crisis to confront Britain in the post-war years – that in Iran – illustrates this. Its immediate cause was oil, but its resolution depended on other factors.

The principal actor, Mohammad Musaddiq, was a wealthy Iranian landowner. As such he seemed an unlikely agent of radical change, and the incongruity was compounded by his appearance and habits. Sir Francis Shepherd, the British Ambassador to Iran, showed his disdain by describing Musaddiq as:

> both cunning and slippery . . . He looks rather like a cab horse and is slightly deaf so that he listens with a strained but otherwise expressionless look on his face. He conducts the conversation at a distance of about six inches, at which range he diffuses a slight reek of opium.[8]

Added to this Musaddiq's 'tendency to faint in public and his habit of negotiating from his bed wearing pyjamas', and it was hard to take him seriously. Ultimately, however, the crisis which resulted in the forced nationalization of AIOC's Iranian assets resulted not so much from underestimating Musaddiq – although he proved a clever and effective politician – as from miscalculating the whole tendency of opinion in Iran.[9]

Iranians had come to hate AIOC because they construed it as the next worse thing to a colonial power. In many ways this construction was unfair. AIOC's ancestor, the D'Arcy company, had taken all the risks in the early days of exploration, and its successor Anglo-Persian, which became AIOC, had spent large sums on providing welfare services to its large Iranian staff, in the form of houses, schools and hospitals. But to the Iranians, AIOC's British staff seemed aloof, while AIOC had made big profits, especially in the late 1930s. The perceived financial inequity was exacerbated during the war. Royalties were based partly on AIOC's dividends, but wartime dividends were limited by the British government. This continued after the war while at the same time AIOC's profits reached new levels on the back of a firm oil price. So money which the Iranians perceived as theirs was used to build up AIOC's Kuwait production and its cash reserves – or went to the British government in tax: its receipts from AIOC were around double those of the Iranian government's between 1945 and 1950.[10]

Financial inequity stirred up nationalist feelings which had been exacerbated by Iran's wartime and post-war treatment. The Allied wartime occupation was followed after the war by Soviet reluctance to vacate northern Persia and pressure from them for oil concessions. In response the Majlis (the Iranian parliament) passed a law which prevented the further grant of oil concessions to foreigners but also, in an even-handed way, called for the restoration of 'national rights' where they had been 'impaired'. In other words, it called for a rewriting of the agreement with AIOC. In 1949 the two sides began negotiations.[11]

   As Iranian grievances built up, international developments pointed to a possible solution – the 50/50 profit split first established in Venezuela and rapidly spreading through the Middle East. And the existence of this formula of course stoked up Iranian expectations. But Sir William Fraser, the new AIOC chairman, strongly resisted it even though AIOC argued that the draft agreement hammered out in 1950 gave the Iranians a similar result. When the Majlis, now dominated by Musaddiq's National Front party, rejected the agreement, the British government effectively took over negotiations; but they had no more success.[12]

   There have been various attempts to apportion blame for the breakdown. Fraser himself has often been accused of a narrow-minded obsession with profit which led him to ignore the bigger picture. Steve Marsh has recently argued that the British government was as or more culpable as it could have steered AIOC's policy if it had really wanted to. The government was wont to lament its inability to control AIOC in spite of its majority shareholding but there is little doubt that if it had held a gun to AIOC's head, for instance by threatening to withhold diplomatic support, AIOC would have been forced to follow the government line. One likely reason why the government initially did very little was that it tended to share AIOC's view that Iranians had weak characters and would eventually give way. Shepherd's disdainful comments on Mussadiq illustrate this Eurocentric viewpoint. It was given a semblance of support by the 1933 settlement, when after years of disagreement Iran suddenly conceded after a firm stand was made by the British government. But in 1933 the old Shah had much more power than the new one in 1950. The latter felt less able to challenge the stronger nationalist feeling of the post-war era or the resurgent Majlis. This points to one other factor – the intransigence of Iranian attitudes because of the country's own flawed political development. This intransigence was a reflection 'of the discontent with the ruling classes, of the disequilibrium in political, social and economic affairs inside Persia, and of the fear that dictatorship would be reimposed with foreign support'.[13]

   A lack of American support for the British position did not, from the British point of view, help. The United States was concerned about the possible growth of communism in Iran, and Mussadiq was thought a lesser evil. But whatever the American attitude, agreement would have been difficult. To Mussadiq, the chief danger was that any agreement, however favourable the terms to Iran, would be seen by his fellow countrymen as a climbdown. By mid-1951 Iran had unilaterally nationalized AIOC's assets in Iran, although AIOC personnel were still in occupation. In October 1951 AIOC evacuated its staff. The US accepted the British position that the nationalization was illegal and US oil companies joined the British in boycotting Iranian crude – a course of action made easier by the rapid increases in production elsewhere in the Middle East. As 1952 came and went the US began to accept Britain's long-standing argument that agreement would never be reached with Mussadiq. Mussadiq's own moderate support declined as the boycott of Iranian oil worsened the country's economic situation, forcing him to turn to extremists. America began to view him as a menace rather than an amusingly eccentric nationalist and he also fell out with the Shah. In 1953 the CIA instigated a coup in favour of the Shah which, after some hiccups, dislodged Mussadiq. While unquestionably an American-led affair, the British gave it enthusiastic support. Anthony Eden, the British Foreign Secretary, was likely to have favoured a cautious approach but was ill and Churchill, in his last fling as Prime Minister, took control of foreign policy. He was hardly going to turn down the chance to regain control of Iranian oil, his old hobbyhorse.[14]

There were two main results. However incompetent Mussadiq was in upholding Iran's real interests – since an international boycott of Iranian oil was clearly against these interests – his was a government with some legitimacy. It was replaced by a newly emboldened Shah who thereafter maintained an authoritarian regime. From the narrow perspective of AIOC, however, the result was as good as it could expect. The company's and Britain's losses from the initial confiscation were far less than were feared in 1951. Burgeoning oil production from AIOC's Kuwait and Qatar interests, and a boom in world trade, had restored both the company's and the country's financial position. Although the Iranian assets remained nationalized, a deal was struck: a consortium was set up which managed production and sold the oil. Financially, it was in the same position as if a 50/50 profit split had been effected. AIOC received compensation for its assets and a 40 per cent share in the consortium. (Shell received 14 per cent, CFP 6 per cent, and five American companies 40 per cent).

While oil was clearly a critical factor in the dispute, important aspects of the ensuing action were not about oil. The US government changed its attitude to Mussadiq because it came to perceive him as inimical to a firm anti-communist line. After his overthrow, the American oil companies were not at all keen to get involved in Iran. There was no worldwide shortage of oil so resuming Iranian production would simply create a potential surplus. But the US and British governments now needed the country to be economically stable, while it was still politically impossible for AIOC by itself, or an AIOC dominated consortium, to re-enter it. So US oil company participation was necessary to make the consortium acceptable, and governmental pressure was applied to them to ensure their compliance. Once that occurred and Iranian oil flowed once more, the focus of political instability in the Middle East moved elsewhere.[15]

THE MOMENT PASSES: THE ARABS, ISRAEL AND OIL

Anthony Eden, the British Prime Minister in 1956, had enjoyed one of the most glittering political careers of the twentieth century. He had become Foreign Secretary in 1935 when he was not yet 40; had gained a reputation for opposing the appeasement of the dictators following his resignation in 1938; and had returned to the position in 1940. His career's trajectory had slowed a little subsequently, as Churchill clung on to the Conservative leadership. But even so Eden still cut a dashing figure when he became Prime Minister in 1955. In November 1956, his health broken and his career ruined, he flew to Jamaica to convalesce. He had been brought down by the Suez crisis; and the Suez crisis was, in part, about oil.

Suez was about other things as well. It involved Britain's conception of the Middle East as a strategic area in the containment of the USSR, as discussed in the previous section. It also involved Egyptian nationalism. Nationalism formed the bedrock of the thinking of Colonel Gamel Abdel Nasser, who had become Prime Minister of Egypt following the overthrow of King Farouk in 1953. Nasser was distrustful of Britain, and insisted on it pulling its troops out of the huge Suez base. This was not in itself a major issue as Britain had other bases in the region, but it and other actions made the West reluctant to supply him with arms. He turned to the Soviets, ringing alarm bells in Washington and London. Then America and Britain, having raised Nasser's hopes that they would finance the Aswan dam, refused to do so. As an assertion of independence and for its revenue, in July 1956 Nasser unilaterally nationalized the Suez Canal Company. This had been owned by French and British shareholders, including the British government, and its operation was governed by international conventions. With the rapid growth of Middle Eastern oil production, the region was now fulfilling the major role in European oil supplies which even five years earlier had been only latent. Around 60 per cent of Britain's oil came through the Canal.[16] It became increasingly clear, however, that Nasser posed no threat to the Canal's smooth running. The mainly conservative Arab rulers pressed him not to disrupt oil supplies, while compensation to shareholders at a fair price was promised. The situation bore few analogies with the Iranian nationalization of AIOC's assets except that both Mussadiq and Nasser were essentially nationalists and not Soviet sympathizers.

That, however, was not how Eden or the French government saw it. Not only had Nasser interfered with their countries' commercial interests and challenged Britain's Middle Eastern defence strategy, but his anti-colonial stance threatened to destabilize each country's African colonies. And to Eden, Nasser's control of the

Canal also threatened Europe's, and Britain's, oil. Nasser, Eden believed, had 'his thumb on our windpipe'.[17] Harold Macmillan, his Chancellor of the Exchequer, was if anything even more obsessed with oil. He believed that Britain would lose both the oil and the oil companies' profits, which made a major contribution to Britain's overseas earnings: 'the conclusion is clear – without the oil both the UK and Western Europe are lost'.[18]

Many of those involved with oil were sure that Eden and Macmillan were wrong. Most senior Foreign Office staff were appalled at the idea of action against Nasser. Earlier, Shell had anticipated the possibility of nationalization and suggested to the Canal Company that they could arrange a leaseback deal with the Egyptians, thus maintaining management control but satisfying the aspirations of the latter. The Canal Company were not interested. After nationalization Shell's planners thought that problems would be settled by negotiation as 'No civilised nation will choose military action if it can avoid it.' Subsequently Shell, BP and other oil companies suggested to the government another scheme involving the leaseback of the Canal, this time to a new operating company.[19]

Doubts as to the need for military action are reinforced by analysis of the economic impact when the Canal was finally closed. Petrol in Britain rose in price by about 34 per cent. Two-thirds of this was a tax increase and one-third attributable to higher freight charges. In other words, the economic cost to Western Europe of canal closure was a relatively small rise in the price of petrol and other oil products, which in 1956 made a relatively small contribution to total energy supply. British oil companies' sales of 'sterling' oil did make a substantial contribution to the balance of payments but the closure of the Canal would not have wiped them out. Shell made much of its money outside the Middle East. BP had substantial African markets and, because Middle Eastern oil was so cheap, could have absorbed the extra freight to Europe and still made money. Eden and Macmillan's judgement exposes their economic naivety, particularly culpable in the case of Macmillan who fancied himself as an economic expert. They failed to understand the power of modern economies and large firms to substitute – coal for oil, longer sea passages for shorter ones and new markets for old.

Rational Shell planners were wrongfooted by panicky politicians, and the result was the Suez adventure. The British and French governments had no obvious excuse for the military action they both considered necessary. So acting clandestinely, with many ministers in the dark, the two governments cooked up a plan with the Israelis. Ever since Britain had relinquished its League of Nations mandate over Palestine in 1947 and Israel had become an independent state, both its boundaries and its very existence had been a matter of contention with the Arab world. The plan called for Israel to attack Egypt, on the pretext of taking reprisals for attacks by Arab irregular forces based in Egypt. British and French forces would then occupy the Canal Zone, ostensibly to safeguard it, and call on each side to withdraw. It was anticipated, rightly, that the Egyptians would refuse (the Zone lying within their own borders) and military action would then be taken against them.

While the military action was successful, the operation otherwise was a fiasco. Practically every country condemned it and the United States was particularly hostile. Domestic American politics played a part in this, but it also stemmed from the realistic assessment made by Eisenhower, the American President, that Nasser was not a Soviet stooge. With the Canal now closed after the Egyptians had sunk blockships in it, two things happened, both resulting from American disapproval of the Franco-British action. First, the Americans refused to allow their emergency oil allocation committee to be constituted. Without it American companies were reluctant to act together because they feared anti-trust action and so Britain could not rely on a reasonable physical allocation of American oil. Second, the Americans refused to support sterling on the foreign exchange market, necessary because its parity was at that time fixed against other currencies and selling pressure could destabilize it. Britain's financial position was weakened, partly because oil companies' foreign earnings fell due to the short-term disruption in the market. In trying to avoid a long-term problem whose effects they had exaggerated, Macmillan and Eden had created a massive short-term one. Sterling came under attack and the related crises precipitated Eden's collapse. Britain climbed down, the troops were withdrawn and the Americans immediately became cooperative. The crisis quickly eased and, although petrol rationing was instituted for a short time, things soon returned to normal.[20]

Suez had many results, most of which are peripheral to our concerns. It drove a wedge between the British and the French, who had wanted to defy world opinion and continue the operation. Britain's relations with most of the Arab world were damaged and Saudi Arabia broke off diplomatic relations. Eden resigned as Prime Minister and was replaced by Macmillan whom many saw as holding almost as much responsibility for the fiasco. Most importantly, Suez accelerated Britain's reappraisal of its position in the world and led to a more realistic assessment. To reduce her commitments, Britain had to decolonize more quickly than had been anticipated; and it needed the US as a permanent worldwide ally. As a concomitant of this, Britain's role in the Middle East was set to reduce. This reduction posed problems for Britain in the future conduct of its diplomacy in the region.

In spite of the efficient operation of the Canal once it had been reopened in spring 1957, Britain remained nervous. Dislike and distrust of Nasser was still a predominant view in government, not just because he controlled the Canal but because of his possible influence on other Arab leaders. Thus in 1959 the Americans still took the view that the biggest threat was of increased communist influence, Iraq now being the perceived target. Britain, on the other hand, saw the worst possibility as control of Middle Eastern oil falling into the 'hands of one man, namely Nasser'.[21] Britain was relatively sanguine about Iraq, in spite of a successful *coup d'etat* by Abd-al-Qasim against the pro-British regime in 1958, and was initially willing to cooperate with Qasim. Qasim's increasingly erratic behaviour, however, overturned Britain's friendly attitude. Ten years after Mussadiq, another threat to Britain's oil loomed as Iraq activated its claim to Kuwait.

Kuwait was a small principality on the north-west coast of the Persian Gulf. It had been *de facto* independent of the Ottoman Empire for many years and in the late nineteenth century had become, with other small Gulf states, a British protectorate. Small though Kuwait was, by the late 1950s the consortium in which BP had a 50 per cent interest was pumping out of it one and a half million barrels a day, or 15 per cent of the Seven Sisters' output. Shell also benefited because Gulf, BP's consortium partner, lacked markets and so Shell took half its output in a profit-sharing deal. The principality was also important to Britain because the Kuwaiti ruling family were happy to keep their surplus earnings in sterling.[22] Iraq, however, had a long-standing claim to Kuwait based on their mutual descent from the Ottoman Empire. Kuwait was due to become formally independent in June 1961. Conscious of the Iraqi threat, Britain strengthened Kuwait's armed forces before independence. Oil was at the forefront of British minds. In 1961 a Foreign Office minute stated that 'our fundamental interest in Kuwait [and other Gulf states] . . . is that they should continue to have an independent oil policy of their own and their policy should not fall under the control of any [hostile] Power'.[23] Britain's interest here was not just in the supply of oil to Britain. It was also in the assets and earnings of British oil companies and in the willingness of the Gulf rulers to keep their financial reserves in sterling.

Unlike the Gulf crisis of 1990–1, the episode 30 years earlier turned out to be a mouse. Immediately after independence, fears grew of Iraqi aggression. It is not clear whether Qasim really intended to invade Kuwait, nor whether his sabre-rattling resulted from a long-term plan to invade or a mere whim.[24] Britain's prompt action in providing military support, together with support from Saudi Arabia and Jordan, neither of which had much time for the Iraqi regime, headed off whatever threat there was. It also led to Britain mending its fences with Egypt and Saudi Arabia, as it would otherwise be left friendless in the Arab Middle East apart from Jordan and the Gulf States.[25] Qasim was overthrown in 1963 and, although the Baathist regime which replaced him eventually gave rise to Saddam Hussein's dictatorship, this change was at first welcomed in the West. By the mid-1960s concerns about oil supplies from the Middle East were much less acute. Although OPEC had been formed in 1960, it appeared weak.[26] And then came the Six Day War of 1967.

The Six Day War, from 5–10 June 1967, owed itself to the continued Arab hostility to Israel. Israel responded to growing pressure with pre-emptive strikes against the forces of a number of Arab countries. Nasser was one of the lynchpins of the anti-Israeli coalition and, as Israeli victory loomed, Egypt once more blocked the Suez Canal. In addition, Arab states embargoed oil supplies to countries deemed sympathetic to Israel – notably the United States and Britain. Western oil supplies were further reduced by civil war in Nigeria over the secession of Biafra, the oil-rich eastern province. Oil now constituted 40 per cent of Britain's energy supplies, as against 15 per cent at the time of Suez, and the novel weapon of embargo seemed to threaten a crisis far greater than that caused by Suez.[27]

Yet the ultimate results of all these threats were small. The Canal closure and embargo were mitigated in a variety of ways. Since the latter did not extend to many countries, Persian Gulf oil could be redirected elsewhere and Britain and America supplied from non-Arab sources. The US itself had reserves of production which it could activate in time of need – 'shut-in' oil – an arrangement which dated back to attempts to control overproduction in the 1930s. Some had been pumped after Suez, and it was exploited again in 1967.[28] Iran and Venezuela, two key non-Arab producers, were also busy pumping more oil. The embargo itself was honoured more in the breach than in the observance. The ruler of Kuwait told the British ambassador that he had to impose the embargo to satisfy Arab opinion, and he accepted that tankers might be rerouted at sea – he just did not want to know about it.[29] Finally, the impact of the Canal closure was further reduced by an impending change in the economics of ocean transport. The old limit on tanker size imposed by the Canal was being breached as shippers realized that it would be technically feasible, and more economic, to build giant tankers (Very Large Crude Carriers or VLCCs) – even if they had to sail round the Cape of Good Hope on their voyage from the Persian Gulf to Europe. Such tankers were already on order so, although the closure led temporarily to a sharp increase in freight rates, it was soon alleviated.[30]

In fact, the Canal was to remain closed until 1975 with decreasing effects on world trade. But the embargo was soon called off as Arab states realized that they were suffering from the loss of oil revenues more than were Britain or America from the reduction in supply. Harold Wilson, the British Prime Minister, argued in his memoirs that the additional burden of dollar oil and higher tanker freights led to sterling's devaluation in October 1967. In reality the weak underlying position of sterling has a better claim to be the real cause, even if devaluation was hastened by the Six Day War and its aftermath.[31]

The relatively easy substitution of other oil supplies and the swift resolution of the crisis fostered complacency among policy-makers and oil companies. The British government set up working parties to examine the possible effects of future interruptions. Their findings, however, were relatively sanguine. They concluded that several major suppliers would have to cease supply simultaneously for there to be major problems and they noted oil companies' ability to divert supplies from non-embargoed countries. They advocated increasing oil stocks but relatively little was done (see Chapter 6 'Government and oil').[32] So any sense of alarm in government quickly dissipated, and this extended to the companies. As late as 1969 Jersey Standard anticipated no major supply issues in the foreseeable future, anticipating that production from the new or prospective fields of Libya, Alaska and the North Sea would meet rising demand.[33]

The events of 1967 marked one, by now largely symbolic, caesura. Britain's 'moment in the Middle East' ended as the Labour government came to the conclusion that there was little purpose in retaining armed forces in the Gulf to guard oil supplies from which Britain had, at least technically, been denied access because of the embargo. The moment was likely to have ended sooner rather than later anyway, as Britain's last imperial commitments were wound down. But as it was, British forces were gone from the Gulf by the early 1970s.

WIDER HORIZONS

In spite of the ever-increasing flow of Middle Eastern oil, the companies were anxious to diversify their supplies. The locations involved included the exotic and unexpected, together with those which had long been either oil producers or seen as prospects.

Shell continued its long-standing interest in North American oil, drilling over 1,000 wells per annum in the USA in the mid-1950s, and it was still involved on a smaller scale in Trinidad. More adventurous was its push offshore. Shallow water offshore wells had been drilled off the coasts of California and Lousiana before the war. Shell started offshore drilling in a big way after the war, and by 1955 they had 200 such wells off the coasts of Louisiana and Texas, and others elsewhere such as Borneo and Lake Maracaibo in Venezuela. In the 1950s, Venezuela, where Shell accounted for around one-third of production, was still the Klondike of the oil world as it had been in the inter-war years. From 1955, when the country's total output exceeded 100 million metric tons (tonnes) per annum, to 1959 it produced 132 million tonnes a year on average. This was well above the combined production of Saudi Arabia and Kuwait. By the 1960s, however, they easily outstripped Venezuela as its growth rate slowed. Shell's offshore exploration, however, continued unabated around the world and by the 1970s it had the greatest commitment among the majors to offshore production.[34]

Shell's most successful new area was Nigeria. Coincidentally, the oil producing area of the Niger delta had once been named by the British the Oil Rivers Protectorate – but then it was palm oil not mineral oil which gave it the name. Shell and BP had jointly explored in Nigeria from 1937 and oil was struck in 1956, four years before Nigeria's independence. During the 1960s production mounted rapidly, apart from a drop at the beginning of the Biafran war in 1967–8, reaching 54 million tonnes a year in 1970 of which the two companies produced 70 per cent. Nigerian crude was valuable for two reasons. It was low in sulphur, ensuring low refining costs. And it was close to the USA, hungry for imports, thus minimizing freight costs.[35]

Nigeria was always a Shell-led operation in which BP participated. Until the late 1960s BP had a poor post-war discovery record. It had been signally unsuccessful in North America, with no major discoveries in spite of much exploration in Canada. Its epicentre was still the Middle East – Kuwait, Iran and Iraq and on a smaller scale Qatar, where oil was discovered in 1939 and brought into production after the war. Its only other big find was Libya, where it had a joint venture with Nelson Bunker Hunt. Even here, BP's original concessions were not productive and its big discovery was on one of Hunt's concessions which he had lacked the capital to develop. BP obtained a 50 per cent interest. Shell had had no success with its exploration in Libya, but took crude from there in a profit-sharing deal with a smaller company, Amerada.[36]

Smaller British companies had a mixed record. Trinidad Leaseholds, renamed Trinidad Oil, possessed an important brand in its Regent petrol as well as a fair-sized refinery in Trinidad. But the latter was reliant in part on fuel bought in from Venezuela, while the company was also vulnerable because it sold product in Britain made from relatively high-cost western hemisphere petroleum, when its competitors could access cheap Middle Eastern crude. Because of this Trinidad was not making enough money to finance further projects such as a UK refinery. In 1956 it sold itself to Texaco which was, via Caltex, already a partner in Regent. Burmah Oil had pursued a very different path. Its assets in Burma were nationalized in 1963 and, although it retained some interests in India, the writing was on the wall for these too. Without changes its future was as an investment trust receiving dividends from its large BP shareholding and a smaller, but still substantial, holding in Shell. This was not much of a future at all, since it was likely to lead to pressure for its break-up. The directors decided instead on a policy of expansion. In 1962 Burmah bought Lobitos, with production in Peru and a small refinery in north-west England, and then in 1966 Castrol, a lubricants manufacturer. (Castrol House in Marylebone Road became the 'head office' of Mogul, the fictional oil company in the late 1960s television series 'The Troubleshooters'.) The acquisitions had some logic as Lobitos also produced lubricants at its refinery, but Burmah was taking itself far from its origins.[37]

In 1975 it lost its last foothold on the Indian subcontinent when the old 'Burmah-Shell' venture in India, a product of the cartelizing drive of the 1920s, was nationalized. At much the same time a similar cooperative arrangement between BP and Shell in southern and eastern Africa, formed in 1928, was unravelling. The companies split up the South African operation between them and much of the rest of the 'Consolidated' area was eroded by nationalization and virtually wound up by 1981. In truth, these parts of the world had become, relatively speaking, economic backwaters. The action was in the rapidly growing countries of Europe, in Japan, and as always in the United States. Shell continued to have a strong position in both Europe and the US, as it had before the war, and also in Japan, where it became a major natural gas supplier from its Brunei field. Natural gas was a Shell strength worldwide. It had a 30 per cent share in the huge Dutch onshore Slochteren field, discovered in 1959. This led to North Sea involvement, discussed later, while by moving early into the transport of liquefied natural gas (LNG), which required temperatures of −165 Centigrade and therefore sophisticated tankers to transport it, Shell could also exploit remote gas fields such as Brunei.[38]

Shell's success points up BP's continued lag in product sales. By 1970 Shell was close to Jersey Standard in worldwide product sales, at around five million bpd – around four times its sales in 1950. (Jersey Standard still led Shell slightly on refining runs, and comfortably on crude output.) BP's product sales, by contrast, were around two million bpd in 1970.[39] This disproportion was not just a matter of Shell's earlier start, although of course that came into it. It also reflected a systemic failure by BP to build an effective image. Thus in the mid-1960s surveys showed that consumers in England, France and Germany saw BP as a dull and old-fashioned organization. Only in Italy did BP score more positively as it was thought to epitomize 'Swinging London'![40] BP did make two big strategic moves, however, in an attempt to remedy its downstream weakness. In 1968 it bought the 10,000 petrol stations of Sinclair in the eastern United States after Sinclair had been taken over by ARCO, which was forced to divest the stations by anti-trust legislation. The next year BP swapped the Sinclair stations and its Alaskan assets for a 25 per cent stake in Sohio, the stake increasing as Alaskan production increased. Sohio was yet another descendant of the original Standard Oil. It was a large company in its own right but with no crude assets. After this series of moves BP had a major position in the US market, albeit an indirect one via its Sohio shareholding.[41]

BP's strength, however, was still in crude production on the back of burgeoning output in Iran – once the new consortium got going from 1954 – Kuwait, and by the late 1960s Libya and Nigeria. It was the third largest crude producer in 1950 and 1970, but the raw statistics conceal a down and an up. It had dropped to fourth behind Gulf in 1955 with the loss of its Iran monopoly, and had only just edged ahead of Gulf again in 1965. But then its crude output accelerated faster than any other major, and its third place in 1970 was a comfortable one. Indeed at three and a half million bpd it was not far behind Shell. Much of BP's oil had to be sold elsewhere: for instance, in 1972 it supplied over 8 per cent of Japan's crude. With all this oil already, BP suddenly seemed on the verge of producing far more, for its reputation for giant discoveries was about to be salvaged. One mighty find was below the North Sea and is discussed in Chapter 8. The other was in Alaska.[42]

Interest in Alaskan oil had been sparked off by a find in southern Alaska in 1957. BP joined with Sinclair, whose petrol stations it was later to acquire, and looked towards the Alaskan North Slope. Behind this, as BP's historian points out, was a distinctive exploration strategy, established in the company's culture by D'Arcy's discovery in Iran 50 years earlier: early entry into new 'frontier' areas where oil had not necessarily been found previously and which held the possibility of giant fields because they were large exposed anticlines.[43] In practice, as had been the case with the company's original Libyan exploration area, the North Slope was disappointing. BP and Sinclair then acquired a large acreage on the flat coastal plain where the anticline was hidden. This too disappointed but BP had, alone, acquired further acreage in the Prudhoe Bay area. And then, just as in Iran in 1908, it was lucky. By 1968 it was planning to pull out when the other operator in the area – a consortium consisting of ARCO and Humble Oil – struck oil. BP decided to keep going and early in 1969 it, too, found its black gold. Total Prudhoe Bay production, shared between BP and Arco/Humble, would eventually reach 1.5 million bpd and some 13 billion barrels have now been extracted. Although BP ceded ownership to Sohio, it retained a major stake in Alaskan oil via its Sohio shareholding.[44]

Oil had been found, but not in a very convenient place. Prudhoe Bay is well north of the Arctic Circle and it was virtually impossible to get the oil out by tanker. Humble at huge cost reinforced a VLCC, the *Manhattan*, and sent it through the Northwest Passage to test the waters. The tanker suffered considerable damage and, anyway, the difficulty of building an oil-loading terminal in the shallow waters of Prudhoe Bay was enough to scupper the project. The only feasible method seemed to be a pipeline, 800 miles long from Prudhoe Bay to Valdez, an ice-free port on Alaska's south coast. It was to be built by the Trans-Alaska Pipeline System, or TAPS, a consortium of BP, ARCO and Humble. Burying a pipeline in the permafrost (permanently frozen sub-soil), as TAPS initially proposed, presented major problems. The oil would be pumped hot, for technical reasons, which would melt the less stable 'warmer' permafrost further south. In addition much of the line ran through an earthquake zone. In spite of the oil companies' later efforts to boost their environmental credentials, at first they had little grasp of the environmental problems. Their feeble response came up against a surge of interest in the environment in the late 1960s in America. This was compounded by the fact that many saw Alaska as the last pristine wilderness in the United States. As a result the project was stalled, beset by opposition and by its own inadequate planning.[45] Richard Nixon, elected President in 1968, was at first sympathetic to environmental issues but in the early 1970s the rapid shift in the balance of oil power to OPEC, and America's perceived need to free herself from reliance on imported oil, led to a comparable shift in the administration's attitude. It became a strong supporter of the pipeline. Soon after the Arab oil embargo of October 1973, with the project greatly amended – it was now to be built above ground – the pipeline bill was finally authorized. Oil started to flow in 1977.[46]

Nixon's brave words of 1973 about achieving energy independence were to be swept away by continued American profligacy in oil use. The environment, however, did not go away as an issue for oil companies. As early as 1970 BP had acknowledged its importance to the public perception of oil companies, announcing in advertisements that, 'when BP Alaska touches the wilderness, we try to touch it gently'.[47] In spite of that claim, there is little doubt that the combination of oilfield, pipeline, loading terminal at Valdez and workforce has been environmentally damaging.[48]

CARTEL OR COMPETITION?

Oil companies have always attracted a lively reaction from critics. Early on they were branded as trusts which worked against the interests of the public to raise prices. Then between the wars the left accused them of corruption and political machinations. After the war those accusations were made less often but the allegation that the oil majors formed a cartel persisted. It persisted partly because, before the war, it had been solidly grounded in reality. The 'As-Is' agreement had produced a cartel, with all its concomitants: allocation of market share, the control of production and common pricing – that is, the price f.o.b. at US ports on the Gulf of Mexico, then the epicentre of world exports.[49]

The allegation that the oil companies were still a cartel became prominent in the findings of the Federal Trade Commission report of 1952, which in turn instigated a major US anti-trust investigation since such agreements, at least under US law, were illegal.[50] However, subsequent to the report posted oil prices did not change much for a number of years and continued to yield the oil majors large profits, leading to the suspicion that they still controlled the market. Whether or not they did is a question that has now faded away as an issue of current concern. First OPEC, and then a variety of other factors, have eroded whatever powers they might have had. For 25 years after the Second World War, though, the oil companies' influence on prices was a central question among oil economists. But the discussion becomes, unavoidably, a little technical, so the reader who cannot stand that sort of thing should jump to the conclusion of this section.

My discussion of the subject has been heavily influenced by the 1968 book by Edith Penrose, who was a distinguished economist in other fields besides oil. After the war prices rose sharply from their wartime controlled levels of $1.36 f.o.b. Gulf of Mexico, but Gulf of Mexico and Persian Gulf prices had deviated, with a new basing point established on the Persian Gulf. By 1948 Gulf of Mexico prices reached $2.68 per barrel, and Persian Gulf $2.18. Some of this reflected quality differences – Middle Eastern crude is often sulphur heavy, more expensive to refine, and therefore less valuable – but most was a real price difference. It enabled prices to be roughly equalized in London, since the haul from the Persian Gulf is considerably longer than from the Gulf of Mexico, and hence tanker freight charges are higher. From then on the price ratio of one to the other continued to decline, with intermissions. In 1950 the standard Saudi Arabian marker crude, Ras Tanura, was only 63 per cent of the Gulf of Mexico price, but this was followed by a period of intermittent ups and downs. By 1959 the relative price was falling again, to just 55 per cent by 1961. Actual prices at that stage were $3.28 per barrel f.o.b Mexican Gulf, that is a modest increase over 1950, and $1.80 per barrel f.o.b. Ras Tanura – about what it had been in 1950.[51]

A brief explanatory narrative suggests that standard economic theory can go a long way to explaining the long-term course of prices. From the late 1940s Middle Eastern oil flowed with increasing abundance on to the world market. But a series of demand and supply shocks, superimposed on the natural rapid increase in demand, kept up prices for much of the 1950s. First there was the Korean War, which overlapped with the Iranian expropriation. They were followed by Suez. However, the long-term ratio of the Middle Eastern crude price to the US price was downwards because the US rapidly shifted from being an exporter to an importer.[52] Initially it was Western Europe which started to take crude from the Middle East as well as from the western hemisphere, and hence the equalization of prices in London. Then as US oil imports increased, some had to come from the Middle East. But it incurred heavy freight charges since it had to be hauled halfway across the world. In this situation the ratio of Middle Eastern f.o.b. prices to US prices inevitably fell, since prices would now be equalized in the Mexican Gulf. The actual cuts in Middle Eastern prices were not inevitable. If oil worldwide had been in short supply, the opposite would have occurred. All prices would have risen, or US prices would have risen and Middle Eastern remained static. But there was no underlying oil shortage. In these circumstances Mexican Gulf prices modestly increased but Middle Eastern crude prices fell.

Reasonably convincing although this 'competitive' story is, the conspiracy, or cartel, theorists still have some strong arguments. First is the high level of profits up to the late 1950s. Second is the relative slowness of price adjustments. In a competitive market, one would expect constant fluctuations in prices such as are evident today.

Penrose put forward various mutually reinforcing arguments to explain the stickiness in pricing. Because As-Is had introduced common pricing procedures which continued even after the agreement had become obsolete, the majors had a clear price marker which encouraged them to voluntarily forgo frequent price changes. They tended to follow price 'leaders' and only initiated price cuts slowly and reluctantly. This state of affairs, very common in markets with a few large companies such as the car industry, is 'oligopolistic' competition. A full-blown cartel such as 'As-Is', in contrast, will coordinate all its pricing decisions. Prices will not be merely sticky but will change in lockstep – which the oil companies' prices from the 1950s did not.[53] However, the companies did have tangible ways in which supplies were controlled, thus preventing too much downward pressure on prices. These were the offtake agreements where consortia controlled fields. In some of them, notably Iraq, Saudi Arabia and Iran, there were agreements by which companies wishing to take more than their quota paid the other companies a premium over the cost of production. Clearly this discouraged companies from taking more oil unless they really needed it, and in particular discouraged lifting it and then selling at a discount.[54] The American companies were able to get round US anti-trust laws here because the US government was keener to have an American influence in the region than it was to punish the companies for cartel-like activities.[55]

The other aspect of the oil majors' structure which Penrose thought critical was their vertical integration. Most oil was transferred within companies. Prices did not have to change on a day-to-day basis but there were still pressures which kept them roughly in line with 'natural' or market prices. Totally artificial pricing would inhibit the efficient allocation of capital within companies. Pricing crude excessively low would be counter-productive because companies received favourable tax treatment on their Middle East profits (see 'Seven Sisters'), while selling it cheaply on the open market would encourage competition in the products market. Conversely, executives running downstream activities in Europe would object to paying excessively high internal transfer prices since these would make it harder for their units to show a profit.[56] Having said that, there was a persistent tendency for the companies to make more money upstream than downstream, suggesting that posted crude prices were usually higher than the market rate would have dictated.

Penrose saw more evidence of collusion in European product prices, which did not initially fall. However, by the late 1950s competition in product markets was pushing down prices here too. As noted earlier, this period saw the beginnings of discounts on posted prices, opening the way for independents to buy cheap crude and undercut the majors' product prices. Between 1958 and 1965 product prices in Europe fell by 25 per cent. Penrose saw 1960 as marking the end of the era when the majors had any significant influence over prices, even though posted prices remained until the early 1970s. BP's history adds more substance to this analysis. As the company with the biggest crude surplus, it was constantly concerned with 'volume push' – in other words, with selling crude in increasing quantities.[57] The nature of two of the major consortia with which it was involved added to the pressure. In Kuwait, there were no financial constraints on the amount which either member of the consortium – BP and Gulf – could lift. They simply paid cost and reimbursed the other partner for any extra investment needed. In Iran, although there were financial constraints on individual members of the consortium lifting extra, there was constant pressure from the Shah for overall increases in production. BP had 40 per cent of the consortium and was therefore the recipient of 40 per cent of the additional output – which it had to sell.[58] So BP was something of a maverick among the majors, with its crude surplus adding to the downward pressure to prices. In the 1960s a further competitive element was added by those companies which came to the European market on the back of Libyan production, notably Conoco and Occidental.

The conspiracy theorist might still point to high oil company profits. But it did not need a conspiracy to achieve high profits during much of the 1950s. Demand conditions were favourable. The restrictions on offtaking undoubtedly helped to limit supply, but they were not enough to keep prices up in the long term. So it was the series of temporary shocks, as noted above, which were crucial in removing enough oil from the market – or in the case of the Korean War boosting demand – to ensure that prices held up. But from the late 1950s Middle Eastern crude prices fell, product prices followed them down, and the oil majors' profit margins declined (see 'Seven Sisters'). A final and telling argument is that the oil majors' rate of return over the whole period 1948–60 was no higher than that of large US manufacturing companies.[59]

By the late 1960s, therefore, the world oil market had shifted from a fairly organized one in which, without deliberately colluding, the majors had considerable control over prices, to one which was much more competitive. European prices were subject to constant downward pressure on the back of what seemed almost limitless new production in the Middle East and elsewhere. What then happened is revealed in Chapter 7.

6

Age of Optimism: The British People and Oil 1945–73

USING OIL

I learnt to drive in the mid-1960s in a Ford Popular made about ten years earlier. It looked dated, and indeed was, with a three speed gearbox and exiguous boot. Like most cars then it lacked syncromesh on first gear, and my abiding memory is the difficulty of changing down to first on hills, as with three gears and little power one often had to. The Ford was being fast overtaken technically, as it frequently was on the road. Morris Minors with their fashionably bulbous shape emerged in 1948 and the original Minis in 1959. They and the Ford all occupied the cheaper end of the rapidly expanding car market. In the 1930s cars had sold to two main groups of buyers, those who needed their car for business or work, and the upper middle classes or those even wealthier who could afford one for leisure use. By the late 1950s real incomes were rising steadily, widening the field of potential buyers; but many of these buyers could only afford cheaper vehicles. The Minor and then the Mini showed how economy could be achieved through better design and not just, like the Ford, by simplicity and crudity. As increasing disposable income met better products, the car market expanded rapidly. At its pre-war peak in 1937, 320,000 cars had been sold. In 1970 over one and a half million were.[1]

Favourable conditions for car ownership interacted with the increasing flow of oil, which helped to keep down the real price of petrol. Then as now, tax increases meant that the pump price rose, but after initial steep rises in the immediate post-war years petrol prices rose more slowly than inflation. Premium grade petrol was 4/8d (23p) per gallon in 1953. By 1970 it was 6/8d (33p) per gallon, an increase of 43 per cent, while all retail prices in the period had increased by 71 per cent.[2] There were, therefore, only limited incentives for greater fuel efficiency. Engines improved, but the gains tended to be eaten up by higher speeds. The hopeless performance of the Ford Popular was not much bettered by my own first car, a Standard Eight also made in the mid-1950s, which occasionally reached 60 mph on a long downhill stretch. By the 1960s, however, even the puniest new car could usually exceed 70, although it was not always wise to do so. The Standard's sluggishness meant that it, at the larger end of the small car spectrum, turned in around 40 mpg. The tiny Mini was much livelier but this meant that it used petrol at a similar rate, and medium-sized family cars rarely bettered 30 mpg.

These factors set the scene for a rapid growth in petrol consumption from the mid-1950s. By 1956, pre-war petrol and derv consumption of five million tons had grown to eight million and by 1970 consumption of the two fuels together was 19 million tons.[3] From the late 1950s road transport was given another spur by a big increase in government spending on new roads. Hitherto it had been easy enough to keep spending down, as road traffic only modestly exceeded pre-war levels. But its continuing growth, and particularly the growth of freight transport by road, increased public pressure for new construction. This dovetailed with a shift in government priorities. Lagging economic performance relative to the Continent and Suez's final blow to imperial dreams pushed economic modernization to the forefront. It is a little simplistic to see motorways as a substitute for Empire, but there is something in the idea. The first, the Preston bypass (now part of the M6), was opened in 1958. By 1972 over 1,000 miles were open.[4]

Petrol, and diesel for road vehicles (derv), were only a part of the vast increase in post-war oil use. And whereas in the inter-war period rising petrol consumption, and to some extent fuel oil and diesel for shipping, had been the main component of increased oil use, by the 1950s there were many big users, actual or prospective. There were several reasons for this.

One was rapid post-war economic growth, not just in Britain but worldwide. As a result, total energy consumption rose far faster than before the Second World War. Up to the mid-1950s coal remained the main source of energy but, even so, industrial steam raising and furnaces took over five million tons of fuel oil by 1956 compared with less than 500,000 tons in 1938.[5] By 1970 these, together with fuel oil's new use in electricity generation, took 40 million tons. In the same year petrochemicals took over 10 million tons. Some uses, however, had already reached their peak or even passed it because of a new competitor, natural gas from the North Sea. Oil had briefly become a popular fuel for gas manufacture in the 1960s but its usage peaked in 1969. Fuel oil consumption by industry peaked in 1970, and oil for central heating in 1973. Total oil use in Britain, around 10 million tons in 1938 and 30 millions in 1956, grew to 98 millions in 1970. In that year, it overtook coal as the biggest provider of energy.[6]

The impact of economic growth on increasing oil consumption was strengthened by the fall in the real price of oil. The rapid shift in the cost balance in favour of oil which occurred in the late 1950s did, however, lead to government intervention in the form of various taxes and other disincentives to oil use in the 1960s, explicitly in order to protect the coal industry. These are discussed in more detail later in the chapter. What is notable is how oil use grew in spite of their application.

To price, therefore, must be added technical change as a factor in promoting oil use. Petrochemicals were a major example. Before the war the petrochemical industry in Britain was virtually non-existent. The main raw materials, ethylene, propylene and butylene, were produced from natural gas or as a by-product of cracking petroleum. Oil firms in the USA – including Shell's American subsidiaries – had made some progress, as they had both natural gas and a need to crack petroleum to produce gasoline, but these conditions did not obtain in pre-war Britain and chemicals were produced mainly from coal. After the war, however, the growth of refining in Britain, discussed later in the chapter, together with the development of cracking technology, made the growth of a petrochemical industry almost inevitable. But of course, continuous technical change was also needed, both in production techniques and in the invention of new applications. There were other factors in petrochemicals' growth. The larger share of product taken by the heavier fractions such as fuel oil meant that British refineries were faced with a potential surplus of light distillates and one of these, naphtha, could be cracked to produce petrochemicals. In the late 1950s another incentive emerged: tax payments to producing countries could be offset against British tax liabilities, but BP at least did not make enough profit in Britain and therefore had available unused tax allowances; petrochemical profits, it was thought, were a way of using these.[7]

The two British oil majors, Shell and BP, inevitably played a large part in the development of petrochemicals in the UK. Shell's global growth in chemicals was such that by 1967 it was around the tenth biggest chemical company in the world, producing by a small margin more chemicals than Jersey Standard. In Britain itself, however, it fell behind BP. Up till 1967 BP's wholly owned production had concentrated on intermediates but in that year it took sole ownership of a large joint venture it had had with Distillers, the drinks firm, which had got into chemicals through the use of alcohol as a feedstock. BP now had large wholly owned petrochemical production facilities at Grangemouth, in Scotland, where it had a refinery, and Baglan Bay in South Wales which was fed by its Llandarcy refinery. However, the British chemical giant ICI was actually the largest UK petrochemical producer, building its own crackers and then in the 1960s, jointly with Phillips Petroleum, a refinery at its vast Wilton site on the River Tees. As a result of this, ICI petrol was for a time a familiar sight, especially in the north of England.[8]

Much technical change was less spectacular than that manifested in the pipes and columns of petrochemical plants. Instead it involved the working out of technologies which had already been established. Internal combustion engines were the chief example. The continued improvement of lightweight diesels helped road freight transport go on eroding the railways' share of freight carriage, which was reduced to relative unimportance by the 1970s. On the railways themselves improvements in diesel engine design meant that by 1968 diesel locomotives had taken over from steam, except for electrified lines. Improved internal combustion engines also helped air transport grow rapidly after the war, although here many other improvements, for instance in airframes and navigational equipment, were important. (This was one area where the war clearly accelerated development; in others, such as automotive technology, it probably retarded it.) Within a few years, however, a new technology, the jet engine, was to dominate air passenger transport and lead to a revival in the importance of kerosene, the product on which the international oil industry was founded in the nineteenth century.

While developments in oil-using technologies were important, as important were the inherent disadvantages of coal as a fuel compared to oil. Its bulk and the difficulty of handling it would inevitably prejudice its use as labour became more expensive relative to capital. Its polluting qualities led to Clean Air Acts, the first in 1956, which increasingly inhibited its use. Perhaps most important, coal supplied power through raising steam, and steam engines are inherently inefficient compared to internal combustion engines. As the latter, more than a hundred years younger than steam technology, were refined their latent advantages became more and more evident. Even over the last 30 years or so, when the relative price shift in favour of oil has been reversed, coal has failed to win back the markets it lost. Sadly, steam locomotives, steam lorries and the domestic hearth have all failed to make a comeback and hardly seem likely to. So one must conclude that coal for most purposes besides large-scale steam raising for electricity generation was on its way out whatever the exact price relativities. The temporary period of very low oil prices, from the late 1940s to the early 1970s, accelerated a decline which would have happened anyway.

SELLING OIL

The 1950s and 1960s were decades when consumerism in Britain reached well beyond the middle classes. In the same years oil entered into consumption in ways old and new: directly as petrol or lubricating oil, indirectly in older by-products or the new wonders of the petrochemical industry. The businessman's Sunbeam, humming along as it took him to a meeting, would, of course, be fuelled by petrol – perhaps Esso Golden Extra if he thought his engine deserved a higher octane than normal. In the 1950s its lubricating oil might be Millers Pistoneeze, but by the 1960s he might be using one of the new multigrades such as BP's Energol Visco-Static. His wife, meanwhile, could choose a skirt woven with ICI's Terylene and by the 1960s she could add a handbag made with BP's Geon, which might also be used to trim the Sunbeam's seats. Then she would return home, perhaps to waft Shell's Vapona flyspray at an errant insect while reflecting how she could persuade her husband to stop using Brylcreem, a petroleum by-product dating back to the 1930s. She might need to soothe her skin, irritated by too much contact with artificial fibres, with Vaseline, another well-established by-product. And by the early 1970s she might even finish her day by cooking pork or chicken which had been fed on Toprina, BP's protein derived from oil.

Until the early 1950s, though, that age of consumerism and most of its products still lay in the future. Instead, an almost wartime austerity still ruled. During the war all petrol was, by government fiat, low octane 'pool' and brand names were disallowed. There was no change to this in the immediate post-war years and, although petrol rationing was discontinued in 1950, the government still restricted sales to 'pool'.[9] In spite of this restriction a radical change was soon under way in petrol retailing, which laid the foundation for the pattern which is still familiar today. Up to the war larger petrol stations had usually sold two or more brands of petrol, thus maximizing their sales by catering for motorists who had different brand preferences. After the end of rationing, however, Esso destabilized the system by offering dealers an inducement to take their petrol – still at that time unbranded pool – solely from the company. A variety of factors lay behind this move. Esso had long held the second position behind Shell Mex/ BP (SMBP) which had had a joint marketing agreement since 1931. But before the war Esso's strength had lain in sales of standard-grade petrol to commercial users – many light lorries, as well as most vans, then having petrol not diesel engines. With work on the Fawley refinery well under way, the company would soon have large quantities of premium-grade petrol to sell, which it would have to market through retail outlets. Premium-grade sales were still not allowed in 1950, but the easing of controls meant that the ending of all restrictions could be anticipated at some stage. By moving quickly to tie up stations with sole agent agreements, Esso could improve its market position. The new arrangements also, of course, saved substantially on the company's transport costs as the number of locations at which its road tankers had to call was reduced. But since this advantage accrued to all companies which chose to follow Esso's policy, it seems unlikely that it was its main motive.[10]

Esso's first targets were mixed stations which also took petrol marketed by Regent, a substantial concern but not one with the resources of SMBP. Regent tried to stem the flow rather than going with it. As a smaller company, it was liable to be squeezed through such competition, since it was likely to end up with widely scattered stations rather than having, as pre-war, at least one pump in many locations. When SMBP joined the rush to exclusivity in 1951, however, Regent had to join in since otherwise most stations would soon be tied to one of the big two. By 1956, 89 per cent of stations had 'solus' – as the new system was called – arrangements.[11]

Before the war dealers had been adamantly opposed to the solus system and had successfully resisted it, so their apparent willingness to change also needs explanation. From the dealers' point of view, while the relaxation of restrictions on brand names could be anticipated at some stage, they did not know when. Until it occurred, they gained nothing from having different companies' pumps. The oil companies' financial inducements to become sole agents would thus have loomed larger in their calculations. The eventual outcome of the shift in the companies' relative strengths was predictable. Esso achieved its aim and together with its Cleveland brand, then quite strong, had almost 30 per cent of the retail market in 1956. SMBP had acquired National Benzole in 1957 and together they had about 50 per cent. Until 1956 SMBP had protected its smaller brands, Dominion and Power, by keeping their pumps at the sites it controlled. After 1956 it moved to a brand-exclusive policy and this meant that the smaller brands, with fewer stations, declined and eventually faded away. National Benzole survived although it ceased to add benzole, a coal by-product which had enhanced the octane rating of petrol but had become redundant as a result of technical improvements. SMBP's new exclusivity policy also meant difficulties with petrol station owners who preferred to sell Shell because of its much stronger image. Since SMBP – partly owned by BP – was committed to supporting the BP brand, some garages had to be persuaded, or leant on, to sell the latter.[12]

Regent fought hard to maintain its position and in the mid-1950s had almost 15 per cent of the market. But the expense of obtaining sole agency in large numbers of stations may have contributed to the takeover in 1956 of one of its parents, Trinidad Oil, by Texaco. Texaco already had a share in Regent via

Caltex, the other parent, and when Caltex subsequently split its operations, most of Regent's stations went to Texaco and were rebranded.[13] The Texaco takeover throws an interesting sidelight on the continuing influence of the British Empire on political discourse – as did the Suez crisis only a few weeks later. The takeover was greeted with an outcry from a number of Conservative MPs and from professional troublemakers such as Lord Beaverbrook, the proprietor of the *Daily Express*. Macmillan, the Chancellor, who was responsible for clearing the takeover, was accused of 'selling out the Empire'. Unlike with Suez, his adroit handling calmed the storm.[14]

The only other operators of any size at that time were Mobil and Petrofina (Fina). Mobil was the British subsidiary of Socony-Vacuum, one of the majors but hitherto only a seller of lubricants in Britain. Mobil's new refinery at Coryton also produced petrol, however, so it set up a sales network and ended the 1960s with 10 per cent of the market. Fina was based in Belgium and had achieved a fair market position although it did not have a British refinery. From 1961, however, the situation changed again. A small independent station operator, Jet, was bought by Conoco which was on the way to becoming a large producer in Libya. With its low transport costs to Europe, Libyan oil gave Conoco a competitive advantage. Jet was already a discounter and Conoco continued the policy, which had virtually disappeared from the British retail petrol market since the days of Russian Oil Products in the early 1930s, on a larger scale. By 1970 Jet and other new entrants had 22 per cent of the market, achieved at the expense of SMBP, Esso and Regent/Texaco.[15]

Not all the new entrants were discounters, since some large international companies such as Total of France also moved into the British market but largely adhered to the majors' prices.[16] So non-price competition remained extremely important, as it had been before the war. The problem for the majors in following the discount route was that petrol prices were transparent. Any price cut could be quickly emulated locally and no significant volume gain would result from it. The alternative policy was to spend the money on giving consumers convenience and better facilities. Since the majors retained by far the largest part of an expanding market, it was obviously quite successful.

As control of pumps had been the majors' biggest weapon before the war, so under the solus system it was control of stations. The solus agreements themselves could last up to 20 years but the companies felt the need to make their control even more secure and moved into ownership. By the mid-1960s the established companies' directly owned stations contributed a quarter of petrol sales.[17] Control of station sites was important because new ones had to get planning permission and, most of all, existing stations were likely to occupy favourable positions near road junctions, by main roads on the outskirts of towns and so on. Out-of-town-centre supermarkets with their opportunities for new station building and increased competition had not yet arrived.

The majors' control of sites was backed up by other forms of non-price competition. In theory companies competed on station quality although Duncan Burn, writing in the late 1950s, noted that 'It is widely felt that service in the United Kingdom is by international standards low.'[18] He was discussing how solus arrangements might improve matters but, even so, my memory is that most petrol stations in the 1960s were still pretty grotty. Nevertheless there were innovations. Pumps became squatter and squarer, more akin to today's shape, and in 1966 BP introduced mixer pumps in Britain. And Shell had introduced self-service in 1963, although the move was more about cutting costs than improving quality.[19] As a small recompense this was the heyday of the petrol company road map, given away free or sold for a small sum. Ian Byrne's website, devoted to these, also has a vast amount of information about the history of brands, both large and small. The impression given is that company maps were never as important in Britain as on the Continent, perhaps because of our excellent Ordnance Survey maps. But the website shows that, for example, Esso maps looked much smarter than the more limited offerings from a discounter such as Jet.[20]

Mainly, though, the majors relied on advertising, underpinned by subtle product differentiation. Standard grade petrol in the early 1950s was still an astonishingly low 74 octane, only a couple of points up on pool petrol, and premium when it was reintroduced in 1953 was around 92 octane – below today's standard grade. One tactic of the majors was to shift octane ratings up from time to time. This was a genuine, not just a factitious, improvement since higher compression engines needed higher octane petrol. But in 1956 the big companies introduced a third, 100 octane, blend, 'BP Super Plus' being the first. Such an octane rating was almost entirely unnecessary in practical terms but demonstrated the companies' technical competence and implied a connection with high-performance racing cars. Additives with possible or real beneficial effects on engines were another way of demonstrating a company's scientific prowess. Thus, in 1954 Shell introduced 'ICA', which was meant to keep sparking plugs in better condition. (It was called TCP in the United States, but as this was a well-known antiseptic in the UK Shell renamed it.)[21]

Advertising itself was very important although it seems likely that it reinforced images which had been built up over a long period. Thus Shell may have benefited from its heavy investment since the 1930s in posters of the English countryside, commissioned from well-known artists, and its high-quality 'Shell Guide' series of county gazetteers. These gave it an up-market image, complemented by other advertisements which, by being catchy and amusing, were themselves a talking point.[22] It also benefited from its long-established slogan 'You can be sure of Shell'. Esso's tiger was a long-standing company mascot and in the mid-1960s Esso capitalized on it with its famous cartoon tiger campaign. Two and a half million tiger tails were sold to hang from petrol filler caps (then usually exposed) and myriads of bumper stickers proclaimed that 'I've got a tiger in my tank'. By contrast BP, in spite of spending two-thirds as much on advertising as Shell and Esso, was not able to shift its negative image. Thus a mid-1960s opinion poll found that BP purchasers were perceived as 'notably lower-class and economy minded'. Confronted with a free choice of brands, Esso and Shell were each chosen by 30 per cent of purchasers, BP by only 6 per cent.[23] BP therefore was particularly reliant on SMBP's control of stations to protect its market share against new entrants. Shell and Esso could also rely on their much stronger image and, although their market share declined in the 1960s, much of the loss came from the decline of their minor brands, Cleveland (Esso) and Power (SMBP).

Retailing oil products to motorists was not just about selling petrol. Diesel cars were still almost unknown, but lubricants were a major part of the retail market. Most people under 40 or so, used as they are to having the engine oil changed at services and not doing much about it in between, would be amazed by the amount of oil consumed by cars in the 1950s and 1960s. With frequent service intervals – typically every 3,000 miles in the 1960s, and engine oil was usually topped up in between – lubricating oil was big business. The biggest specialist firm was C. C. Wakefield, who sold under the trade name 'Castrol', but the big oil firms attacked the market vigorously in the 1950s and 1960s. In this they were aided by the solus policy which enabled them to stock only their own oil in company-owned stations, while solus agreements might also restrict the lubricants stocked by non-company owned outlets. As a result of a long-running campaign led by Wakefield, the Board of Trade referred the petrol and lubricants market to the Monopolies Commission in 1960. With the celerity one expects of such an organization, it reported in 1965. Its judgement affected more than just the lubricants market. It restricted solus agreements to five years and mandated that such agreements should allow retailers to sell competing brands of lubric-ants, accessories and so on. It also prevented companies with more than 15 per cent of their business through owned outlets from acquiring a larger number of outlets – although they could dispose of old ones and acquire the same number of new ones. The judgement, therefore, must have done something to improve the position of new operators in the wider petrol market. Since the lubricants market had also been opened up further, fierce competition continued in it and another company, Duckhams, came from almost nowhere to win 26 per cent of the market in 1970. BP bought the company in 1970 to strengthen its position in lubricants.[24]

Competition also increased when SMBP was broken up, a move agreed in 1971 and completed by 1976. The prime mover here was Shell which, although it had 60 per cent of the shareholding and quota, was sure it could do better on its own. BP would also lose because its refineries were more export orientated and not linked by a pipeline running through the Midlands, as Shell's were. Under the SMBP arrangements, products under either brand might be supplied by any of the companies' refineries, thus allowing BP to take advantage of Shell's potential for low-cost distribution. Agreements were made to ensure that BP still obtained these advantages for twelve years after the SMBP dissolution, while BP also acquired National Benzole and most of its 'National' brand stations to bring its share up to 40 per cent.[25] BP's *quid pro quo* for the break-up of SMBP was the winding up of the old 'Consolidated' marketing area in Africa, another partnership with Shell, which BP disliked as being under Shell's sole managerial control (see Chapter 5, 'Wider horizons').

While petrol sales were and are the public face of oil companies' business, they were, of course, only part of their overall sales, which also comprised increasing amounts of diesel, fuel oil, kerosene for jet fuel and other products. Most of these sales were either to wholesalers or direct to large end-users.[26] The market was always more competitive than the petrol one but, Duncan Burn thought in the 1950s, not particularly so. Most sales were made at fairly standard published prices, with quantity rebates. There is plenty of evidence, though, that competition in the oil world in general increased from the late 1950s (see Chapter 5, 'Cartel or competition?'). It is likely that sales of products other than petrol then saw more discounting. Unlike petrol retailing, such discounts would not necessarily become public and could therefore be selective. However, hard evidence is lacking. Sales departments also relied on their technical expertise in the best use of oil products, which was likely to give the big companies an advantage.[27] Some companies also specialized in lubricants where specification might be as important as price. Mobil, for instance, only sold lubricants in Britain before it built its refinery. Lobitos, which had a small refinery for lubricants and by-products, was another example.

An increasing volume of sales, of course, were of petrochemicals and here too the big companies were mainly concerned with sales to other businesses and so escaped the complexities of the retail market. The petrochemical market, however, had other characteristics which made it difficult in other ways. Investment was 'lumpy' because scale economies meant that only very large units could economically produce the basic chemicals. As a boom developed, prices would rise and at that stage several companies would decide to invest. For example in 1965 British Hydrocarbon Chemicals, the BP/Distillers joint venture, started work on a 250,000 ton ethylene cracker at Grangemouth which exceeded the capacity of all its existing crackers there. Then a few months later ICI planned a 450,000 ton cracker for its Wilton site. The resulting overcapacity drove down prices, and profits, in the late 1960s. But to cut back investment meant losing economies of scale and therefore eventually becoming uneconomic. BP suffered particularly in this period, making a net loss in petrochemicals between 1967 and 1973. Then in the 1970s the increases in oil prices cut back the growth rate in petrochemicals and the years of glorious, if not always profitable, expansion came to an end.[28]

Over the long term, chemicals never delivered quite the returns which more optimistic oil company executives had once anticipated. Shell, early in the field because of its US interests, is still a major chemical company but has only a modest presence in the UK, as has Exxon.[29] BP's oil-derived protein, Toprina, was an early casualty of the oil crisis. Large-scale production was planned at an Italian joint venture, but it was difficult to obtain Italian approval of Toprina's safety. This was driven in part by genuine environmental concerns, which were compounded by Italian bureaucracy and political infighting. It was not helped by a culture clash, BP's nutrition manager not being the best choice to liaise with the Italian Ministry of Health. He wore 'a bowler hat [and] monocle . . . and shouted at the Italians. Constantly referred to . . . World War II and the Italians' part in it'. There were as a result endless difficulties, but in the end closure in 1978 was forced by the simple fact that increased oil prices meant the process was unlikely ever to be economic.[30] BP finally sold its chemical interests, including the Grangemouth refinery, to INEOS in 2005. The Baglan Bay chemical plant and the Llandarcy refinery which supplied it had been closed a few years earlier. ICI, by far Britain's biggest petrochemical producer, had its own refinery at Wilton on Teeside. But eventually, like the British Empire from which the company took its name, ICI's was dismantled piecemeal. The rump of the company was taken over in 2007.

REFINING AND TRANSPORTATION

On the morning of 11 December 2005, starting at one minute past six precisely, a series of huge explosions ripped apart the fabric of an oil depot and industrial estate a few miles north of London, at Buncefield in Hertfordshire. During the night, a level gauge in a petrol storage tank had failed. The tank, fed by a pipeline, continued to fill but the level gauge did not record it. A protection system, which should have cut off the supply to the tank when overfull, also failed to operate. As the petrol overflowed a vapour cloud built up and finally ignited. It was a series of accidents, which made the British briefly aware of the infrastructure which provided them with petroleum products. Buncefield was the terminus, or on the route, of two pipelines from coastal refineries and was a major distribution depot. For a few days, while fires raged, it remained a centre of attention. But fortunately there were no fatalities, although 40 people were injured, and fairly soon the nation forgot about it again.[31]

Before the Second World War most oil came into Europe as refined product and large refineries were located, like Abadan, in or near the centres of oil production. This had been logical when exploitation outside the US started, because a large proportion of product was fuel oil for ships' bunkers or paraffin which had a worldwide market, and therefore importing crude oil to Europe to be refined and then shipped out again was not sensible. Between the wars petrol consumption in Europe had grown substantially but it was still relatively small and economies of scale dictated that refineries remained in their original locations. A dramatic illustration of such economies is that Abadan's annual throughput was equal to the UK's pre-war oil consumption – although the illustration is not quite typical as Abadan was the largest refinery in the world.

After the war, numerous large new European refineries were built. As a result there was a significant change in Britain's coastal geography. Since refineries needed considerable amounts of land, new ones were often located in previously rural coastal regions. Refineries did not employ large numbers of workers relative to the capital investment they absorbed, but nonetheless they opened up significant employment opportunities as well as impinging on the landscape. And they provided the feedstock for petrochemicals, bringing in a further land-hungry and obtrusive new industry. Why did this shift from a long-established pattern of oil company operations occur?

While there was some government pressure to extend refining in the UK, changing circumstances meant that the shift also suited the oil companies themselves. Extrapolating from pre-war patterns of growth, it was clear that demand would increase steadily after the war. In the event, of course, it increased rapidly. Since post-war Europe was desperately short of dollars, it was also clear that non-dollar oil – which mainly meant Middle Eastern oil – would be the means of meeting that increase. But much of the additional oil would come from countries such as Kuwait, Bahrain and Saudi Arabia whose oilfields were hardly developed before the war. There were, therefore, few refineries apart from

Abadan and to construct new ones in the producing areas was expensive, since the materials and much of the labour had to be imported. Finally, oil company planners were starting to think about using much larger tankers. But these might be too large for the ports where products were delivered. New refineries with deep-water anchorages would accommodate them. Meeting additional demand by building new refineries in Europe made sense to both governments and oil companies.[32]

The post-war Labour government's eagerness for new refineries was not deflected by concerns, expressed by the armed services, about their vulnerability in another war. At a time when the need for dollars was acute, the ability to save dollars, both by refining Middle Eastern oil and by keeping within the UK the added value of such refining, overrode other priorities. The government had a panoply of controls over capital expenditure so its approval for individual developments was vital. It had reservations over two major planned refineries, Jersey Standard's (Esso) at Fawley and AIOC's (BP) on the Isle of Grain in Kent. They were not in development areas, that is the areas of heavy pre-war unemployment. And, in an early example of environmental concerns over oil, Fawley was also criticized because it would impinge on the New Forest. Esso adamantly refused to build its refinery elsewhere, however, and it was thought invidious to insist on BP doing so when it was committed to expanding another refinery, Llandarcy, which was in a development area. These and other expansion plans were approved in August 1947, although the refineries took a number of years to build.[33]

In the final peacetime years before the war, just 2.4 million tons of oil were refined in Britain – about one-quarter of consumption. By 1953, with the first stages of refinery expansion more or less complete, 25 million tons were refined and capacity virtually matched domestic consumption, although in practice a proportion of products were imported and a similar proportion of those refined in Britain were exported.[34] Apart from Fawley and the Isle of Grain, there was another big new refinery, Socony Vacuum's (Mobil) at Coryton on the Thames Estuary. Shell carried out major enlargements, amounting effectively to new builds, of its existing establishments at Thornton (now Stanlow) in the north-west and Shellhaven on the Thames next to Coryton, while BP did the same at Llandarcy and Grangemouth.[35] Refinery building fell back after these projects were completed in the early 1950s, but then picked up again in a second wave of investment in the 1960s.

Investment in refining was necessary not just to increase capacity but because of rapid changes in technology. Thermal cracking had been adopted in the inter-war years and enabled companies to vary the types of product they produced. It was particularly valuable as it enabled the yield of petrol from a barrel of oil to increase. In the late 1930s catalytic cracking was developed, again initially in the US, and eventually superseded thermal cracking for most purposes. Platinum reforming or 'platforming', by which low-octane products could have their octane ratings enhanced, was another important process first developed in the 1940s. All these processes took years, and heavy investment, to become commonplace and themselves were constantly improved. The combination of technical development and demand growth meant that, as well as the building of new refineries, older ones were subject to continuous upgrading and expansion. Then in the 1960s there was a trend towards building refineries in locations where giant tankers could offload. The estuary of Milford Haven in west Wales became a particularly popular site for this reason, with three refineries around the town of Milford Haven itself and one on the opposite side of the estuary near Pembroke Dock. There were also two on the Humber estuary near Immingham. New refineries and the expansion of old ones meant that by 1970 over 90 million tons of oil was refined in Britain.[36]

Along with the changing location of refineries went another change – the rapid growth in the size of oil tankers. The standard tanker in the big oil companies' fleets was around 10,000 to 12,000 tons for a remarkably long time, from the 1920s to the early 1950s. It was a size suited to the carriage of products to ports all over Europe. BP was already anticipating larger tankers in the 1940s, when it started planning coastal refineries, and by the early 1950s its new 28,000 tonners were arriving. Broadly speaking, the larger a vessel the less the freight cost per ton due to economies of scale. Flexibility was reduced, but big tankers dedicated to carrying crude only needed to go to a limited number of destinations – the refineries. The logic of scale meant that tanker size then increased rapidly and the word 'supertanker' was coined. BP had a 50,000 tonner delivered in 1959 and Shell a 71,250 tonner in 1960, and by now tankers were equalling the tonnage of the previous maritime record holders, the great ocean liners. Beyond that size tankers could not pass through the Suez Canal fully loaded. They could, however, go through with a part load and then top up, either from oil bought through the Canal by smaller vessels or from one of the pipelines which terminated on the Mediterranean coast – the Tapline from Saudi Arabia or the Iraqi pipeline. Tankers rapidly grew to over 100,000 tons and by the mid-1960s a new term, Very Large Crude Carrier (VLCC), was used for the 200,000 tonners plus that were being considered. The plan was for these tankers to make their entire loaded voyage to European destinations round the Cape, although they would return via the Canal. In the event, the Arab-Israeli war of 1967 and the eight-year closure of the Canal was to prove the new giant tankers irreplaceable. Even using the Cape route in both directions, they were a cheaper means of transport than using

80,000 tonners via the Canal. A huge ordering boom resulted as the oil companies converted to VLCCs. With ships of this size, direct access to many refineries, even some newer ones, might be impossible. Oil companies therefore established offloading points where there was particularly deep water. Here oil could be transhipped to smaller vessels for the last part of its voyage. The technology was then refined so that oil could be transferred at sea.[37]

In the early years of the oil industry in the USA, Rockefeller's control over transportation had been an important element in his ability to control the market. Shell had emulated this in the 1890s with their ability to undercut others by efficient tanker transportation through the Suez Canal – although at that stage they were shipping kerosene from west to east, rather than crude oil or products the other way. From then on large oil companies had taken it for granted that they should also own ships. By the inter-war years, however, a breed of independent tanker owners had come into existence. At that time Norwegian owners were predominant although they were later joined by the Greeks. The majors' fleets, therefore, were not an essential part of their control of the market since independent oil firms had access to tankers. But their fleets gave the majors considerable security in the light of their vast demands for shipping, particularly at times of crisis such as the Suez Canal closures. Nevertheless the capital which was tied up in ships was large even by their standards, and by the 1960s they increasingly chartered vessels from specialist tanker owners, both to meet short-term fluctuations and on long-term charters.[38]

Transport within the UK also needed considerable investment. By the late 1950s volume was building so much that large commercial pipelines, supplementing the government's wartime network, became economic. A product pipeline from Fawley to a depot near Heathrow was started in 1960, while BP had already installed a crude oil pipeline from Loch Finnart on the west coast of Scotland to Grangemouth on the east and was building one from Angle Bay in Milford Haven to Llandarcy, thus linking both its old refineries to deepwater harbours. In the light of concerns over this new (for Britain) means of transport, the government passed, remarkably quickly, a bill to regulate pipelines. A product pipeline was then built linking Stanlow in the northwest with Shellhaven and Coryton in Essex, with various branches. It was this pipeline which ran via Buncefield, from where there was a branch delivering kerosene to Heathrow. Later Total built a pipeline to Buncefield from their Lindsey refinery near Immingham. The modern pipeline network can be viewed on the Linewatch website. Pipelines notwithstanding, other forms of transport remained important. Given the close-ness of most of Britain to its coastline, it is not surprising that much product is still distributed initially by ship, which is the cheapest means of transport, and then by road from coastal terminals. Bulk rail distribution grew in the 1960s and Esso actually pulled out of the cross-country pipeline consortium because it found rail cheaper, although subsequently rail's share has declined.[39]

OIL AND THE ENVIRONMENT

At 6.45 a.m. on Saturday 18 March 1967, Captain Pastrengo Rugiati was woken up with the news that land had been picked up on the radar. With 120,000 tons of BP's Kuwaiti crude aboard his supertanker, Rugiati was almost at the end of a four-week voyage from the Persian Gulf via the Cape of Good Hope. The land on the radar was the Scilly Isles, and his ultimate destination was the BP jetty at Angle Bay in Milford Haven, a sheltered anchorage in south-west Wales. From there the oil would be pumped to BP's Llandarcy refinery. The Scilly Isles, however, were on the port (left hand) bow, not on the starboard as Rugiati had planned. The current had set the tanker slightly to the east of the route he had plotted. The first officer, on watch, swung the vessel slightly to port, ready for Rugiati to get her back on to her original course west of the Scillies.

But getting her back would take time, and Rugiati felt that he did not have it. He must arrive at Milford Haven by 11 p.m., or wait another five days for a tide which would furnish the depth of water needed to enter the Haven. The tanker could easily get there in time with normal steaming, but Rugiati needed to trim the tanks, which would reduce the tanker's draught. To minimize the risk of spilling oil, he did not want the vessel moving quickly while this was being done. Rugiati decided from his cabin to revert to the course the tanker had been on a moment before, which would now take him east of the Scillies, between the islands and Land's End at the tip of Cornwall. Then he dressed and went to the bridge.

Going between the Scillies and Land's End is not the best route for a large supertanker travelling at 16 knots, or about 18 miles per hour. But it was perfectly possible on the existing course, which would take the ship east of the Seven Stones, a group of rocks about six miles east of the Scillies. Rugiati, however, adjusted course slightly to port, to aim for the gap between the Scillies and the Seven Stones. It was a mistake. Six miles is not a lot of space, there were fishing vessels in the way, and fixing the tanker's exact position was difficult. At the point where Rugiati wanted to make a further port turn to take him safely past the rocks, a fishing vessel prevented the manoeuvre. Tension on the bridge was mounting. Clear of the fishing boat, Rugiati ordered the helm hard to port, but the ship did not immediately respond. The selector control was in the wrong position. Rugiati remedied the problem and helped the helmsman swing the wheel. The ship started to turn, but just too late. She impaled herself on the Pollard Rock, at the north-west tip of the Seven Stones.[40]

The ship was the *Torrey Canyon*, and it was the aftermath of its dramatic wreck which has made it so famous. Other, more recent, tanker disasters have receded into local memory only. But most people to whom I've mentioned the *Torrey Canyon* have heard of it.

With oil washing out of the vessel and drifting towards the Cornish coast, a Dutch salvage company attempted to tow it off the Pollard Rock, a hazardous enterprise in which a member of the salvage team lost his life. Remarkably, no one else was seriously hurt throughout the whole affair. On Sunday 26 March a Cabinet meeting was held. With Harold Wilson, the Prime Minister's, usual instinct for publicity, the venue was Culdrose Royal Naval Air Station in Cornwall. There Sir Solly Zuckerman, the Cabinet Office's Chief Scientific Adviser, recommended that the tanker should be set on fire.[41] The original plan to put men on board to blow open the decks in order to introduce fire-raising compounds to the oil tanks was far too hazardous, and when on Tuesday 28 March the tanker was formally abandoned by the owners the decision was taken to bomb the vessel. I had thought, from my vague memories of the incident, that the idea of bombing came from Wilson himself and was another publicity stunt. But actually newspapers had suggested such an action as early as Tuesday 21st and Zuckerman had put the possibility firmly on the government's agenda by Wednesday 22nd.[42] On the afternoon of the 28th, Royal Navy Buccaneers dropped high explosive bombs to crack open the decks, and RAF Hunters followed up with tanks of aviation fuel to accelerate the fire. 'The wreck was completely enveloped in flame and black smoke was seen to rise to a height of 3,000 feet.' How much oil was actually destroyed in the bombing was never satisfactorily established, as no one knew how much was released earlier. About half the original cargo, or 60,000 tons, was a contemporary estimate. Certainly the wreck ceased to shed oil and there seems little doubt that, without bombing, the entire contents would ultimately have escaped.[43]

As the *Torrey Canyon*'s washed on to Cornwall's beaches, it dramatized to the British people the potential environmental hazards of oil. But concern about this was not new. Earlier perceptions of the problem posed by oil pollution, however, tended to be limited to specific hazards, some of which the oil companies dealt with themselves, and the wider environmental implications of man's disturbance of nature were not yet major issues.

A few years earlier, in the 1950s, my family's holidays in South Devon were marked at the end of the day by an application of methylated spirits to childish feet in order to rid them of the tarry deposits picked up off the sand. Perversely,

I enjoyed this process and remember it more vividly than most other things about the holidays. The deposits came from oil which was discharged by tankers flushing out their tanks on leaving European ports for the voyage back to the Middle East. The problem became much worse after the war because tankers were increasingly laden with crude rather than products. The latter, being lighter and more volatile, either evaporated or broke up in seawater more easily. International conventions introduced in the 1950s to prevent discharges were not working and Shell took the lead in devising and adopting the 'Load on Top' system. In this the oily residues, rather than being immediately discharged, were concentrated in one tank. During the voyage the water used for tank cleaning separated from the oil and could then be discharged with little contamination. BP supported Shell's efforts. Jersey Standard, and eventually other American companies, followed. Later the system was replaced by 'Crude Oil Washing', in which the crude itself was used for tank cleaning.[44]

Another significant, but now almost forgotten, environmental concern of the 1950s and 1960s was the non-biodegradability of synthetic detergents, leading to a build-up of foam on rivers and canals. Here too Shell, ahead of most other companies, produced improved formulations. The visibility – and unattractiveness – of the problem meant that public opinion was a real force in promoting change. Much more intractable was the issue of air pollution. It was legislated on in Britain by the Clean Air Act of 1956 but was a major continuing concern of both governments and the public. Oil polluted the air in three major ways. Lead, an anti-knock additive in petrol, was discharged by car engines. Sulphur was discharged from burning heating and fuel oil. And refineries themselves were a localized source of a variety of emissions. Up to the early 1960s, however, coal burning, at least in Western Europe, was a much worse agent of pollution; the 1956 Act was largely directed against it. Shell had set up an Atmospheric Pollution Committee in the same year, but it was moribund by 1960. In 1963, however, Shell and BP jointly established an industry-wide committee on air and water conservation, which within a few years represented 75 per cent of Europe's refining capacity. But Shell's official history points out that efforts to combat pollution still tended to focus on solutions to individual problems rather than being built into planning at the start. Thus to reduce localized refinery emissions at Shell's Dutch refinery at Pernis, a 700 feet (215 metres) high emissions stack was built – which merely spread the problem over a wider area. Some progress was made, for instance improved desulphurization techniques were introduced from 1955. Even so, sulphur emissions remained a big problem in the United States where far more oil was used for heating and legislation forced oil companies there, including Shell, into further desulphurization measures.[45]

Anticipation of legislation against lead in petrol drove research from the late 1960s – including research into hybrid petrol-electric cars, an anticipation of their recent prominence. The problem for oil companies was that car manufacturers also had to participate as engines would need to be modified. Only in the 1980s were cars built with engines which could run on unleaded petrol. From 1993 all cars sold in Britain had to have such engines, although leaded petrol itself was only finally banned in 2000.[46]

The environmental problems which had the most fundamental impact on public awareness in the long run were those caused by pesticide residues. The pesticides concerned were the products of petrochemicals, and Shell was particularly involved in their manufacture. The details of the problem will not be dealt with here, partly because there are plenty of other sources and partly because the subject is too large to do it proper justice. However, it needs mentioning because of the importance of the book *Silent Spring*, by Rachel Carson, published in 1962. Carson's book, a scientifically based criticism of modern pesticides, was one of the key building blocks in the modern consciousness of the environment. In spite of its long-term significance, however, the public initially was less concerned with pesticides than with the more visible problems mentioned above. With governments slow to act, chemical companies had no strong reason to do much about pesticides in the 1960s, especially as there was controversy about their exact effects.[47]

The *Torrey Canyon* incident added large-scale oil spills to the list of public concerns about oil pollution. Such spills caused the highly visible oiling of seabirds, and of course had a potentially deleterious effect on the holiday industry. In fact the authorities' clean-up efforts were prompt and reasonably efficient.[48] But they relied heavily on detergent to emulsify the oil thus making it break down quicker in seawater. The detergent was highly toxic and killed off much of the delicate marine life on the foreshore. A survey made two months after the incident for the Nature Conservancy compared two beaches which had been affected by moderate amounts of oil. One, Trevellas Cove, was treated with detergent, while the owner of the other, Trevaunance Cove, refused to use it and manually removed the oil. Marine life at Trevaunance was hardly affected, while at Trevellas it suffered badly. Oil is a product of nature, and in small quantities is a nuisance rather than a major environmental hazard. Eventually, weather and water will break it down. Nevertheless the *Torrey Canyon* episode taught some useful lessons on how, and how not, to deal with such emergencies and clean up afterwards – including using less toxic detergent or not using it at all. It also led to Britain lobbying for improvements in the oversight and design of tankers, many of which were eventually adopted. It took a number of years, however,

for major improvements to be mandated as they depended on agreement between maritime nations.[49]

Unfortunately, the aftermath of the episode saw a surprising degree of
complacency as to the likelihood of something like it occurring again. The *Torrey
Canyon* was registered in Liberia – a 'flag of convenience country' – which held a
Court of Inquiry, generally thought to be less than thorough. Union Oil, which
had the ship under a long-term charter and was effectively responsible for it, was
cleared of any blame. Instead, Captain Rugiati was found wholly responsible.
Certainly Union Oil could be exonerated on several counts. Rugiati was an
experienced and, until the disaster, a respected officer and all his crew were
Italian, so there were no language difficulties. The ship was well looked after. But
there had been omissions and problems – small, but possibly vital for the *Torrey
Canyon*. The Admiralty's *Channel Pilot* made it clear that no large vessel should
steer between the Scillies and the Seven Stones, but the ship was not issued with
a copy. The steering gear mechanism could, too easily, be put into the disengaged
position which is why the ship did not immediately respond to Rugiati's last
desperate course change.[50]

But even these were specific to the disaster and, it could be argued, were not
likely to be repeated. What seems to have not been fully grasped is that, when
there were so many large tankers steaming about in northern European waters,
sooner or later someone else would make a mistake or some accident of weather
or current would occur. Only three years after the *Torrey Canyon* two medium-
sized tankers, the *Allegro* and the *Pacific Glory*, collided off the Isle of Wight.
The *Pacific Glory* grounded and was only salvaged with difficulty. Not much
oil was spilt, but there were 14 fatalities as the vessel caught fire. A few years
later the *Amoco Cadiz* sinking occurred off the coast of Brittany (see Chapter 9,
'Beyond the environment'). In 1993 the *Braer* lost engine power due to salt water
contamination of fuel off Shetland and was wrecked, shedding 85,000 tons of
crude. Fortunately most missed the coastline but it took over seven years before
all the restrictions on fishing in the area could be lifted. Then in 1996 came an
oil spill which, in hindsight, had been waiting to happen for 35 years.[51]

It took place at the entrance to the *Torrey Canyon*'s intended destination,
Milford Haven. The tanker was the *Sea Empress*, carrying around 150,000 tons
of North Sea crude to the Texaco refinery near Pembroke Dock. As with the
Torrey Canyon visibility was good. The wind was brisk but not gale-force. The
Sea Empress was being piloted into Milford Haven when, according to the Report
of the Chief Inspector of Marine Accidents, the pilot was surprised by the tidal
flow setting to the east – towards the Haven – and ran aground on rocks in the
middle of the channel at the entrance to the harbour. There was then a saga of

refloatings and subsequent groundings before the ship finally came free, having lost over half her cargo – 72,000 tons. The accident was bad enough. But behind it lay an ignorance by the Milford Haven Port Authority (MHPA) and some of the pilots of the complex nature of the tidal pattern at the mouth of the harbour. In addition, there were reservations about the quality of pilot training while relations between the pilots and the MHPA were poor. Since the harbour had been used by tankers since the first refinery was opened in 1960, it seems something of a miracle that such a serious accident had not happened earlier. Fortunately around 90 per cent of the oil which escaped was carried to sea. Of that, it was estimated that around 40 per cent evaporated and 50 per cent was absorbed into the water with the aid of dispersants. But roughly 5,000 tons came to land, although the eventual impact was quite limited. The subsequent environmental investigation indicated that seabird cleaning was almost certainly pointless, since the vast majority of cleaned birds died soon after; humane destruction of oiled birds would have been better. More positively, huge advances had been made since the *Torrey Canyon* in the effectiveness of dispersants and of beach cleaning, so that the environmental side effects were minimized.[52]

As suggested above, it is unfortunately the case that occasional collisions or wreckings of tankers are almost inevitable. This is not an argument for complacency about accidents, but attention also needs to focus on everyday pollution. A large tanker could discharge up to 800 tons of oil after washing its tanks, so the potential for pollution was actually far greater than from the occasional spectacular accident.[53] In their reaction to wider environmental concerns, oil companies were certainly concerned with costs, and to that extent could be accused of a narrow-minded obsession with the obverse of costs – profits. But cost was not always a central issue with the companies and in specific areas of the environment such as tanker and refinery discharges BP and Shell were willing to act voluntarily and proactively. Oil companies tried, however, to ensure that all or most of the industry followed them so that 'free-riding' was minimized. This was legitimate because free-riders – those who did not follow a costly procedure to minimize pollution – would not just earn higher profits but could also steal a higher market share because of their lower costs, thus reducing the value of anti-pollution measures. But the oil companies were still reluctant to see the environment as a central concern, preferring to treat it issue by issue. By the 1970s a different attitude was slowly emerging, discussed in Chapter 9. As the Alaska pipeline saga demonstrated, however (see Chapter 5, 'Wider horizons'), companies could still be extremely cavalier about the environment while paying lip-service to its importance.

GOVERNMENT AND OIL

In 1976 newspaper reports began to appear of a scandal involving oil companies and the British government. Coming only a few years after the 1973–4 oil crisis had vastly increased oil company profits, a scandal was grist to the newspaper mill even though some of the alleged actions had taken place ten years earlier. The word 'Oilgate' (the Watergate scandal which brought down President Nixon was still recent) was banded around.[54] The scandal was over the supply of oil to Rhodesia, the old name for what is now Zimbabwe. Oil had the capacity to cause problems even when the Middle East was not involved.

In December 1965 the government of Rhodesia, one of Britain's remaining colonies, had made a unilateral declaration of independence (UDI) as it disliked British pressure to alter its electoral system, loaded towards white residents, before independence was granted by Britain. Britain ruled out military action and relied instead on economic sanctions to bring Rhodesia to heel. In the event, Rhodesia lasted 14 years, partly because of the limitations of sanctions. Before UDI, Rhodesia's oil supplies had mainly come through Mozambique, in 1965 still ruled by Portugal. Crude oil was landed at Beira, a port in the north of Mozambique, and piped to a refinery at Umtali in Rhodesia. Oil bound for Beira was easy enough to interdict and this was done by the Royal Navy in the 'Beira Patrol'. Other routes, however, were available, for instance via South Africa. In the era of apartheid, the South African government was technically 'neutral' in the dispute but insisted that oil companies should sell products, without enquiry as to their destination, to any intermediaries who cared to buy. Of course, there was nothing to stop such products ending up in Rhodesia. Products carried overland from South Africa could be railed to the Rhodesian border but then faced a costly road journey, until a rail link was constructed in 1974. But there was an alternative route, direct by rail from Lourenço Marques (now Maputo), Mozambique's southern port, to Rhodesia. Royal Navy patrols could not stop South African vessels bringing oil products to Lourenço Marques, for there was no proof that they were destined for Rhodesia. They might be for Mozambique itself or for the Transvaal, an area of South Africa close to Lourenço Marques and traditionally supplied from it. And Portugal, then with an authoritarian government, was also sympathetic to Rhodesia.[55]

The oil companies' dilemma was that their South African subsidiaries were subject to South Africa law and so could not prevent their customers selling petroleum products to Rhodesia. The direct South African route being expensive, from 1966 Mozambique was increasingly used. Shell was the most directly involved of the British oil companies, because the whole of southern Africa was within the 'Consolidated' area (see Chapter 2, 'Magnates and caudillos'). Shell and BP supplied this jointly but Shell was the manager. Shell Mozambique was a British incorporated company, and as such subject to British law. But there were potential loopholes. If Shell Mozambique supplied a South African company – and in fact a South African company was used as an intermediary to buy oil for Rhodesia – and there was legitimate doubt as to whether the product was heading to the Transvaal or Rhodesia, then should Shell refuse to supply? If it did, it risked the wrath of South African authorities, which might put into jeopardy the whole of Consolidated's South African business.[56]

Shell's dilemma was solved by a variety of stratagems. It took the Bingham Report, which unravelled them, 400 pages to do so and it takes us about two, so some corners will be cut. In brief, from late 1966 Shell Mozambique was supplying Rhodesia direct from its coastal depot, although in doing so it was ostensibly fulfilling South African orders. Early in 1968 Shell and BP's London managements became aware of the situation and discussed it with the British government. But the government had its own reasons for not wanting to make too much of a fuss. Of course it wanted sanctions to be effective, and patently they weren't. But negotiations with Rhodesia were ongoing and South Africa was a potential mediator. Irritating it too much was not thought to be good policy. South Africa was also a good customer for British goods and with sterling in one of its frequent post-war spells in the convalescent ward after devaluation in 1967, the fear of losing foreign exchange earnings was another factor. So the government connived in a face-saving exercise in which the Shell products consigned to Rhodesia were supplied by Total, the marketing arm of the French oil company CFP. In return Shell provided Total with an equivalent value of products in South Africa. The companies and the government could then claim that British firms were not involved in sanctions-busting, which since Britain was the main party in the dispute would be a humiliating admission. In 1971, however, Total became dissatisfied with the financial terms of the agreement – or possibly worried about its legality – and Shell Mozambique reverted to selling to a South African company, with the products again being railed direct to Rhodesia from its Mozambique depot. Shell's senior management, however, remained ignorant of this. By this time UDI had existed for so long that interest in it declined, and the story remained moribund until the involvement of Mobil in supply was exposed in 1976. With renewed media pressure, and with the South African government now more concerned to placate black African states, supply by British companies was finally halted in 1977, although consignments via Mozambique had been terminated by the new independent government in 1976.[57]

It is easy to express moral indignation at the whole episode, and it was partly the moral indignation of David Owen, Foreign Secretary in the late 1970s, which led to the affair being exposed so thoroughly and then ended.[58] But the historian needs to understand the forces at work.

From Consolidated's perspective, refusal to supply Rhodesia would have led to two things. Caltex, Mobil and Total, the other oil companies concerned, would take over Consolidated's business but oil would not be prevented from reaching Rhodesia. Consolidated would also jeopardize its position in Rhodesia when UDI was resolved. Furthermore, refusal to supply South African intermediaries would infringe South African law and possibly jeopardize the whole South African business, as well as putting the South African executives at risk of legal action. This is, of course, a rather kindly way of looking at it. Internationally, both Shell and BP were big enough to absorb all these losses had they been willing to. But both parent companies could claim that their policy was to allow subsidiaries to operate at arm's length, whilst from 1968 they believed that their actions had been cleared by the British government – which they had been, until the Total exchange broke down. Nevertheless the evidence is clear, even though the Bingham Report was very reticent in making accusations, that the parents did not make much effort to discover the true state of affairs. In this BP was less culpable than Shell, the manager, but when the Consolidated arrangement was terminated in the early 1970s BP was eager to get its 50 per cent share of the business – including supplying Rhodesia.[59]

Their approval of the Total exchange throws the spotlight as much or more on the British government as on the oil companies. The government could put forward the economic argument – rather a grubby excuse – and, more cogently, the diplomatic one, both rehearsed above.

One may think that the government and the companies acted immorally or one may think that they had limited options and pursued a justifiably pragmatic path. Whatever the verdict, the whole episode highlights how the government's options were limited by Britain's post-war weaknesses. Military weakness ruled out military intervention, and economic weakness strengthened the felt need to mollify South Africa rather than taking it on.[60] But the oil companies, whatever their international reach and relative strength, were ultimately at the mercy of events too. Their operations in southern Africa ultimately depended on the goodwill of the South African government, which was believed to be willing, and certainly had the capacity, to act if the companies broke South African law. They were also liable to depredations by competitors and, however gentlemanly the oil companies' relations with each other were at times, they would certainly take advantage of weakness.

Closer to home, oil posed governments less dramatic but nonetheless difficult questions. One was the competitive threat to coal. Coal continued to provide the bulk of most European countries' fuel requirements up to the mid-1950s, and until then the biggest perceived energy problem was a perceived shortage of coal. But by 1958, as coal prices rose and oil prices fell, it became apparent that fuel oil was often cheaper than coal for basic steam raising in industry and electricity generation. The problem, for countries with large coal-mining industries, then became one of having too much coal and, consequently, redundant coal miners. By far the biggest coal mining country in Europe was Britain, with an output in 1960 of almost 200 million tons.

Martin Chick has contrasted the approach to running down coal in Britain and France. The French carefully calculated the optimum economic rate at which the industry should decline, making allowance for the cost of retraining workers and for the added insecurity of dependence of imported oil. The policy aimed explicitly at improving France's industrial competitiveness. Britain, in contrast, took a pragmatic approach in which the rundown was slowed in order to avoid excessive redundancies in economically vulnerable coal mining regions such as South Wales and the North-East. To do this, pressure was put on the electricity generating industry, then nationalized, to maximize coal burn at the expense of oil. Fuel oil use in the private sector was discouraged by a duty of 2d per gallon, equivalent to around 25 per cent of the industrial fuel oil price. The result, of course, was to increase electricity prices and industrial costs.[61] In fairness to British governments of the period – both Conservatives and Labour followed the policy – it is worth noting that labour productivity in British mines increased far faster than in French. As a result, between 1960 and 1970 British output fell by 25 per cent compared with a fall of 30 per cent in France, but the British workforce actually declined more rapidly. Furthermore, with far more miners to start with, Britain's problem of labour redeployment was greater.[62]

The decline of coal was a problem which arose from an opportunity – the cheapness of oil which enabled lower costs and therefore higher living standards. But the concomitant increase in oil use produced another problem, that of energy security.

Signs of governmental concern with this surfaced in the mid-1950s, before Suez, but at that point it was associated more with the oil stocks needed for recovery after nuclear war (if such recovery was possible) than with the more mundane contingency of restricted oil supplies without full-scale war. There were some signs of concern about Middle East oil supplies at the time, but in 1955 a prescient memo from the British ambassador to Beirut, arguing that there was too much complacency about the future stability of Middle Eastern oil, seems to have been ignored.[63] After Suez, the focus moved from the aftermath of nuclear war to the stockpiling needed in case supplies were restricted.[64] The Organization of European Economic Cooperation (from 1960 the Organization of Economic Cooperation and Development – OECD) recommended that governments hold a reserve of four weeks supply, which with company stocks would give around four months in all. (Rather neatly, a Mr Stock was one of the civil servants involved in the discussions.)[65]

Initially pressure was put on the companies with some success. Shell-Mex/BP, in particular, kept relatively high stock levels – for instance over 15 weeks in December 1963 – and there seems little doubt that these levels were not just accidental but that the company cooperated with the government. Other companies were less helpful. In September 1961 Regent, now owned by Texaco, was called in for a meeting about their stock levels and in 1963 Gulf's stock levels were regarded as 'unacceptably low'.[66] By early 1967 it was noted that average year-round company stock levels were around 82 days of normal usage, but this was in the context of greater efficiency which had meant a reduction in the normal stock level to only 60 days. The government reserve, however, was still only one million tons which by then meant only five days' worth. Nevertheless total reserves were deemed almost adequate: three months rather than four became the target. The additional stocks almost certainly helped after the Six Day War of June 1967 led to cuts in British supplies. By early August stock levels in the months ahead were still projected at around ten weeks. The crisis sent stocking policy a little way up the political agenda, but not much. Michael Stewart, the Foreign Secretary, remained concerned about the position but Treasury ministers were worried about the foreign exchange implications of building up stocks.[67]

In practice, UK stocks remained quite high compared with most OECD countries. In 1971 only France, of larger European countries, had higher stock levels. By early 1973 the government was anticipating EEC legislation mandating 90-day stocks. Ironically, it was just at this stage that stocks ran down, to 56 days in January. The cause was quite clear – the worldwide shortage of crude which was now becoming apparent. When, therefore, the turmoil caused by production cuts and embargoes gripped the world in late 1973, Britain had little cushion. But although the physical shortage of oil led to minor inconveniences, it had far less economic impact than the miners' industrial action or the rise in oil prices. A few additional days' worth of oil stocks would not have solved these.[68]

The government was by no means inattentive to stocking levels and was quite successful at putting pressure on the companies to keep their stocks up, although the cooperation of Shell and BP was an important factor. BP's apparent recalcitrance over stocks when meeting with civil servants in 1969, noted by Keir Thorpe, may have been the company putting down a marker that it and Shell should not always have to bear the brunt of carrying excess private company stocks. But even so stock levels seem to have remained relatively high until 1972.[69] The essential problem was that holding stocks of 20 or 30 days above normal was not enough to deal with major worldwide shortages, which manifested themselves in higher prices.

7

Crisis: Oil in the 1970s

PRELUDE TO CRISIS

On 21 October 1973 the chairmen of Shell and BP, Frank McFadzean and Sir Eric Drake, met Edward Heath, the Prime Minister, at Chequers, his official residence. The world was in crisis, and one of the roots of that crisis was oil. Following another Arab-Israeli war, the Arab states were both cutting production, and totally embargoing oil supplies to the USA and the Netherlands. At the same time Middle Eastern oil prices were rising at an unprecedented rate. They had already reached $5 per barrel – more than two and a half times the level at the beginning of 1970. Britain herself was suffering increasing inflation and faced the possibility of industrial action by coalminers – domestically mined coal still being used extensively in power generation.[1]

Unlike 1967, Britain was not on the Arab embargo list, although all importing countries were threatened by cuts which would reduce production by 5 per cent each month. But as in 1967, the oil companies tried to deal with the situation by adjusting supplies from non-Arab producers, so spreading the cuts evenly. Whereas in 1967, however, there had been plenty of oil to go round and 'shut-in' US production to add to the supply, in 1973 world supplies were desperately tight and the US was producing to its limit. Spreading the cuts meant pain for everybody. Heath had invited McFadzean and Drake to Chequers to ask them not to spread the cuts but to allocate Britain all its normal supply of oil since it was not one of the embargo targets.[2]

The request was on the face of it understandable. But if acted upon it would open a hornet's nest of problems. Britain had benefited in 1956 and 1967 because oil companies had reallocated supplies to even out shortages. Now Heath, who had taken Britain into the European Community, wanted them to refuse the same treatment to other countries, thus disadvantaging one of the Community's strongest supporters, the Netherlands, and Britain's closest ally, the USA. Furthermore he wanted the companies to break commercial contracts throughout the globe. If they were ordered to do so by the government, then *force majeure* would apply and they would be legally secure.[3] But even in these circumstances, the companies would lose considerable goodwill while the nation would anger its friends and allies. Not surprisingly, the oilmen refused. They would only comply if ordered, and if they were seen to be ordered. But when Drake asked for the instruction in writing, Heath's reply was, 'You know perfectly well I can't put it in writing.'[4]

Heath's request could be construed as the action of a Prime Minister anxious to stand up for his country. Or it could be seen as embodying stupidity, short-sightedness and panicky selfishness in roughly equal measures. His memoirs, in which he spoke of his deep shame at Drake and McFadzean's 'obstinate and unyielding reluctance . . . to take any action whatever to help our country in its hour of need' might further be seen as exhibiting appalling ingratitude since BP, at risk to its worldwide commercial reputation, actually went some way to meet his request. In the utmost secrecy, Drake ordered that some supplies should be covertly redirected to Britain.[5] (It has recently been suggested that Heath suffered from an under-active thyroid gland, a condition likely to impair his judgement and his ability to deal with crises. But this doesn't excuse the entry in his memoirs, since he was well aware of the actions which BP had, in fact, taken.)[6]

Britain's problem was ultimately a detail in the wider crisis of 1973–4. And that wider crisis was caused less by the embargo than by the rising price of oil, which by January 1974 had doubled again, to over $11 per barrel. The apparent cause of that price rise was an organization whose name, up till then little known, rapidly became famous or infamous: OPEC, the Organization of the Petroleum Exporting Countries.

OPEC was born several years earlier. Its parents were the Venezuelan and Saudi Arabian representatives at a 1959 congress of oil producers, which met after the big oil companies first cut their posted prices and thus reduced the oil producing countries' revenues per barrel. At that point the producers did little. But the second cut, in 1960, led to these two countries, with Iran and Iraq, forming OPEC. For a number of years the organization marked time. In spite of their initial indignation against the price cuts, there was strong rivalry between the leading members, particularly Iran and Saudi Arabia. With prices seemingly set by the companies and not the producers, revenues were dependent on volume. So each country put pressure on their respective consortium members to produce more oil. Combined with the new 'elephants' – giant fields – coming on stream in countries which were not yet OPEC members – notably Algeria, Libya and Nigeria – the result was further downward pressure on prices, even though demand was also rising rapidly. In spite of the cuts in posted prices, discounts once more reappeared. As the previous chapter showed, even in 1967 a partial embargo, combined with the Suez Canal closure, did no more than cause temporary inconvenience to consuming countries while the effect on prices was limited.[7]

The situation, however, was gradually changing, partly because Arab countries were becoming increasingly radical. In 1969 the old regime of King Idris of Libya was overthrown, and a young colonel, Muammar al-Qaddafi, seized power. Up till then Libyan oil had been one of the key factors undermining OPEC's dream of stabilizing prices. It was good quality and close to Europe. There was no expensive haul round the Cape or journey in the risky Tapline (the Trans-Arabian pipeline linking Saudi Arabia and the Mediterranean, which ran through Syria). And its volume had been steadily increasing. The effect of oil from Libya and elsewhere in the 1960s is illustrated by the rapid rise of Jet, still a familiar brand especially in Eastern Europe and then a discount brand of petrol marketed in Britain and some other European countries. It was owned by Continental Oil (Conoco), one of the main Libyan producers. Shell and BP were also involved in Libyan consortia. But the company most associated with Libya was Occidental, run by the eccentric Armand Hammer.[8] (His name is rendered memorable by its resemblance to that of an American manufacturer of baking powder and toothpaste.)

Occidental lacked other sources of supply, so it was vulnerable to pressure from Libya. The opportunity soon came. In May 1970 the Tapline was accidentally breached and Syria refused to allow repairs. The result was a sudden increase in the demand for tankers, since Tapline oil now had to be hauled round the Cape, and an escalation of freight rates. Libya's oil went straight to the Mediterranean coast and thus shipping costs were minimized, making its oil more desirable. Qaddafi put increasing pressure on Occidental by ordering it to cut its production. With supplies tight, the company could not easily buy from elsewhere to meet its commitments. In September Occidental gave way. It agreed a price increase of around 15 per cent and a further annual escalation. Most important, it agreed a 58 per cent tax rate. Some of this included a previously voluntary contribution by Occidental, but the rest of it was a real increase. Libya's price breakthrough was not in fact the first – Algeria had actually unilaterally increased prices by more in July. But Algeria's oil went mainly to French companies. Libya's production was greater and it was taken by more companies. And Libya had also made a breakthrough on the hitherto almost sacrosanct (to the oil companies) 50/50 profit split.[9]

With Occidental's cave-in, the same terms were put to the other companies operating in Libya. Shell and BP tried to engineer a common front with the other majors. But most Western governments had no taste for getting involved in a struggle in which Libya's deep pockets would give Qaddafi the upper hand. Furthermore the America majors were concerned about overt collaboration because of anti-trust issues, and so were reluctant to join any such front. The companies gave way and similar terms were applied to them, with a tax rate of 55 per cent. Libya's success encouraged OPEC members around the world. The oil companies quickly accepted the 55 per cent tax rate throughout the Middle East and Venezuela raised its tax rate to 60 per cent. Some Gulf posted prices were raised. In the light of the agreements with Libya and the continued tight oil supply situation these concessions by the companies were almost inevitable. In addition, OPEC members called for a general increase in prices to be achieved by negotiations between the companies and the Gulf producers. But it was further Libyan demands early in 1971 which rang the loudest alarm bells. The companies were faced with demands for an increase in the tax rate to 60 per cent and another price rise. And a political note was introduced: oil companies were told to pressure the US government to change its Middle East policies – meaning, of course, its backing for Israel. This time the companies did form a common front, with the US and British governments supportive. Practically every major and many independents joined in. The front included an agreement not to unilaterally accept Libyan demands but rather to negotiate jointly with OPEC.[10]

Within a year the old order in the oil world had been overturned. Since 1945 the companies had effectively set the posted price and their power to do so had been underpinned by the tendency to surplus which reduced the producing countries' market power. Now there was a shortage of oil and they had to accept that the producers were calling the shots. As a consequence the companies' long-standing belief that OPEC was of little account had to adjust to circumstances. Instead of being spurned, OPEC would be welcomed as the body which could impose discipline on its members and avoid leap-frogging.

No sooner was it formed than the companies' common front was undermined. One reason was the attitude of the Shah of Iran. The Shah attached great importance to Iran's position as one of the largest oil producers and was hyper-conscious, as were many Iranians, of Persia's glorious history. He did not want Iran to be lumped together with the Arab states, particularly radical ones such as Libya. He argued that a common negotiation would result in the Libyan demands becoming universal. The US government was receptive to Iranian arguments because, as Britain pulled out of the Gulf, the Americans had tried to develop new safeguards there against the Soviet Union. They saw Iran and Saudi Arabia as friendly powers, to be cultivated as regional leaders. With US government support for common negotiations not forthcoming, the companies were forced into a makeshift scheme to split negotiations between the Gulf states (Saudi Arabia, Iran, Iraq and the smaller states such as Kuwait) and the Mediterranean exporters (Libya and Algeria, and Saudi Arabia and Iraq again because of their pipelines to the Mediterranean). The companies would then attempt to negotiate simultaneously with each group. The scheme was undermined before it began because the Libyans simply refused to negotiate before the talks with the Gulf producers were completed. The subsequent negotiations with the Gulf states were only a little happier for the companies. The states followed Libya's lead in threatening production cutbacks. Western governments again declined to take a stand, preferring certainty of supply to price stability, and the companies were forced to make further big concessions in the Tehran agreement of February 1971. The states achieved a price rise which, taking all the adjustments into account, amounted to almost 50 cents or around 25 per cent. But at least the companies thought they had stability. They were promised five years in which, apart from a prearranged increase of about 12 cents per barrel per annum, there would be no other price changes, tax increases or leapfrogging.[11]

Libya's earlier silence, however, meant that it had made no promises to avoid leapfrogging. And with even the conservative Saudis willing to delegate the Mediterranean producers' negotiations to Libya, there was no hope of moderation there. The 'negotiation' was almost entirely on Libyan terms. By its close, agreement had been reached to increase Libyan crude prices to $3.45 cents a barrel – a 35 per cent increase. Libyan crude was now far more expensive than Saudi Ras Tanura crude, although much of the differential was accounted for by lower freight rates and by its better quality.[12]

While the Tehran agreement had promised stability in pricing and taxation, it had made no such promises about ownership. In 1968 OPEC had formulated some long-term demands, and one of these was for participation – the euphemism for a shareholding in the concessionary companies or consortia. Participation was interpreted by some in the oil companies as yet another aggressive move but it could be seen as a means of diverting aggression. Aggression was exemplified by Libya, with its price escalation, its leapfrogging tactics, and its forced nationalizations – for instance BP's assets in Libya were nationalized in December 1971. Iraq, where Saddam Hussein was becoming the dominant leader, also nationalized all the northern oil assets of the IPC, the descendant of the old Turkish Petroleum Company which went back to pre-First World War days and in which Shell and BP were participants. Not surprisingly, it was the radical states which pushed for outright nationalization. Demands for participation were led by the conservative state of Saudi Arabia.[13]

The Saudi oil minister was the subtle and intelligent Zaki Yamani, or Shaikh Yamani as he was usually known in the Western media. Yamani's skills in negotiation and Saudi Arabia's importance meant that he became OPEC's lead negotiator in the 1970s, while his ease in the English language and in contacts with the media made him the organization's public face too. Yamani, reflecting the Saudis' basic position, was inclined to moderation, although also alert to other factors which might necessitate him taking a harder line. One of these was Saudi Arabia's jostling for position with Iran as a regional leader in the Gulf area now that Britain was pulling out. The other, always latent, was the hostility between Israel and the Arab states.

By pressing, after the Tehran agreement, for participation, Yamani achieved several moderate aims. He diverted Gulf producers from immediately trying to bridge the wide differential which had opened up between Mediterranean prices and Gulf prices. And by promising moderate Arab states a stake in their oil production assets, he dampened down Arab rivalry with Iran whose production assets were, in theory, nationalized – although in reality the consortium there operated with virtually the same autonomy as in states with no nationalization. Unlike the Iranian situation, however, participation was not an empty formula. Hence it would represent real progress for countries which entered into such arrangements, and hence also the oil companies' dislike of it. In return for the purchase of assets – at a price well below what the companies wanted – countries would gain a share of the still very substantial profits the companies were making from their upstream operations. Furthermore, while, by the agreement which was eventually reached, the companies would initially buy back at a discount most of the participating countries' share of crude production for resale through their own marketing networks, buyback would gradually be phased out. Thus the producing countries would eventually have their own crude supplies and could, if they wished, develop their own marketing networks. The General Agreement on Participation, GAP, was finally agreed in December 1972. It involved Saudi Arabia and two smaller Gulf states, and provided for a gradual increase to 51 per cent participation. Internal Kuwaiti opposition, however, kept that country out. Other OPEC countries followed the model, for instance Nigeria which had only joined the organization in 1971. As a coda to these middle stages of the drama, the Shah was stimulated by the GAP to renegotiate Iran's agreement with the consortium, which of course included BP and Shell. He had been angered because the GAP would eventually give the participating countries 51 per cent, with real control, while his 100 per cent was, in truth, only on paper. By mid-1973 the Iranians had a new agreement which made them not just the nominal owners but the real operators and refiners, and in addition would give them some of the oil to market. The rest would be sold to the consortium. The consortium in practice still managed the production assets, but now as sub-contractors rather than principals.[14]

In all these negotiations – and in some cases unilateral actions by the producing states – Western governments were reluctant to get involved. The complacency over oil supplies which had ruled until 1970 was now punctured. In December 1971 the US State Department had concluded that the West would soon be 'almost completely dependent on OPEC oil' – and that there was not much they could do about it. 'The high trumps are all in the hands of the producing countries and will be for the next twenty years.' In those circumstances the Department advised that the companies should accommodate OPEC's moderates such as Saudi Arabia, for fear of something worse. With the US counselling caution, other Western countries were unlikely to do much.[15]

By mid-1973, with the conclusion of the participation negotiations and Iranian renegotiation, a degree of stability seemed to have returned to the relationship between the companies and most OPEC countries. But with a worldwide boom, the oil market was becoming ever tighter: it was estimated that a maximum of 3 per cent of current capacity was available to meet additional demand, when annual demand increases were routinely more than double this. The US had imposed oil import quotas since 1959 in order to protect the relatively high cost domestic US oil industry. But now the US industry, whose mothballed production assets – 'shut-in oil' – had been activated in previous crises, was itself producing to its limit. In April 1973 President Nixon ended the quotas and there was a further surge in demand for OPEC oil. Significantly market prices, usually at a discount to posted even in the recent years of high demand, went above them. Furthermore the higher posted prices agreed at Tehran in 1971 had already been adjusted upwards, ostensibly to compensate oil producing countries for the devaluation of the US dollar, but in fact because they had the power to impose such increases.[16]

Many of the charges whose explosion was to lead – among many other things – to the meeting at Chequers in October 1973 were now in place. But certain vital detonators had still to be activated.

CRISIS

On 6 October 1973, on the Jewish holy day of Yom Kippur, Egyptian and Syrian armoured forces attacked Israel without warning. To Israelis it was the Yom Kippur War, to Arabs the October War. The result, after initial Israeli reverses, was the throwing back of the Arab forces. But with heavy Israeli losses of equipment, they called upon their long-term supporters, the United States, for new supplies. The US responded with a massive airlift. On 17 October the Arab oil states announced the production cuts mentioned in the previous section as a retaliation. Within a few days these were extended to include total embargoes against the United States and the Netherlands, which had assisted the US airlift. Portugal was included for the same reason. It was these actions which set the scene for Heath's confrontation with Drake and McFadzean, also described earlier.[17]

The Yom Kippur war and the embargo were not just another stage in the cycle of Middle East wars. They were also the result of the increasing radicalization of Arab states. This put pressure on the remaining conservative states, particularly Saudi Arabia, which had hitherto attempted to balance their friendship with the US and their hostility to Israel by acting with restraint. They now felt constrained to choose one or another and chose the Arab countries. The war and the embargo were not directly linked to the pressure on oil prices which was already well underway. But there was an obvious indirect link in that the radicalization of Arab governments had led to some of that pressure, while the embargo and the cuts added a further twist to the price ratchet.

The invasion of Israel coincided with the preparations for a further meeting between the oil companies and the OPEC negotiators, scheduled to be held in Vienna on 8 October. OPEC had observed the tight market conditions and the consequent rise of market prices above posted. The radical Arab states had also observed it and added their impetus. So in spite of the promise at Tehran in 1971 of five years of stability, by September 1973 Yamani declared the Tehran agreement 'dead or dying'. The companies knew they would have to accept an increase in the price of oil and offered 15 per cent. The OPEC negotiators asked for the price to be doubled. The companies felt that they had to consult Western governments over such a drastic increase, with major implications for Western economies, and asked for a recess. The meeting broke up. And the next news the companies, and the world, heard came over the radio on 16 October: OPEC would raise posted prices by $2 per barrel. Arabian Light marker crude, which had risen in the last four years from less than $2 to just $3 per barrel, would go up to over $5 – a 70 per cent increase.[18]

For the companies, the increase meant the final collapse of their virtual hegemony over oil prices in the post-war years. Their control was never complete, because it had been eroded by discounting, but nonetheless it was clear that, within the system, the producing countries came at the bottom of the hierarchy. The events of 1970–1 had established negotiation between companies and producers. October 1973 saw OPEC unilaterally deciding the posted price. Painful though this was for the companies, for Western governments the situation was far worse. The price increase threatened to exacerbate inflation which was already a major problem. The cuts and embargoes threatened more – the disruption of industrial and agricultural production, and a further boost to inflation as well. And international tension, exacerbated by war and embargoes, was reaching a dangerous level. The USA and Soviet Union were both intensely nervous of moves the other might make in the Middle East, and their armed forces were on a high state of alert.[19]

Fortunately sense prevailed. Tensions eased, and there was a ceasefire in the Arab-Israeli conflict. But the economic pressure on the West continued. Although the cuts in production were terminated in November for most European Community states and Japan, the embargoes on the Netherlands and US remained so the overall oil supply situation was still critical. As a result, oil sold outside the posted price system – and this particularly applied to 'participation' oil – was fetching extraordinary prices. In November and December, for instance, lots of Nigerian and Iranian oil sold at around $17 per barrel at auction. The differential between this and posted prices was too tempting for OPEC members. Yamani urged caution. His and Saudi Arabia's concern was that a further large price increase would cause a world depression thus dampening demand – and reducing the prop which high demand gave to prices. But it was not just radical Arab states who were urging such an increase. The Shah had once believed that only increased volume could meet his never-ending need for more money. Now a new El Dorado opened up before him, made possible by increased prices. At another Tehran meeting in December, OPEC once more unilaterally raised postings. From just over $5 per barrel, Arabian Light marker crude went to $11.65 from 1 January 1974. Not only was the increase of about 130 per cent far greater in percentage terms than before, it was hugely greater in absolute terms. Oil exporters' revenues, $23 billion in 1972 – after considerable increases had already taken place – were $140 billion by 1977. The payments of consumer countries were correspondingly increased.[20]

Although much of this vast increase in revenue stemmed from the price increases, it also stemmed from another change which flowed from the logic of OPEC's greatly strengthened position. This was the final dismantling of the concessionary system. Within two years or so concessions in OPEC countries had become endangered species as the countries moved towards outright ownership of oil company assets. Participation, conceived of as a means of moderating 'extreme' demands for nationalization, survived in some cases but proved only a temporary solution in others as the extreme became normal. Kuwait took 60 per cent participation in 1974 and 100 per cent in 1975. The smaller Gulf states either took majority stakes or complete control, as did Nigeria and Venezuela. Iraq predictably nationalized its remaining concessions. In most of these either Shell or BP, or both, had holdings. Compensation was paid to them and other oil companies for their assets, but this was relatively small in proportion to the profits which had flowed from them. Most crucial to world oil supplies was Saudi Arabia, although here the only direct interest was American. The Saudis had taken 100 per cent control by 1976. In many cases the companies continued in an important role as subcontractors, with 'buyback' rights to oil. But the proportion of revenue which they took from crude sales was now greatly diminished. Frequently, the oil producers now sold direct to the market. The proportion of such oil rose from 8 per cent in 1973 to 42 per cent in 1979.[21]

In less than four years not only the oil supply system, but one of the foundations of the West's rapid post-war growth – cheap oil – had undergone radical readjustment. What was the impact – on the West, on the companies, and on Britain?

TURBULENT YEARS: 1974–80

After the rigours of 1974, even a government beset with as many problems as Harold Wilson's fourth administration might have expected to have a peaceful Christmas. Wilson's Labour government had replaced Heath's Conservatives early that year as the latter wrestled unsuccessfully with a miners' strike. Labour did not initially have a Parliamentary majority, but had been re-elected with a small one in November. The miners' strike had been resolved and, although inflation was mounting, the oil price was now stable after its dramatic rise. But at 6.30 on the evening of 23 December the Chancellor, Denis Healey, was in an emergency meeting with the Governor of the Bank of England. The meeting was called because of a crisis in the oil industry. Burmah Oil was about to go bankrupt.[22]

We left Burmah in Chapter 5, pursuing an active diversification policy. The policy was continued and indeed stepped up in the 1970s. The company had become involved in North Sea oil and had recently acquired Signal Oil and Gas, a US producer. It had also discovered that, as demand soared and freight rates increased, tankers offered an apparently easy route to wealth. In 1973 Burmah made £18 million from playing the spot market for freight – multiply by about ten times to reach present-day values. Then in 1974 it all went wrong. As the oil price rises bit, demand stagnated, tankers were in surplus and freight rates fell.

Burmah estimated that it now faced an £18 million pound loss on its tanker operations for 1974. And there was another aftershock of the crises of 1973–4 – a dramatic decline in the UK stock market, taking with it the value of Burmah's BP shares. Because of its tanker losses and the declining value of its assets, Burmah was about to break covenants on two separate loans – one of them a $600 million loan it had taken out to buy Signal. Burmah's total assets comfortably exceeded its liabilities. But with intense nervousness in financial markets, the chances of its renegotiating the covenants were slim, especially as its management had hidden their heads in the sand and kept their merchant bankers at arm's length, giving the latter no chance to prepare the markets. Without renegotiation Burmah would become insolvent. In itself, the bankruptcy of a medium-sized oil company would be serious but not catastrophic. But to Healey at the end of 1974, the implications were catastrophic. Britain was in a desperate financial position. North Sea oil, and its revenues, was not yet flowing, and the country was likely to need large dollar borrowings. So default on what was by the standards of the day a vast dollar loan was an appalling prospect, because of its effect on American confidence and willingness to lend.[23]

Burmah was saved, but at a painful cost to its shareholders. The Bank of England, acting on behalf of the government, took practically all the company's BP shares in exchange for cash to settle its immediate financial problems. With the London stock market in January 1975 at its lowest point for many years, the government paid £2.30 per share. This was better than £1.90, which was the lowest BP shares reached, but it compared with the £6.00 they stood at in 1973. Burmah slowly recovered, even though its tanker losses in 1974 eventually turned out to be £32 million. But it had to sell many of the assets which it had so optimistically acquired. Signal went, and the government, at the height of its nationalizing ambitions, picked up most of the North Sea oil assets for its British National Oil Corporation. Only in 1979 did a slimmed-down Burmah return to the dividend lists.[24]

The government forced Burmah to swallow a bitter pill, but the company mostly had itself to blame. Its expansion might have gone on merrily, however, if it had not been for the oil crisis and its multiple impacts. One of those impacts was the fall in oil consumption which led to Burmah's tanker problems. Production in 1974 was virtually the same as in 1973, but of course in early 1974 it had been necessary to make up for the late 1973 cutbacks. By late 1974 demand was declining as economic growth world wide slowed or even went into reverse and users began to economize, and 1975 saw the first worldwide decline in oil production on a yearly basis, apart from during the war, since the 1930s depression. But then consumption started to grow again and by 1979, at 3.2 billion metric tons, production was about 10 per cent above 1974 levels. Growth was well down from the heady annual rates of over 7 per cent seen in the 1960s, but apparently even at much higher prices demand was still increasing.[25]

The underlying reality was very different. Price has a major effect on demand, with oil as with everything else. But because of the fixed nature of much demand for petroleum products, it takes time for that effect to become manifest. Perhaps the most striking example is the demand for petrol – gasoline – in the USA. US petrol prices have always been low by European standards, and in the heyday of the big American car in the early 1970s new cars, on average, did just 12 mpg. The oil crisis was a wake-up call. Buyers turned to small cars while politicians, seriously alarmed by America's growing reliance on foreign oil, mandated a legally effective target of 27.5 mpg to be reached in 1985 by all car manufacturers selling in the USA. The latter makes it difficult to determine the pure effect of price on demand, but the overall results were dramatic. By 1983 new cars in America averaged 22 mpg, an increase of 85 per cent. But it took longer for this to significantly affect the average for all US cars. Between 1973 and 1985 the efficiency of the whole US car fleet rose by only 30 per cent, because there were still plenty of older models around.[26]

Examples of efficiency increases which took time to work through could be multiplied. For instance, ships became far more economical as diesels were installed in bigger vessels, hitherto reliant on steam turbines. But as with cars, ships could not all be replaced at once. The initial oil price increase reduced the capital value of less economical units, whether cars or ships, bringing their total costs into line with more economical ones. It was only as they grew older and maintenance costs mounted that they would finally go to the scrapyard. Multiplying this effect across the economy means that the short-term impact of price increases is much smaller than the long-term one. Economists talk about price elasticities – meaning the percentage that demand for a product will fall if prices rise (or vice versa). Around 1990 the short-run price elasticity of demand for energy was estimated at between 0.2 and 0.5, meaning that a 1 per cent rise in price will lead to a decline of between 0.2 per cent and 0.5 per cent in consumption. However, price here means the real price, adjusted for inflation in the general price index. This helps to explain why demand kept on going up in the mid-1970s. In nominal terms, oil prices between 1974 and 1978 were still rising, from about $12 to $14 per barrel. But these were years of high US inflation which meant that real oil prices were actually falling.[27]

The other reason why oil consumption kept rising also explains why, eventually, it would fall. It was those old ships and cars which were still operating but would eventually be phased out. The long-run price elasticity of demand for energy has been estimated at 1.25. So a sharp increase in the oil price in real terms will eventually lead to a very substantial fall in the demand for oil – but it is a long 'eventually'. In the meantime, other factors will change too. In particular, economic growth means that the underlying demand for oil will rise if its price remains the same – or will mute the fall in consumption associated with a price increase.[28]

In the mid-1970s, the continued rise in consumption meant that OPEC retained considerable pricing power and a fresh outbreak of turbulence in the Middle East proved the catalyst for a further price shock. The Shah's pro-Western stance increasingly irked Iran's religious leaders. Strikes and demonstrations, starting in late 1978, brought about the Shah's overthrow in January 1979. The word 'Ayatollah' became familiar in the West, and the rule of Iran's paramount Ayatollah, Khomeini, began. Output was disrupted for a considerable period and Iran's new rulers were willing neither to rebuild the old relationship with the consortium which had operated in Iran since 1954, nor to pump the same quantities of oil. Then in 1980 the Iran-Iraq war started, causing further disruption. Output in the two countries together, almost 20 per cent of world petroleum output in the late 1970s, ran at under half the previous level for several years. With so much oil off the market, official OPEC prices rose again, briefly reaching the heady level of $35 per barrel in 1979 and remaining at over $30 for several years. In retrospect, the 'Second Oil Shock' seems less important than the first, which was associated not just with the price increase but also with a transformation in the ownership of oil assets and control of the oil market. At the time, partly because the tension over Iran went on so long, it seemed just as traumatic. In the short term, price spikes in 1979 took spot oil prices as high as $45 per barrel.[29]

In spite of the turbulence of the 1970s, Burmah's travails were not typical of the other oil companies. Burmah's problem was that it was not fully integrated but a conglomeration of diverse assets. The tanker arm was far larger than the company's own needs dictated and the unfortunate juxtaposition of the tanker problems with the stock market fall dragged the company down. For Shell and BP the oil crisis posed huge challenges but brought certain immediate advantages. Ironically, given that oil companies had fought against it, the biggest immediate bonus was the price shock in 1973–4. This brought a vast windfall profit as the companies' stocks, acquired at old prices, rose in value. Shell's 1974 profit of almost one billion pounds was the highest in real terms that it ever achieved in the twentieth century. Such profits were not repeatable, of course, although there was another but smaller peak in 1979 after the second big price increase. But profits remained quite high throughout the 1970s and into the early 1980s, even though the companies had been stripped of much of their crude oil production

– and crude had traditionally been where the big profits lay.[30] Part of the reason why profits remained high was very simple. The companies were producing less but what they did produce made far more money. The effect was magnified because much of the production they retained was high cost. At pre-1973 prices it would have been marginally profitable. Now Shell's US wells suddenly started to make lots of money, although less than they might have done because US domestic oil prices were controlled between 1973 and 1981, averaging about $5 per barrel less than OPEC prices.[31] For BP, its two great areas of promise became vital to it in a way which it could never have anticipated in the days, not so long ago, when its biggest problem was getting rid of its surplus crude at a decent price. North Sea oil trickled in 1975, its first year of production, and was producing in substantial quantities by 1977. In the latter year the Trans-Alaska Pipeline was completed and Alaskan oil too began to flow. The companies had survived in a very different world from the one they bestrode in the 1950s and 1960s. But major changes had to be made. The loss of much of their crude oil meant that they were less integrated and less able to make up for losses in one part of their operation with profits in another. These changes are explored in Chapter 9.

THE OIL CRISIS AND THE BRITISH ECONOMY

The problem of Burmah Oil was as nothing compared to the wider economic problems which confronted the country. By far the most serious and intractable was inflation. Over the decade from 1970 to 1980 retail prices in Britain rose almost fourfold, the rate of increase peaking at 24 per cent in 1975.[32] The inflation of that decade is only history to many people now, but others who were adults at the time remember it well. And as inflation was not fully controlled until the 1990s, ensuring that it does not happen again is still a major policy objective of governments, economists and bankers.

In popular memory, the oil price rise and the wider inflationary spiral tend to be associated. Clearly there were connections. But what were they exactly, and what impact did the oil price rise have on the other major economic problems of the 1970s: the sharp slowdown in the developed world's rate of economic growth and the increase in unemployment?

The obvious subject with which to start is the oil price itself. OPEC, ostensibly the genesis of its rise, has often been described as a cartel – an organization whose constituents collaborate in setting the terms of supply of whatever they produce. In economists' language, if a cartel is effective it acts as a monopoly.

Can an OPEC monopoly explain the oil price rise, as the press and the public at the time often assumed?

As 'Prelude to crisis' explained, the price rises began in 1970 in Libya, which was acting unilaterally. This initial rise was largely a function of the improved market position of Libyan oil consequent upon the closure of the Tapline. It also seems likely, given that some of the firms producing in Libya had been discounters in Western European markets, that Libyan oil was underpriced before the rise. Then between 1970 and 1973 other OPEC countries, and Libya, continued with incremental rises. If OPEC hadn't existed, these would probably have been made in a less uniform way, but there seems little doubt that they were essentially market related in the context of rapidly tightening oil supplies. We saw earlier that by 1973 the US was producing at full capacity, and (see Chapter 6, 'Government and oil') that British oil stocks had fallen to unprecedentedly low levels early in 1973. The lifting of US oil import quotas in April 1973 was the final straw in an already very tight world supply situation. With market prices above posted, even after the recent increases, there was a clear signal that, irrespective of OPEC, posted prices were set for a further rise. But was it simply demand that dictated a rise to almost $12 per barrel?

Almost certainly not. If there had been numerous oil producers selling in a competitive and well-supplied market, the price of oil should settle at the cost of production, plus overheads and normal profit, of the most expensive barrel entering into supply (the marginal barrel). Prices had risen between 1970 and 1973 partly because the marginal barrel was no longer coming from the cheap oilfields of the Middle East but was being squeezed out of expensive American fields. And the infrastructure for future expansion was being built at even greater cost in Alaska and the North Sea, but was not yet producing. For a short time in late 1973, the marginal barrel was somewhere in a tanker on the high seas, subject to intense competition from buyers. Even so, in anything other than the very short run it was not, in a competitive market, likely to be priced at anything near $12. To that extent, the commonsense explanation that much of the oil price rise was due to OPEC acting as a monopoly must be correct. However, its monopoly power was partly dependent on the tightness of oil supplies. If there had been more supply from non-OPEC sources and higher stocks, an attempt to impose rises of the 300 per cent achieved in late 1973 could have been resisted by buyers for a considerable period – probably enough for the weaker, that is less well-off, OPEC producers to break ranks. More likely, the moderates such as Saudi Arabia would have had the whip hand at the beginning and never allowed such an increase. So ultimately, while the magnitude of the increase was undoubtedly the work of OPEC, the underpinning which allowed substantial rises in the first place was the rapid growth of demand in the preceding years, along with a slower growth in potential supply. In the early 1980s when demand had fallen sharply OPEC was arguably – for a time – at its most effective in terms of keeping prices above the market level. It used another weapon of the monopolist, the limitation of production, to enable it to sustain those prices for a number of years.

Understanding the role of demand in the oil price rise gives us a start in understanding the effect of oil prices on inflation generally. Burgeoning demand for commodities and labour, and limited potential supply, were characteristics of the developed world's economies by the early 1970s. As a result, inflation had been picking up from its relatively low level between the mid-1950s and the mid-1960s. By 1970 it averaged around 5 per cent in OECD countries. And Britain was suffering more than most. In 1970 and 1971 retail prices increased at an average of 8.5 per cent per annum before the rate of increase temporarily moderated.[33] As these figures imply Britain seemed more vulnerable than most countries to the factors at work. Some economists have seen monetary policy as the root of the problem in Britain and certainly British interest rates, while high in nominal terms, were sometimes lower than the rate of inflation. This meant negative real interest rates and hence over-incentives to borrow. Many economists, though, considered that changes in the labour market and in the relative power of trade unions and employers were more important. Loose monetary policy then accommodated the resulting wage rises, which fed their way into prices. Price rises were also stoked up by devaluations of the pound, in 1967 and then when it floated in 1972, which raised import prices in sterling terms. But subsequently commodity prices in general, not just oil, kept on rising – non-food raw materials doubled in price between 1972 and 1974.[34] Finally, the devaluations had made British goods cheaper abroad and this meant that employers were less concerned about holding down their costs and more likely to accede to wage demands. This litany suggests that there are plenty of culprits likely to be involved in Britain's inflationary decade as well as oil.

The initial impact of oil on price rises can be measured simply, if crudely, by taking the proportion of spending on oil before the price rise and the proportion after. According to Heal and Chichilnisky the initial proportion in OECD countries averaged around 1 per cent and rose to 3 per cent, that is a rise of 2 per cent. My calculations suggest that these figures are too low for Britain, where they are more like 1.7 per cent rising to 5 per cent. So in Britain 3.3 per cent of national income after the first price increase was accounted for by that increase, and was the initial inflationary impact. Added to this were the feedback effects on wages, through increased wages on other prices, and so on. Heal and Chichilnisky suggest that the initial inflationary impact should be multiplied by about three, which gives us about 10 per cent for Britain. To this should be added the impact of the 1979 increases. Oil was now a larger slice of national income and its price more than doubled, so on the face of it the inflationary effect should have been as bad or worse. However, falling demand and the substitution of gas for oil, already factors in the late 1970s, were even more evident by the early 1980s. They reduced the inflationary impact, and in fact by 1982 oil accounted for less than 5 per cent of national income. So the first oil shock was the most severe.[35]

These price effects seem substantial. But set against the increase in the price level over the whole decade, and the further 40 per cent between 1980 and 1985, they were quite small. It may be that the juxtaposition of the 1973 price rise – and the oil embargo which exacerbated shortages – with the miners' industrial action, which started in November 1973, increased the price rise's impact in Britain, because it put the miners in a position to pursue their wage claim more vigorously. Their success in this helped to break down Heath's wage limitation policy and possibly helped to bring the Labour government to power in the ensuing election. But how far these events exacerbated inflation in the long run is quite speculative and, anyway, the miners' success cannot be linked too closely with the oil shortages. They were successful partly because their picketing of power stations was successful and more plentiful oil supplies wouldn't have prevented that.

The oil price rises also had an impact on output in the developed world. As with inflation, the mid-1970s marks a major break with the previous trend, in this case one of seemingly inexorable growth. And as with inflation, it is tempting to see oil as closely involved with this change.

The immediate effect was a transfer of purchasing power to oil producers. Again the sum involved is, more or less, the difference between consuming countries' spending on oil before, and after, the oil shocks. In Britain's case, however, North Sea oil made it a net exporter by the time of the second oil shock in 1980 so no transfer took place that time. And although the effect of the first oil shock was substantial, it was a one-off subtraction, not a continuous brake. Such a transfer should result in a temporary, not a permanent, reduction in growth rates. Furthermore the oil producers eventually spent a great deal of their windfall with developed countries, thus mitigating the medium-term impact. In the short term, the transfer of such a large sum to countries which were not immediately able to spend it disrupted economic mechanisms in various ways and thus exacerbated the effect. In addition, governments' and central banks' concern about inflation raised interest rates, while attempts to economize on oil consumption diverted capital spending which might otherwise have raised output. The replacement of steam turbines by diesels on ships is an example. But these effects would all have worked themselves out in time. Instead, growth rates in the developed world remained far lower in the 1980s and 1990s than in the 1950s and 1960s. In spite of the estimates above which suggest a limited impact, were oil prices still in some way to blame?

There is another and more plausible explanation for the break in the trend rate of output growth, and the one which most economists favour. Rapid growth in the 1950s and 1960s was to a large extent the result of the technological lead which the USA had established over Western European countries and Japan at the beginning of the period. Given relatively high levels of skill and education in these countries, favourable demand conditions, and the ability to acquire US know-how and technology, over the next two decades they grew rapidly until they caught up with America. This helps to explain why the US's own growth rate was relatively slow in the period. Britain's was lower than the rest of Europe's, but economically it was less far behind the USA than most other countries in 1945. Cheap oil helped to speed the West's, and Japan's, growth between 1945 and 1973 but it was only one factor among several.[36]

If cheap oil does not play a major part in explaining Western post-war growth then the oil shock, dramatic and important though it was, only explains part of the turmoil of the 1970s. In fact, the oil shock can be better seen as part of a more general crisis in a period in which rapid growth was coming to an inevitable end. Growth slowed partly because the production of raw materials – including oil – was being outstripped by demand, with consequent price rises. This demand/supply imbalance was superimposed on the end of the era of technological catch-up. Other factors, particularly an increase in the power of labour and a consequent rise in its share of national income, may also have been at work. OPEC increased oil prices above the level at which they would otherwise have risen, therefore exacerbating inflation, and reducing growth, by more than would otherwise have happened. But it was stoking a fire which was already burning.

In the first half of the 1980s, British unemployment averaged over 12 per cent and several of the factors discussed above, particularly lower growth and changes in the labour market, help to explain this rise. In addition to those factors, a shift in government policy associated with the Conservative administration of Margaret Thatcher, who came to power in 1979 and who took a stronger line than her predecessors on government spending and monetary expansion, may have played a part.[37] One final factor in the unemployment of the early 1980s, however, was driven by oil. This was its impact on the exchange rate of sterling. In the mid-1970s, before North Sea oil came on stream, Britain's balance of payments deficit, already high, ballooned upwards because of the need to pay for expensive imported oil. One result was that sterling, already in the international doghouse, became even more unpopular and collapsed in value. As a consequence in 1976 the Labour government had to cut government spending sharply and seek an international loan to prop sterling up. By 1980 the situation was very different. North Sea oil was on stream and sterling became regarded as a 'petrocurrency'. Such popularity was not an unmitigated blessing. Most people in Britain became better off, but manufacturing industry suffered as British goods became less competitive. High unemployment owed itself partly to this as well as to longer-term factors and government policy. So ironically, while Britain did not suffer a transfer of purchasing power to oil producers during the second oil shock, because by then it was one itself, oil was not an unmixed blessing.

8

The North Sea

GAS AND GEOLOGY

The origins of Britain's North Sea oil and gas go back about 300 million years. We will cut the story short and start in 1959: not in Britain or the North Sea, but in the Dutch province of Groningen.

There was a certain amount of drilling for hydrocarbons in the Netherlands in the 1950s, and it was a well drilled in a field of sugar beet near the village of Slochteren, in Groningen, which first struck gas. The Groningen gas field was a giant, and encouraged oil companies to believe that gas might be found in similar geological formations in the southern North Sea. Oil mainly originates from the decay, burial under sediment, and subsequent heating under pressure when they are deep in the earth, of marine algae and bacteria; similar processes at work on the remains of land plants produce coal and, if they are buried more deeply and become hotter, methane gas. The Groningen gas came from the same Coal Measures which produced Britain's coal, buried more deeply as they sloped under the southern North Sea. These, together with geological changes which allowed the gas to seep into sandstone over which was an impermeable salt layer, produced gas fields.[1]

At much the same time, coastal states acquired the mineral rights of their adjacent continental shelf to the 200 metre depth – or in localized areas deeper – by the Fourth Geneva Convention of 1958. This was ratified in 1964 and Britain passed its own Continental Shelf Act in the same year. In 1965 Norway and Britain agreed a division of much of the North Sea, most of which is less than 200 metres deep. It was a favourable settlement for Norway in that the Norwegian Trench, a rift of up to 700 metres deep near the Norwegian coast, was ignored in the division even though, strictly speaking, it bisects the Norwegian part of the shelf and is therefore, from one perspective, its outer limit. Britain was anxious to establish boundaries which could allow exploration to commence and Norway could have delayed this for years by appealing to the International Court of Justice.[2]

Britain's urgency was in part because of the perennial problem of the balance of payments. Whether oil or gas was discovered – and attention initially was focused on gas – it could substitute for imported hydrocarbons and thus reduce the import bill.

With the international legal framework in place, the government could begin licensing. The initial round in 1964 was in the final year of a Conservative government but Labour, which came to office in that year, did not change the policy significantly. The British policy was to allocate licences by administrative fiat rather than by auction. Auctions can maximize financial returns to the government, if oil companies consider the prospects attractive, but may conflict with other aspects of public policy. Licensing allowed such policy imperatives – for instance the participation of British companies – to be accommodated. Equally important, licensing allowed the government some control over the rate of exploration through the specification of working programmes. The system of licensing is also important. Britain and Norway both opted for small licence blocks and detailed specifications for their working – an obvious contrast to the vast concession areas once common in the Middle East.[3]

Britain's first licensing round in 1964 predictably sparked a rush to the southern North Sea. It was relatively shallow and weather conditions not extreme, so offshore experience gained – and equipment used – elsewhere was easily transferable. BP found the first traces of gas in the British sector in September 1965 and, after deeper drilling, the West Sole field off the Lincolnshire coast was confirmed. Tragically, on 27 December, just a few days after confirmation, the drilling rig responsible, the *Sea Gem*, capsized. The rig was a 'jack-up', a barge with extendable legs which stood on the sea bed when drilling. Hangers securing the deck fractured and the deck shifted, causing two of the legs to collapse. The rig sunk in a few minutes although a nearby ship, the *Baltrover*, was able to pick up some of those who escaped. Even so there were 13 fatalities. Soon after this discovery Conoco found the Viking field, to the south-east of Sole. The Shell/Esso consortium which had discovered Groningen was drilling a little further south still, and in 1966 they discovered Leman Bank, one of the largest offshore gas fields in the world. The North Sea is relatively narrow at this point and it was only an accident of geology millions of years ago that placed the fields in the British sector and not the Dutch one, which in this area is adjacent.[4]

Two other giant fields, Hewett and Indefatigable, were discovered in the same year and the same general area as Leman. The largest proportion, by volume of gas, of Britain's pure gas fields were discovered within a period of about 15 months. Subsequently many smaller fields were found, and the isolated Morecambe field in the Irish Sea (1974) was a giant, although much smaller than Leman. The complex of fields around Leman, off the north Norfolk coast, briefly made Great Yarmouth the centre of the British hydrocarbon industry until the drilling action moved further north.[5]

Much gas now comes from the central and northern North Sea where it is usually found in conjunction with oil and has a different geological origin. But it took a considerable time for this gas to be extensively exploited. The Gas Council, later British Gas, then a nationalized monopoly and therefore the only buyer, paid very low prices which discouraged investment in gas collecting infrastructure. Cheap gas had a number of major, but now taken-for-granted, effects on Britain's energy consumption patterns. The old coal-gas industry finally expired and gas manufactured from imported oil, which had experienced a brief boom, also quickly declined. But gas's share of the total energy market rose substantially. The death-knell sounded for the domestic grate and coal-fired central heating as gas central heating became increasingly common. Gas was still prohibited as a fuel for power generation in order to protect one of coal's remaining markets, but industrial fuel users started converting to it. My stepfather ran a small paper-mill in the Wye valley east of High Wycombe in Bucks and his mill and others in the valley, all previously coal-fired, converted to gas in the early 1970s, as I recall, except one which had gone over earlier to fuel oil.[6]

The oil price rise of 1973–4 further increased the attractions of gas to consumers but, conversely, also increased the attractions of oil exploration and led to a shortage of gas. British Gas was forced to offer much higher prices in the mid-1970s for Norwegian gas, to fulfil its commitments and to get exploitation in British waters started again. Subsequently gas's market share went on growing, as most new houses had gas central heating. Then in 1990 the power generation market was opened to gas and by the late 1990s took roughly one-third of production, which peaked in 2000 at the equivalent of over 100 million metric tons of oil.[7]

The oil companies' focus of attention from the early 1970s were the central and northern parts of the North Sea. Here the geology is more complex. Most oil comes from the Kimmeridge Clay. If such oil-bearing strata are buried more deeply, and therefore become hotter, the planktonic remains in them are gasified. Some gas in these sectors also comes from coal seams laid down at periods when the underlying rock was lifted and the surface was land or swamp. Since the geology was different, the gas discoveries in the southern sector were not critical in persuading companies to look for oil further north: there was already some interest in the area. As a result, in both the British and the Norwegian sectors, licences were issued in 1964 and subsequently, although in some cases it took time before drilling started.[8]

OIL!

2/4–1AX seems a set of unrelated letters and numbers. But to oilmen they identify an historic well: the first in the North Sea to find commercial quantities of oil. What the drillers had struck, in December 1969, was the giant Ekofisk field in the central North Sea, roughly equidistant between Dundee and northern Denmark. Ekofisk and the numerous fields subsequently discovered around it were, however, actually in the Norwegian sector. Most of Britain's oil lay further north.[9]

The first oil to be discovered in the British sector came soon after – Amoco's Montrose Field, east of Peterhead. Ekofisk and Montrose transformed interest in the central North Sea and further north still, in the areas lying east of the Orkneys and Shetlands. BP had originally had no great hopes of finding oil but had applied in 1965 for some blocks. It was only under pressure from the Ministry of Power, the government department responsible for licensing, that it agreed to drill two wells rather than one. Then came Ekofisk and Montrose. BP's licence had only two years to go, and it rushed to get its rig *Sea Quest* into position. Peter Kent, the company's chief geologist from 1966, was more interested in the northern basin than his predecessor and had suggested earlier that Block 21/10, a few miles north of Montrose, might be promising. But this had eventually been rejected and *Sea Quest* first drilled elsewhere. That well yielded only a small quantity of oil and the rig was moved to 21/10. In October 1970 oil was found, although because of a violent storm the rig was then cut off for a week. When the storm eased the news was confirmed. BP had struck the Forties field, the first British giant.[10]

By the time the latitude of Forties was reached – 58 degrees north – the weather in the North Sea is apt to become rough: '. . . winds of 125 miles an hour, waves 100 feet high . . .'. It was further north still, off the Shetlands, that in June 1971 a Shell/Exxon consortium made a strike in Block 211/29. The discovery was kept secret because it came just before an experiment in the auctioning of blocks. At the auction in August the consortium startled everybody by bidding, with neat symmetry, £21 million for the nearby block 211/21. Next year, as rumours started to leak out, the consortium announced that it had discovered another giant – Brent. The blocks around also yielded Cormorant (the consortium favoured bird names for its fields), partly in 211/21. A whole raft of others were then found in the East Shetlands area, some owned by Shell and Exxon and some by other consortia.[11]

Finding and exploiting the oil posed huge technological challenges. Exploration drilling necessitated rigs which could be moved, since the well might be dry. Floating platforms with retractable legs – 'jack-up' platforms such as *Sea Gem* – were adequate in the southern North Sea, if they were well built, since it was shallow. Further north the semi-submersible was the rig of choice. This floats but, when in position, is semi-submerged to keep it more stable and is held in place by giant anchors. 'Dynamic positioning' in which propellers around a floating rig controlled by computers keep it in position in spite of waves and weather have also been used but it is expensive in fuel to hold such a rig against strong winds. *Sea Quest* and *Staflo*, which discovered Brent, were both semi-submersibles.[12]

Once the extent of a field was proved through further drilling, then permanent platforms would be installed. Platforms hold a derrick for the rig, accommodation modules, and miscellaneous facilities such as laboratories. A number of wells are likely to terminate on it, their associated valves and pipework sprouting out to form the 'Christmas tree'. Associated gas is separated from the oil here. Apart from fuelling the gas turbines which provide power, in the early days it was often flared, but now it too is likely to be piped ashore. Some early platforms were vast monsters made of concrete which, when in position, would be ballasted and sunk. Chambers in such platforms gave them buoyancy so they could be towed into position, and could also be used to store oil. More common was the steel jacket platform, a giant Eiffel Tower-like structure pinned to the seabed with steel piles. In deeper water tension leg platforms have been used. In these jointed legs are kept in tension, and therefore stable, by ballast adjustments. From a platform directional drilling – drilling away from a vertical axis – radiated out a number of wells, which might tap parts of the reservoir several miles from the platform. At its peak Forties had five platforms and over 120 wells.[13]

Although the Norwegians had landed oil from Ekofisk in 1971, it was not until 1975 that British North Sea oil first came ashore. Production then built up rapidly and by 1985 reached its first peak of 127 million tonnes. The oil price collapse led to a rapid reverse. Exploration activity fell and the development of marginal fields which had already been discovered was put on hold. Production declined as some of the big early fields had already passed their peak and in 1988 the *Piper Alpha* disaster put one substantial field out of action for three years. By 1989 production was around 90 million tonnes and there was considerable pessimism about future prospects. Projections saw production falling to around 75 million tonnes in 1995 and under 50 million by 2005. But over the years there had also been a host of technical changes. These and a limited recovery in the oil price were to transform North Sea prospects.[14]

Developing North Sea oil in the 1970s was enormously costly. One reason was simply the perceived need for great strength in the production platforms and other undersea equipment such as pipelines. North Sea weather imposed other costs too. Platforms and pipelines could only be installed during 'weather windows' – periods when reasonable spells of calm weather were likely, which in practice meant during the early summer. Shell originally thought that developing Brent would be three times as difficult as developing an offshore field in the Gulf of Mexico. In practice it was ten times as difficult. Another factor in driving up costs was the inflation of the 1970s but this was more than matched by the rising price of oil so it was not, to the oil companies, an increase in real terms. But the sheer demand for equipment and labour in the period forced up prices over and above normal inflationary increases. Ross Leckie, as a student working on the rigs in the late 1970s, earned an incredible £1,286 for a fortnight's work. The average male manual worker at this time earned a bit over £80 per week.[15]

By the 1980s costs were coming down rapidly. Enhanced computing power meant that three-dimensional seismography gave a far better picture of the probable oil-bearing strata, refining the accuracy of exploratory wells and reducing the need for appraisal wells which test the limits of a field. Improved directional drilling techniques widened the area which could be tapped from a platform. Platforms themselves became much lighter: Gannett in 1992 weighed 5,000 tons, but only five years earlier a similar structure would have been 15,000. One of the most labour intensive oilfield operations, the insertion of new pipe to extend a drill, was being partially automated by the 'Iron Roughneck'. Fewer workers meant less accommodation and lower associated platform costs. Off-field costs were also lowered as the government trimmed tax rates from 1982. By the 1990s it was relaxing licence terms and the taxation regime still further with the explicit aim of encouraging exploration. And with greater competition among suppliers, the excessive cost-inflation of the 1970s was brought under control. Ross Leckie earned far less for a spell on the rigs in 1987–8 than he had ten years earlier, in spite of a doubling of the average British wage in the period.[16]

These cost-reducing factors continued into the 1990s and one result was a pick up in exploration and development even though there was only a modest recovery in the oil price. As early as 1990 the *Petroleum Economist* greeted increased exploration with the headline 'Good Times Returning' and after small production increases between 1991 and 1993 a big leap saw Britain's offshore production break its 1985 record in 1995. Fittingly, given the period covered by this book, the peak of 137 million tonnes was reached in 1999 – one year before gas production peaked.[17]

Complex fields such as those west of the Shetlands could now be worked. The earliest, Clair, had been discovered in 1977 but the depth of water – 1,500 feet or more – and fractured oil-bearing formations made exploitation uneconomic. Two more fields, Schiehallion and Foinaven, were discovered in the early 1990s and subsequently all the fields were developed. Schiehallion and Foinaven are worked via another innovation, subsea clusters – well-heads on the sea bed into which a number of wells feed before the oil is piped to the surface. Then the oil flows to 'Floating, Production, Storage and Offloading' (FPSO) vessels, anchored like semi-submersibles, from which it is periodically collected by tanker. No fixed platforms or pipelines are needed and horizontal drilling – wells drilled more than 80 degrees from the vertical – enables the oil in the fractured reservoirs to be captured. BP is the operator although a number of companies have interests. BP gained a good deal of experience in horizontal drilling, a logical but challenging extension of directional drilling, in Britain's biggest onshore field – Wytch Farm in Dorset.[18]

Dorset had been a gleam in the eye of British oil prospectors for many years (see Chapter 3 'Britain's own oil'). The small Kimmeridge field was discovered in 1959, and the village actually gave its name to the Kimmeridge Clay, the 140 million year old shale which extends into the North Sea and is the source of much of Britain's oil. Wytch Farm was discovered in 1973 and production started in 1979. It was originally operated by British Gas, the nationalized gas company, but was sold to BP in 1984. The field is, in fact, mainly offshore, since most of the reservoir lies under Poole Harbour and further east, under Poole Bay off Bournemouth. It counts as onshore since it is exploited from the land, desirable in an environmentally sensitive area. This made horizontal drilling, in a sophisticated form using steerable tools in the drill head, essential to reach the outer limits of the reservoir. BP broke a world record in 1999 when Well M16 reached 10.7 kilometres horizontally from the well-head.[19]

Britain has other onshore fields in the Wessex-Channel Basin in southern England which hosts Wytch Farm, some yielding mainly oil and others mainly gas. In the East Midlands the fields around Eakring in Nottinghamshire, discovered just before the Second World War, are now worked out (see Chapter 4 'Britain's Oil supplies') but there is a field currently being exploited near Gainsborough in Lincolnshire. With the exception of Wytch Farm all of these are small by North Sea standards. Much more important are the gasfields of the Irish Sea, which also produce some oil. The gas here is a product of the Coal Measures, as it is in the southern North Sea. The Morecambe fields (often inaccurately called

Morecambe Bay) were discovered in 1974 and developed in the 1980s. The area had been prospected by Gulf but it had let its licence lapse and it was John Baines, a geologist with British Gas, who saw the area's potential. Morecambe was followed by the Liverpool Bay complex of fields including Hamilton and Douglas, which came on stream in the late 1990s, as did some fields near the Cumbrian coast. The reserves in all these fields are extensive but shallow and, again, sophisticated directional drilling has proved invaluable in exploiting them economically.[20]

Technological change has been essential in the continuing development of the North Sea and much of this change has arisen through experience – 'learning by doing'. But in order to learn people had to do, and the harsh, often dangerous and sometimes fatal experience of working in the North Sea is the subject of the next section.

WORKING IN THE NORTH SEA

On 6 July 1988, maintenance work was being carried out on *Piper Alpha*, the platform for the Piper field north-east of Aberdeen. It was owned by Occidental Oil, run by the legendary Armand Hammer. The maintenance work, on a pressure valve, meant that one of the two pumps which compressed gas for transport to the mainland was switched off and the pipe temporarily sealed. The fitter had filled in a form stating that the pump was out of action and should not be switched on and, as the supervisor was busy, had gone off duty leaving the form in the control centre.

At 9.45 p.m., the operating compressor failed. No one saw the form stating that the other pump should not be turned on and at 9.55 p.m. it was restarted. Gas immediately leaked from the temporary seal and in two minutes had exploded. Production stopped but by then further explosions had occurred and a major fire had broken out. The electric fire-fighting pumps were disabled and the back-up diesel pumps, which were designed to cut in automatically, had been switched to manual operation because divers were working around the platform. Now, because of the fire, no one could reach the controls. With no instructions being given, many of the crew moved to the fireproofed accommodation below the helicopter deck. But no helicopters could land. Then at 10.20 a gas line from the Tartan field, which ran close to *Piper Alpha*, exploded. A fireball now engulfed the platform, which subsequently collapsed. The accommodation module sank with most of those inside. The total number of dead was 167.[21]

The consequences of the disaster were profound. The entire North Sea safety culture changed, as discussed below. The disaster enquiry, chaired by William

Cullen, had revealed some basic flaws. Some were endemic to the industry, such as the constant pressure for production which impinged on the judgement of supervisors and managers. Some were, perhaps, more specific to Occidental which was heavily criticized. It 'adopted a superficial attitude to the assessment of the risk of a major hazard' and 'failed to ensure that emergency training was being provided as intended'. Even if the fire-fighting system had been switched on, many of the deluge heads would have been blocked with scale. The inspection regime, administered by the Department of Energy, was also a target: inspections were 'superficial to the point of being little use as a test of safety on the platform'.[22]

Of the 62 survivors, many came through only because they chanced the leap through debris to the North Sea. Even so, many survivors suffered long-lasting mental scars, as of course did the families of those who died. Some survived only because of heroic efforts by co-workers or rescue boats. 'Younger workers gave older colleagues life-belts salvaged from the wreckage', while two crew members on the rescue tug *Sandhaven* were killed as it manoeuvred directly underneath the rig when the gas line exploded. A total of seven George Medals were awarded, several posthumously.[23]

Over 20 years before *Piper Alpha* there had been another, though smaller, North Sea disaster – the sinking of *Sea Gem*, mentioned earlier in the chapter. The circumstances were very different. Kevin Topham, who was a driller on the *Sea Gem*, does not refer to excessive pressure of work but rather good accommodation, excellent food and the provision of stewards for the crew. Where 'hurry, hurry, hurry' – his words – had operated was in the preparation of the rig for North Sea work. Welds were inadequate and hence the fracture of its legs, which precipitated the disaster.[24]

Sea Gem may have operated in a more gentlemanly fashion than a 1970s rig drilling for oil, but that did not mean there was a developed safety culture – rather the opposite, as Topham remembers it. This existing lack of safety awareness was exacerbated by the high-pressure world of 1970s drilling, with the weather in the central and northern North Sea putting a premium on getting the job done on time. Maurice White worked his way up a drilling crew from roustabout – labourer – to roughneck, who manipulated the pipes as drills were extended or pulled out of a hole, to driller in charge of the drilling process. Later he became a toolpusher, overseeing the entire drilling crew and responsible for the logistics of the operation. He too uses the words 'hurry, hurry, hurry', this time to describe the pressures on the crew. People were not unaware of safety, and drillers and toolpushers cared about their crew. But the culture was one in which it was assumed that people should look after themselves – and that accidents would happen. White himself slipped on the pipe deck and broke his leg. He was in close proximity to far more serious accidents: a man falling 90 feet to his death from the derrick which hoisted the drill pipes (30 foot drill pipes were screwed together in 90 foot lengths); another man losing his foot when a pipe dropped from a derrick. In sober statistical terms, the risks of being killed in an offshore installation in the mid-1970s was eleven times the risk in the construction industry, itself hardly the safest type of work. White, by now a manager, became involved in developing the new safety culture which emerged after *Piper Alpha*. There was more cooperation between companies and contractors, who performed much of the work on drilling rigs and production platforms; and most of all more emphasis on planning for operations, in which planning for safety – the safety case – was a critical part. These and other safety improvements mandated by the Cullen Enquiry were expensive. But technical advances and better planning meant that North Sea costs actually continued to decline.[25]

In spite of the dangers, North Sea work was attractive to many young men. Money was part of it – the enormous wage earned by Ross Leckie was mentioned in the previous section. But there was also a sense of excitement. Maurice White had seen drilling in his first job as an oil equipment salesman: the self-reliant crew – 'quite tough guys' – the driller who was responsible for putting thousands of feet of pipe in the right place, the 2,000 horsepower engines, all generated an image which helped to lure him on to the rigs.[26]

They were tough guys because it was tough work. Drilling would go on even in atrocious weather when platforms would move 'quite alarmingly', although White points out that fishermen in small vessels were actually much more vulnerable to the weather. Much of the work, especially for the roustabouts, was simply dull and hard, shovelling mud in an all-steel environment and living in basic accommodation. In his early days it was also a very 'macho' environment. Some drillers would shout and bully and that meant the occasional confrontation, although with strict rules on fighting and alcohol this rarely became physical. If it did, there was instant dismissal. Although drillers and toolpushers in the early days were often Canadian or American, crews were not highly cosmopolitan. Some people had a past to hide, but most were 'straightforward guys', and British. Back in the 1960s when gas was the target, some crews had come from the Eakring field in Nottinghamshire which was then running down. Kevin Topham himself took this route to the North Sea, and he also remembered 'Fifers' – Scottish crews who had worked in the Middle East. This was a time when oil companies such as BP, which ran Eakring, often did their own drilling. Later specialist contractors became the norm. Maurice White worked for KCA, a rare British drilling firm.[27]

Drilling needed considerable skill, although the skills were usually acquired on the job rather than by formal training. Work which may now be electronically controlled was still dependent in the 1970s on experience. 'Kicking-off', for instance – altering the direction of a drill – was vital when drilling production or gas injection wells which might need to penetrate the reservoir rock miles from the platform. (Once a field had been found, such wells were drilled from the production platform rather than from a specialist drilling rig.) To do this a driller needed the ability to 'think in three dimensions'. They also needed 'mechanical sympathy' – the ability to sense, for instance, when a drill bit might be about to stick. Not all of them had it, and Maurice White thought that some drillers never really understood what was happening in the well. The penalties for failure could be harsh. With only a little provocation, a driller who fell foul of an oil company representative could be 'run off' – fired. This met with little resistance because union activity was very limited. The companies opposed it, while perhaps the ethos of a typical crew member was not very sympathetic either. It was only after *Piper Alpha* that unions gained more of a foothold offshore.[28]

North Sea work called on many other skills. Sometimes, as with drilling, these were learned on the job, but often they involved specialist training. One such, dangerous as well as highly skilled, was diving. In the early North Sea days many divers were ex-Navy men, since the Royal Navy was a world leader in diving techniques. While technology developed to allow divers to work at much greater depths, simultaneously diving work, like that on the surface, was being automated by 'Robot Operational Vehicles' – unmanned mini-submarines. Another specialist skilled occupation involving long training – and not one which has been automated, as yet – is that of the helicopter pilots. But as with other support jobs – for instance the supply vessel crews – numbers have diminished in recent years because automation has reduced the number of those working offshore. By 2000, 19,000 were employed, about half the numbers in 1990.[29]

BRITAIN AND NORTH SEA OIL

So far North Sea oil and gas have been discussed from technological and human perspectives and their impact on the wider political and economic scene has barely been mentioned. But clearly such high levels of production must have had economic effects. And anyone with some interest in politics would suspect a link between the copious flow of oil and Scottish nationalism. As we will see, oil was intertwined with the political scene in other ways too.

The economic effects of North Sea oil and gas can be divided into three: the fiscal, that is its contribution to government revenue and, conversely, the effect of taxation policy on North Sea production; local and regional effects on employment and the economy; and the macro effect – the interactions between North Sea oil and the wider economy. This last is obviously the most speculative. And equally obviously there are no hard and fast divisions between these categories. I have split them like this for convenience.

Prior to 1974 Britain had virtually no taxation on oil company profits. Most of the producing states' share of profits were notionally accounted for as tax payments by the companies and were offset against British tax (see Chapter 5, 'Seven Sisters'). But the persistent tendency for actual sale prices to be lower than posted prices produced an anomaly. Companies transferred crude at posted prices to their own refining and marketing operations, but since these competed with independents who bought crude at actual prices, the prices realized for products were relatively low and produced losses in downstream operations. So companies' huge upstream profits were tax-free in the UK, and their downstream activities accumulated losses which could be set against profits in other UK activities – such as the North Sea. Labour, in opposition, made a lot of noise about this after a critical report from the Public Accounts Committee in February 1973, but in fact the Treasury had been well aware of the implications before then. Anthony Barber, the Conservative Chancellor, announced in the 1973 Budget that the two related issues – transfer pricing of crude and 'ring-fencing' North Sea profits from earlier accumulated losses – would be dealt with. Whether Labour pressure accelerated his announcement is difficult to say from the papers I have seen.[30]

One other major element of Labour policy, Petroleum Revenue Tax (PRT), also came on the agenda during Edward Heath's Conservative government. In 1973 ministers debated various measures and it was agreed in October that what was initially called 'Excess Revenue Tax' would be brought in. By November its familiar name had been adopted. It fell, however, to Labour's Edmund Dell, who was largely responsible for the Public Account Committee's report, to introduce legislation on transfer pricing, ring-fencing and PRT. PRT was originally 45 per cent on profits, once development costs had been reclaimed, net of royalties of 12.5 per cent, operating expenses and various other deductions. PRT effectively became bipartisan, continuing under the Conservatives when they returned to power under Margaret Thatcher in 1979. Labour had raised it in 1978. In 1980, with the second oil price rise increasing profits still further, the Conservatives did so again, to 80 per cent. Labour's other key policy, participation, is discussed later. This too had been discussed in 1973 by the Conservatives, although as an alternative to PRT, rather than additional to it.[31]

By 1982, with the oil price slipping, PRT was eased for small, high-cost fields.

Nevertheless with production increasing, the government take from North Sea taxation was £12 billion in 1984–5 or 8 per cent of total tax revenue. The oil price fall of 1985–6 reduced this drastically, however. One part of the government response was to reduce taxes further. PRT was abolished in stages on new fields in 1992–3, royalties having gone earlier, and PRT on old fields was reduced to 50 per cent in 1993. By now the government tax take had fallen to just one billion pounds. New fields were only subject to normal corporation tax and Labour, in power from 1997, accepted this. When the oil price rose in 2002 a supplementary corporation tax of 10 per cent on oil profits was introduced, but all royalties were abolished; subsequently corporation tax has been increased again.[32]

In the early days gas was another example of an essentially bipartisan approach, whilst also illustrating that governments were not pushovers for the oil companies. As already noted ('Gas and geology') Labour in the late 1960s imposed a low price on the producers – well below what they asked, and 10 per cent or more below the average price for Groningen gas at the Dutch border. I can still remember my stepfather lamenting the decision, presumably because he had shares in Shell or BP – although later on his paper-mill was to benefit from low gas prices. The Conservatives did not change the policy and, as Richard Toye points out, at that time they also accepted the underlying fact that gas was a nationalized industry. It was Labour in the mid-1970s who were forced towards more market-based pricing by the disequilibrium which would result if gas prices fell excessively behind those of oil, and by the need to meet increasing demand by importing Norwegian Frigg gas.[33]

Important though gas was to the British economy it only had limited employment effects. There was a brief boom in Great Yarmouth, the main supply centre, while the gas fields were being developed but once they were established that was it. Gas is much simpler and less labour intensive to extract than oil and the production platforms are nearer the coast, thus reducing the need for supply networks. But when oil exploration and development started, on a far larger scale than gas, the employment effect was still muted because Britain had a miserable record in building drilling rigs and supply ships. Platform construction was more successful, but this was partly because platforms were such enormous affairs in the early days that their potential sources of supply were limited. What lay behind this failure?[34]

From the 1950s to the 1970s, Britain's record in shipbuilding, much heavy engineering, and in building major civil engineering projects was dismal. Whatever the reasons for these failures – not our concern here – they help to explain why much of the heavy North Sea construction work eluded Britain; or, as with production platforms, why it was consistently late and expensive. A number of specialist sites were developed, with government help, to construct platforms. Nigg Bay in the Cromarty Firth was one which became notorious for poor labour relations and poor workmanship. Many of the workers had come from unrelated local occupations such as farming or, as incomers to the sparsely populated area, lived in unsatisfactory temporary accommodation. In the rush to develop oil in the early and mid-1970s, the hunt for platform sites got out of hand. Portavadie on Loch Fyne on the west coast, in the middle of nowhere, cost the government £15 million, partly because 200 houses were built for the workforce. No workers ever came and the site lay empty for years until it was sold for £7,500.[35]

If this had been all, then the impact on the British economy of North Sea development, as opposed to production, would have been both nugatory and temporary. In fact the overall position was better than this implies. Firms making specialist products, such as pumps and valves, were reasonably successful from the beginning. As time went by other specialist manufacturers have repeated this success. For instance Wellstream, a Newcastle firm, has a quarter of the world market for underseas flexible pipe. Another success story is the Wood Group, based in Aberdeen. This grew from the old-established firm of John D. Wood which diversified quickly into rig supply. It now provides a huge range of services and manufacturing and employs 25,000 people worldwide, many in North America. A recent estimate is that the subsea sector, in which both these companies play a leading part, employs 40,000 people in Britain directly and indirectly, mostly in Scotland and north-east England.[36]

However, we should not be too optimistic. Andrew Cumbers found in 2000 that, although small and medium-sized firms in the Aberdeen region had moved over time into manufacturing for the oil sector, they carried out relatively little research and development. Many firms did not source locally and, although there were industry-based networks, there seemed a curious lack of the social networks so important in California's Silicon Valley. On a more positive note a number of international firms have their European headquarters in Aberdeen. But one wonders how long they will stay as North Sea output shrinks. At the moment, though, Aberdeen remains, as it became in the 1970s, a prosperous city and the economic benefits of oil diffuse to a lesser degree around Scotland's east coast. North-east England is not so prosperous – but without North Sea oil its economy would probably be in even worse shape. The biggest economic gain of all, in proportion to size, went to the Shetland Islands. With great prescience, the clerk (chief executive) of the Islands' council, Ian Clark, obtained for it the power to own and run an oil port in one of the main island's sea-lochs, Sullom Voe. Shetland grew rich on the income from it.[37]

Why has there been more success in oil-related manufacturing in the last

25 years than in the first 15 or so? An initial impetus came from the Offshore Supplies Office founded by the government in 1973 to 'coordinate and stimulate deliveries of UK produced goods and services'. But on quitting office in 1980 its director-general was still bitterly critical of British industry, while as time went by European competition rules put such favouritism off limits. A more likely reason for today's relative success is simply the longevity of the North Sea, combined with its role as the most consistently testing area for underwater oil recovery. More efficient local firms have had a long period in which to develop, while branch plants established by foreign firms produce 'learning-by-doing' effects among their local suppliers.[38]

Of course the North Sea's economic impact has not been confined to supply, since it also encompasses those employed on the rigs. Total North Sea-related Grampian region jobs peaked at 50,000 in 1985 and, after a fall, reached a slightly higher peak in the early 1990s before drifting down again. To these should be added jobs in the north-east and, in the 1970s and 1980s, production and head office jobs on Clydeside. However, quoting specific figures for the UK as a whole is very hazardous. This is because oil's overall impact on jobs must take into account its macro-economic effects.[39]

The starting point for measuring these effects is the proportion that North Sea output of hydrocarbons bore to national income. As production built up, this reached 5.8 per cent in 1984.[40] When prices fell in 1985–6 it declined sharply and remained at a much lower level for the rest of the twentieth century. Where does this money end up? When prices have been high, so has been the tax take and therefore the government has been one beneficiary. Profits have also flowed to British shareholders but much of the profit went to the foreign oil companies which had invested in the North Sea. Finally, most operating expenditure went directly to production workers, or to British supply firms and their employees. Development expenditure went to British firms too but a big slice, especially in the early days, went abroad.

However, to simply tot up oil's contribution after deducting payments abroad is not enough. On the one hand, there was a multiplier effect: workers' wages have been spent in Britain thus creating further employment. On the other hand, there was an opportunity cost to spending on the North Sea. If the oil and gas had never existed, the capital would have been invested elsewhere and the labour would have done something else. Capital might have made a lower return and some of the labour might have been unemployed or employed at lower wages. But even so, other opportunities would have existed and so the simple addition of money spent does not tell the whole story.

Oil had another effect. As explained in Chapter 7 ('The oil crisis and the British economy'), sterling's new status as a 'petrocurrency' forced up the exchange rate in the early 1980s. This hit exports and pushed up unemployment, although it helped to cut inflation. Subsequently oil and gas contributed to maintaining a higher exchange rate. This helps us towards a summing up of the economic impact of gas and oil. A higher exchange rate meant cheaper imports. In addition there were enhanced employment and profit opportunities, and an increased tax take which meant higher government spending or reduced taxes elsewhere. These all point to a commonsense conclusion. Over their life span North Sea hydrocarbons have made the people of Britain better off. Exactly how much is probably impossible to say. But for most people except those directly employed in the oil industry, the answer is likely to be: a few per cent, but not more.

This conclusion begs a question which is essentially political, and perhaps ethical, rather than economic. Should the governments of the day have retained more of the oil earnings for posterity by exploiting the resources more slowly? And that, of course, leads to another vexed question – was it really Britain's oil or just Scotland's, as the Scottish National Party asserts? Interestingly, Christopher Harvie suggests that the initial upsurge of nationalism in the early 1970s owed only a little to oil. The further upsurge in support for Scottish Nationalism more recently also seems to have various causes, although the potential of oil as a replacement for transfers to Scotland from the overall tax take must be an attraction.[41]

Harvie's entertaining book about North Sea oil has other serious messages, including a broad thesis about its effects within Britain. To Harvie, British policy has been to exploit oil to the maximum and this, of course, has meant making a choice in favour of the present over the future, a choice with which he clearly disagrees. But Harvie also sees Britain as, all too often, simply messing things up. Initially British industry failed to respond adequately. He gives better marks to Labour's policy in the 1970s. But then the Conservatives sold off Britain's hydrocarbon assets and reduced the tax take from the North Sea rather than using the windfall to reconstruct British industry. In all this he contrasts Norway favourably with Britain.[42]

British industry's early failure is indisputable. But the Norwegian perspective on his other criticisms, and on his praise of Norway, is rather different. Oystein Noreng, a Norwegian academic, pointed to the many similarities between the two countries' approaches. He broadly approved of the policy, which both adopted, of administrative allocation of small blocks (see 'Gas and geology'). Auctions might bring in more money initially but gave governments less control. And if there were excess profits, governments could vary the tax take to siphon them off. When assessing the details of licence allocation and tax policy, Noreng gave slightly better marks to Britain. And he pointed out that, while Norwegian indus-try appeared to be more successful in its initial response to the opportunities presented by North Sea oil, by the late 1970s this led to a full-blown economic crisis in Norway as demand fell.[43]

Noreng's book was published in 1980 and, over the next decade, British policy shifted towards lower taxation while participation, one of Labour's key policies, was abandoned. By this the British National Oil Corporation (BNOC), set up in 1975, could negotiate the right to 'buy back' up to 51 per cent of a field's produc-tion. In practice this was usually sold back again to the companies to refine. The exercise was initially profitable. BNOC also acquired direct stakes in fields. In the 1980s BNOC's holdings were hived off into Britoil and then privatized as was British Gas's Wytch Farm. Then British Gas itself was sold. Participation ceased to be profitable in 1983 as the oil price slid and BNOC was wound up in 1985 as the price fell further. In the circumstances it was an understandable decision, while privatization, however controversial at the time, is now accepted by most political actors, right or left. And reducing tax rates was explicitly designed to stimulate continued exploration in the context of a falling oil price. In line with this, the Conservative governments of the 1980s retained Britain's licence alloca-tion policy and hence considerable influence over the pace of development. But they did not see their role as the active reconstruction of British industry. The oil supply industry, however, would benefit from continued development of the North Sea and, as noted above, this seems to have happened.[44]

As the post-1990 resurgence in production shows, the policy of encouraging exploration and development was successful. But was the entire policy of rapid exploitation wrong?

Rapid exploitation was favoured initially to solve Britain's balance of payments problems, which were seen as a major handicap in the 1960s and 1970s. So the initial rapid exploitation may be excused, but did the acceleration of depletion up to the mid-1980s, the subsequent reduction of tax take to encourage further exploration, and the encouragement of gas use in power stations from the late 1980s, just pander to our desire to consume now at the expense of future generations? Harvie compares British policy with Norwegian, which imposed limits on the rate of development. But the conditions were very different. For Norway with a population of under five million, oil had far more potential to destabilize the economy if rapidly exploited through the over-commitment of resources to the oil sector. In spite of Norway's limits on exploitation, this is exactly what happened in the late 1970s. To Britain's far larger economy, oil and gas were important, but not overwhelmingly so. In that case, decisions over depletion rates come down to two basic considerations. Practical – if we wait, alternative technologies may be developed which reduce the value of oil. This has not happened so far, and maybe it was always an over-optimistic argument. But there is a legitimate point. The other is ethical – should we privilege ourselves over future generations? To do so seems selfish. But arguably future generations will enjoy much better technology, and much higher standards of living, than we do now. If this is the case, the argument for giving them most of the benefits does not sound so compelling. Of course climate change is one other factor. But North Sea oil is only a fraction of total world oil supply, so its contribution to global warning via its impact on oil consumption is not likely to be large.

9

Age of Uncertainty: Oil After the Oil Crisis 1980–2000

BEYOND THE OIL CRISIS

In 1982 BP took a 270,000 ton tanker out of lay-up in Brunei Bay where it had been for six years, a victim of the decline in long-distance haulage of Middle Eastern crude. BP then removed the ship's steam turbines and substituted more economical diesels.[1] In the long run, oil consumption was highly responsive to price increases because of efficiency measures like this (see Chapter 7, 'Turbulent years'). But between the first oil shock in 1973–4 and the 1979 price rise there was time to make only the most obvious economies. As a result, following a brief drop during the 1974–5 recession, oil consumption had gone on rising.

The period after 1979 was very different. On the one hand, efficiency improvements started to have a real impact. On the other, the response of Western governments to the trade-off between inflation and recession had changed. Inflation in the 1970s, particularly in Britain but to some extent in all Western countries, had risen so high as to seem a political as well as an economic threat. In part as a response to those perceived threats, several countries had elected conservative governments, which were willing to pursue relatively restrictive monetary and fiscal policies. The best-known exponents of these policies were Margaret Thatcher in Britain and Ronald Reagan in the United States. Between 1980 and 1982, therefore, the Western world experienced a much more significant recession than in 1975, as a renewed upsurge of inflation was met by restrictive policies. Efficiency improvements and recession together caused a much steeper and more lasting fall in oil consumption than had happened in 1975. Worldwide production, which had originally fallen as a result of the Iranian revolution and the Iran-Iraq war, stayed down. From 1981–6 it was 10 per cent or more below the 1979 peak of 3.2 billion metric tons. Only in 1988 was the 3 billion metric tons level exceeded again.[2]

At the same time non-OPEC production was booming. North Sea oil was important, but the single biggest source was Russia, which had stepped up production sharply in the 1970s as the oil price rose, and continued to do so into the 1980s. The result was a squeeze on OPEC. If oil prices were to remain high, its production had to be restricted to match both the decrease in consumption, and increasing production elsewhere. Initially Iran's and Iraq's problems had achieved this but soon the reduction in supply from those two countries was not enough. Other major OPEC producers had to cut production sharply, and the burden fell particularly on Saudi Arabia, which reluctantly accepted a role as a 'swing' producer. But most of OPEC started to feel real pain.[3] Much of the windfall from the oil price increases had already been eaten up: by inflation, which drove up the price of the manufactures OPEC producers wanted to purchase; by increases in consumption in the OPEC countries, which heightened their populations' expectations of further largesse; and sometimes by corruption. Falling oil production was the final straw. Among the less wealthy OPEC producers, there was an increasing tendency to cheat by exceeding their quotas and selling the surplus undercover. Because of the producers' own actions, this was now far easier to do. Once they had acquired control over their own oil production in the 1970s, they had quickly moved to selling much of it, not in long-term deals with the oil companies but on the spot market. Therefore the source of the oil could be easily disguised.[4]

In 1985 Saudi Arabia lost patience. Their production had fallen to little more than two billion bpd. By early 1986 they had increased production to five million bpd and were selling it in agreed deals, but effectively at spot prices. The idea of a standard OPEC price was abandoned, and the organization moved to setting price targets, which were often not met. Spot market prices ruled, and the result of the upsurge of Saudi production was their dramatic fall. Up to 1985 they had been holding at above $25 per barrel, but for most of the next 15 years they would fluctuate around $15, occasionally dipping down almost to $10. Adjusted for US inflation, prices were even lower. At constant 1974 prices, crude oil was consistently under $10 per barrel by the late 1980s, continuing to fall slowly for most of the 1990s. OPEC retained a role in that it kept some restraint on production – although much of that was as a result of self-restraint by Saudi Arabia and a few other Arab countries.[5] But with little restraint outside OPEC, it can be inferred that the oil price was somewhere near the level it would have been if OPEC had not existed and oil was in plentiful supply – as it was.

The one exception was a brief spike up to $30 during the crisis over Kuwait. Iraq had a long-standing claim to the oil-rich emirate (see Chapter 5, 'The moment passes: the Arabs, Israel and oil') and in 1990 it forcibly occupied it, possibly to distract its own population from the failure of the Iran-Iraq War. The resulting opposition to Iraq was almost universal, including Arab countries such as Syria whose usual relations with the USA, the main organizer of the anti-Iraq coalition, were somewhat colder than freezing. If Kuwait had just been a stretch of sand, probably no one would have gone to war, and to that extent oil was obviously a factor. But the unity among Arab nations indicates that there were other well-grounded reasons. Most Arab states, like Kuwait and Iraq, had some connection with the old Ottoman Empire. Precisely because of this, to lay claims to each other's territory on the basis of their shared ancestry would open up a Pandora's box of possible disputes. Iraq was easily defeated and became an international pariah, setting the scene for the American-led invasion of 2003. And the oil price subsided again.

However, consumption had once again begun an upward trend. Economy efforts, particularly in the US, were running out of steam as real oil prices once again seemed to be semi-permanently low. At the same time economic growth in China became a real factor in driving consumption growth, as the Chinese economy was now large enough to consume a significant slice of world output. As a result the oil price recovered in 1999, reaching $25 a barrel in 2000. It was to dip again in 2001–2, but then began a steady climb.[6]

After the first oil crisis the big oil companies faced a series of dilemmas. Within a few years much of their crude was effectively removed from them by 'participation' which often turned into 100 per cent nationalization. The companies often retained a role, and some income, as contractors but this was no substitute for the old 50/50 arrangements. On the other hand, their non-OPEC crude was now far more profitable. But with much less of it they still had to do something about their downstream activities – refining and selling the product – which had traditionally played second fiddle even though they absorbed large amounts of capital.

The problem was most acute for BP. In the 1960s it had been stuck on a treadmill in which it had to satisfy the producing states by driving volume, since with the static oil prices of that period higher volumes were the only way in which it could increase their – and its – revenue. The result of this volume push was twofold. The company was heavily dependent on crude sales to third parties – nearly 50 per cent of its sales in 1970. But it still had to dispose of large quantities of refined products itself, through a marketing network which was poorly developed by comparison with its main rivals in Europe, Exxon and Shell. As a result, in the early 1970s its downstream activities in Europe made losses. Stripping BP of much its crude was, in the end, to be the making of it. But in the first few years of the crisis it faced major challenges. How it met them and what transpired is discussed in the next section.[7]

Shell could afford to take a more measured response. It had extensive operations in North America through its majority interest in Shell Oil. Although North
America had many integrated companies such as Shell itself, it had always had
companies which specialized in upstream or downstream. This divorce of the two
sides meant that the firms engaged in downstream had to be profitable in their
own right. In Europe, most oil companies were integrated and had been able to
cross-subsidize less profitable activities. But even there, Shell's historic strength
in marketing, and its refusal in the 1950s and 1960s to push volume at all costs,
meant that its downstream side was much stronger than BP's. An early 1970s
analysis by BP put Shell at second among the seven majors in refining flexibility,
and fourth in the profitability of its product mix, while BP came seventh and
sixth. Nevertheless Shell still had to take steps to make its European downstream
activities more profitable.[8]

In the long run, it was inevitable that downstream margins in Europe would
rise. All the big companies operating there had been partially 'de-integrated'
through nationalization of their Middle Eastern and North African production.
And so they all became, to some extent, free-standing refiners and marketers. As
a result, these activities had to become profitable in their own right, as they were
in the North American product market. But the transition took time, because
for years the companies were wrestling with surplus refining capacity which was
geared to producing large amounts of fuel oil – the demand for which fell most
steeply as a result of the price increases. So in the early 1980s the further increase
in the oil price combined with burgeoning North Sea production meant that
upstream still made most of the money for Shell. However, the 1986 price fall
changed the picture. In some years, such as 1989 and 1994, Shell's downstream
profits actually exceeded upstream, and between 1980 and 1998 downstream
produced 40 per cent of its oil business profits.[9]

Oil companies also had to radically restructure their shipping businesses, as
the need to haul Middle Eastern crude long distances round the Cape to Europe
in VLCCs fell. The marine business had never made much money. Basically,
the majors had been in it for strategic reasons, to safeguard the middle stage of
their oil supply between production and refining/sales. But now they had lost
much of the production stage and drew more oil from the North Sea or Russia,
both much nearer to Europe with pipeline links. The companies initially laid up
VLCCs or used them for storage, but in the 1980s they were forced to take more
drastic measures. Exxon's fleet shrank from over 25 million deadweight tons to
about two million. Shell also reduced its fleet size, although not by so much, and
in 1986 made all its UK mariners redundant, re-employing those who wished to
come back at lower pay through an Isle of Man company.[10]

Downsizing was essential in marine but, even after the oil price fall, cutting back on upstream activities was a less attractive option. In most cases they were still profitable; but their profitability had declined and this had some beneficial effects. Research now emphasized lowering costs and enhancing recovery rates. Horizontal drilling and three-dimensional seismic surveys, made possible by enhanced computing power, were two strategies which helped. The price fall, however, meant that exploitation of heavier crude, which was difficult to extract, was often put on hold and by 1990 Shell was cutting exploration expenditure more widely. By the end of the century, however, as prices rose so once again did interest in heavy oils. In more conventional oil extraction, apart from the North Sea, the big new hope of the international oil industry was Russia. Its production, then entirely state-owned, had increased after the first oil shock but by the late 1980s lower prices and growing economic chaos led to a reverse. The fall of Communism – and falling oil production – meant that Western oil companies gained some important concessions in the 1990s, and Russia became important to both Shell and BP. The political situation became less welcoming again after 2000, however.[11]

One of the side-effects of North Sea exploration was to encourage British firms other than the oil majors and a few smaller established companies into the upstream side of the industry. In the 1970s new North Sea players included Pict Petroleum and London and Scottish Marine Oil (LASMO), along with the established companies Premier Oil and Ultramar. The 1960s Labour government had also encouraged nationalized industry participation, so British Gas – logically – and the National Coal Board – bizarrely – had stakes. Few of these players became significant North Sea stakeholders, but their participation may have encouraged other entrepreneurs into the industry, with the result that there are now a number of flourishing smaller British oil companies. LASMO, which became a sizeable company and purchased part of Ultramar in 1991, was taken over by the Italian firm ENI – Enrico Mattei's old fiefdom – in 2001, while British Gas's original North Sea assets had been privatized in the 1980s as Enterprise Oil, itself brought by Shell in 2002. Surviving independents include Tullow Oil, founded in 1985 and now producing 75,000 boepd, Dana Petroleum and Premier, which acquired Pict in 1995. They tend to operate by using the cash flow from existing producing assets, often in the North Sea, to explore and develop in diverse locations ranging from India and Pakistan to Africa and Indonesia. They are all tiny by the majors' standards, however, with BP producing 50 times as much oil equivalent as Tullow – one of the larger independents – in 2007. The exception is BG Group, one of the legatees of the privatized British Gas. Its history is dealt with later in 'Oil and gas in changing markets'.[12]

Gas has always been an important component of North Sea production, and became increasingly important elsewhere. Gas which could not be piped to its destination had to be transported as liquefied natural gas (LNG), which required pressurized tanks and temperatures of −165 C. Shell had built up expertise in the late 1960s and when oil prices rose natural gas exploitation seemed an obvious course of action. The two products are not direct substitutes but there is considerable potential for substitution, particularly in heating and power generation, so over the long term gas prices exhibit some correlation with oil prices. But consumption of LNG in Europe was slow to develop because of plentiful supplies of Dutch onshore gas, North Sea gas and Russian gas, all of which could be piped. Nevertheless, with the help of the first two, and LNG sales elsewhere in the world, Shell expanded gas sales throughout the 1980s and 1990s, rivalling Exxon as the world's largest private sector operator. BP was initially a much smaller player, although its production increased rapidly.[13]

Gas became important enough to replace petrochemicals as Shell's second core business after oil. This also reflected the disappointment which chemicals proved to oil companies. By the late 1990s Shell, having for many years swallowed the fashionable chemical company nostrum of diversifying into speciality chemicals, had decided to 'build on basics' – a euphemism for getting rid of much of the speciality business. Even in the late 1980s, when oil earnings were depressed, chemicals never contributed more than 25 per cent of Shell's earnings. Their overall profit contribution over the period 1976–2002 was much less than that. Shell remains an important chemical company, although its interests in Britain have always been quite small. From the 1960s BP produced more chemicals in Britain than Shell, but in 2005 it took even more drastic action, selling its chemical interests, including the historic Grangemouth refinery, to INEOS.[14]

THE RISE AND RISE OF BP

Today, BP vies with Shell for second place among Western oil companies, behind Exxon-Mobil. Behind that position lies 30 years of transformation. 'In the past', wrote BP's chairman, Peter Walters, in his report on 1983,

> the major international oil companies have been likened to supertankers whose momentum requires them to travel a considerable distance to effect a change in their course. I believe BP is today entitled to claim that when the need arises it can be much more flexible and nimble-footed . . .[15]

In truth, in 1983 it was only part way through its transformation. But given its situation ten years earlier, even survival seems an achievement. Before the oil crisis BP was the third largest crude producer but its downstream activities were weak and inefficient. Then between 1974 and 1979 most of its historic reserves in the Middle East and Nigeria were lost. Following that came the global decline in oil consumption in the 1980s which left in its wake overcapacity in refining and ravaged downstream margins.

Survival was achieved partly through luck and partly through judgement. The luck was in BP's traditional areas of strength, crude production. BP was still taking Nigerian crude and 40 per cent of Iranian output until 1979, when the Iranian revolution disrupted production there. Iran eventually took over the management activities of the Iranian consortium while Nigeria nationalized BP's interests, ostensibly as punishment for BP's involvement with South Africa. But by 1979 Alaskan oil and oil from the North Sea, where BP owned the giant Forties field, was pumping in large quantities. Since they only started production in 1977, the replacement of existing sources of crude with completely new ones was a close run thing. In spite of their high costs, high prices made the crude from these sources very profitable, especially Alaskan oil since taxation there was lower. In 1984, the penultimate year before the oil price fell sharply, 50 per cent of BP's profit came from its majority shareholding in Sohio, acquired in exchange for the Alaskan acreage (see Chapter 5, 'Wider horizons').[16]

Luck, however, could not help the downstream activities or make BP's whole operation more efficient. The absence of the company history for the post-1975 period makes it difficult to say precisely what drove the company's transformation in subsequent years, but the annual reports and other sources give some clues.

Clearly cost-cutting was necessary. From the mid-1970s distribution systems were rationalized and the head office streamlined. In 1981 a much sharper axe was taken to costs. Twenty-three per cent of European distillation (basic refining) was closed or slated for closure, including, in the United Kingdom, the post-war refinery on the Isle of Grain in Kent. Simultaneously there were cuts in chemicals' capacity and a 'major reduction' in 'small, unprofitable retail sites'. As with Shell and Exxon, the early 1980s also saw a drastic reduction in shipping capacity, with staff levels falling 45 per cent between 1980 and 1983.[17] Cutting costs, however, was not enough by itself. Readers of earlier chapters will remember that, almost from the beginning, the company was bedevilled by a bureaucratic culture which previous reforms had never effectively penetrated. The reforms of the 1970s were in part designed to remedy this. The 1976 *Annual Report* notes a continuing policy of decentralization and there was a rapid growth in oil trading which was well developed by 1978. The old concept, once common to all the majors, that companies moved their own oil through their own refineries and into their own sales outlets had been quickly broken down. However, it seems likely that much of the company's increased flexibility and nimble-footedness, in Peter Walters' words, were down to his appointment as chairman and chief executive in 1981, at the age of 51. Walters recounted how, back in 1967 during the Six Day War, he had had to instantly take a major decision on chartering tankers and in doing so was forced to bypass BP's complex computer-driven system for allocating crude. The experience had left him with a lasting belief in the importance of rapid decision-making, which meant further decentralization.[18]

By the mid-1980s BP was in a position where the 1986 fall in oil prices could be weathered comfortably, since downstream was now making good profits. BP, however, was still less than half the size of Shell and Exxon when measured by net income. Its relative position improved when in 1987 it acquired the 45 per cent of Sohio it did not own, catapulting it to number three among the oil majors. It consolidated this in 1988 when it bought Britoil, the part-privatized, previously government-owned North Sea oil operator. 1987 was also notable for another reason. The government had originally acquired shares in BP back in 1914, and its stake had reached its peak as late as 1975 when the Bank of England bought Burmah's holding to rescue that financially troubled company (see Chapter 7, 'Turbulent Years'; the Bank of England's stake was technically separate from the government's original holding). Since 1979 the Conservative government had sold some of its holding and in 1987 the last government shares were disposed of. Then in 1989, the final year of Peter Walters' chairmanship, a change which was both symbolic and real was announced. In 1967 BP had moved from its old headquarters, Britannic House, built in the 1920s, to a glass and steel skyscraper which became the new Britannic House. In 1990 the headquarters of two of the major decentralized subsidiaries – BP Exploration and BP Oil (the downstream activities) – moved to their own offices and the slimmed down corporate headquarters moved back to its original home. But in spite of its size, BP was becoming more focused. Over the years, it had become involved in a number of peripheral activities which made little contribution to profits. Like Shell, it had diversified into coal-mining in the 1970s and had also acquired metal-mining interests, but these were all sold in the late 1980s or early 1990. In 1993 BP Nutrition, a relic of the company's takeover of Distillers' chemical interests in the 1960s, also went.[19]

But before that happened there was a stumble. Through acquisitions, BP had climbed the league table in size but it had also piled up a load of debt. This was increased because of the fall-out from the 1987 government share sell-off. Opportunistically, the Kuwait Investment Office had acquired a 21.6 per cent stake in BP. Nowadays that would probably be seen as unexceptional but the government still saw the company as a 'national champion' in spite of their own share sale and disapproved of the holding. In 1989 a solution was found by BP buying back over half the shares to leave the Kuwaiti stake at 9.9 per cent but this put the company further in debt. Then recession led to pressure on margins, closures and write-offs. The result in 1992 was a heavy loss and the sacking of Robert Horton, Walters' replacement. Horton was disliked for his perceived arrogance but the problems, self-evidently, were not all of his making. Of necessity there was a further drive to reduce costs in the main business, with personnel, excluding those in service stations, falling from 68,000 in 1991 to 50,000 in 1993. Downstream activities, benchmarked against major competitors, had been below average in 1992 and were towards the top by 1994. But perhaps the most notable efficiency improvements were in crude production. The average cost of output had been $4, in 1993 prices, in 1989, falling to $3 in 1993 and $2.56 in 1994. The cost cuts occurred, in part, while a new rising star was in charge of that sector – John Browne. In 1995 he became chief executive.[20]

While many of the achievements between the mid-1970s and the mid-1990s were in cost-cutting, BP also had to transform its image for marketing purposes, particularly in petrol retailing. In the 1960s BP's customers in Britain were perceived (presumably by the customers who favoured other brands) as 'notably lower-class and economy-minded'. Its image in Europe was not much better.[21] The process of image improvement is less concrete than efficiency improvement, and its key elements harder to pin down. The 1979 Report noted that 'Progress has been made towards a higher-value added product sales mix . . . and improving retail networks', and these emphases became themes of the Peter Walters' years. They complemented the policy of closing smaller retail outlets and in 1987 Walters noted that average throughput at European petrol stations had risen 71 per cent since 1981. BP was also pushing into the growing markets of Southeast Asia such as South Korea, Malaysia and Hong Kong and even into mainland China. In 1989, to use its own horrible neologism, BP began a huge programme of 're-imaging' its stations worldwide so that they all came under the BP brand, which had a new logo. It had also from the late 1970s polished up its corporate image, winning awards in 1980 for 'best corporate arts sponsorship' and in 1987 for 'International Corporate Environmental Achievement'. There seems little doubt about the positive result of all of this activity although the exact contributions of different elements are impossible to separate. Even before 're-imaging', surveys of brand perceptions showed BP perceived as more 'modern' than Shell, a transformation from the 1960s.[22]

The efforts, both to improve distribution efficiency and to boost BP's image, continued into the 1990s. Average sales per station continued to improve rapidly, while in 1996 BP effectively took over, and rebranded, Mobil service stations in Europe, although it was technically a joint venture. The push into Southeast Asia and China continued and was accompanied by expansion into the new markets of Eastern Europe, with the first BP petrol station in Moscow opening in 1996.[23]

A consistent theme runs through BP's downstream progress from the late 1970s onwards. The inheritance was numerous, often small, sales outlets, inefficient refining and a lame image. Closing small petrol stations and dropping unprofitable lines of business in other fuels cut costs and working capital requirements and enabled investment in the remainder of the network. In petrol retailing this meant bigger and more attractive stations which improved the brand image. This was reinforced by corporate sponsorship. But of course the policy risked reducing sales too much and thus increasing overheads and refining costs per unit sold. This was partly met by the ruthless closure or sale of refineries. By 1988, for instance, there were five in Europe against 16 in 1981. But it was also met by acquisitions which included distribution networks, notably Sohio and later Mobil's European network, and expansion in new areas. This enabled BP to leverage (another awful corporate word for which it is difficult to find a synonym) its now enhanced image into the US, Eastern Europe and Southeast Asia.[24]

It is quite clear that much of BP's transformation goes back to the 1970s and, especially, the 1980s. Costs were cut, peripheral businesses disposed of and the image transformed. However, it still remained to make BP into a company rivalling Shell, the feat with which John Browne is most associated – Exxon managing to stay ahead by merging with Mobil in 1998. BP 'merged' with Amoco in 1998, increasing its profit by about one-third. But it was, effectively, a takeover with Browne remaining the chief executive. The company was BP Amoco for two years but then declared that BP meant 'Beyond Petroleum', reverted to its familiar initials and adopted the Helios logo, replacing its time-honoured shield. A merger with Arco in 2000 completed its hectic few years of expansion but there was one, almost poignant, coda. Burmah Oil had financed BP's early exploration in Persia and was for many years its chief shareholder after the government, before being laid low by rash speculation in the tanker market. Best known in later years as the owner of the Castrol brand of lubricants, Burmah was also bought by BP in 2000.[25]

BP had also been diversifying its reserves, a process carried forward by the acquisitions. In 1980 Alaska and the North Sea had contributed 80 per cent or more of output but by the late 1990s they fell to less than half, with other areas such as the Gulf of Mexico, Colombia and Angola becoming important. Apart from enlarging BP, therefore, the mergers helped it to remain a major crude producer and subsequently its production record has been better than Shell's. BP has also moved rapidly into gas production, in which Shell was traditionally stronger. In 1985 gas was only 7 per cent of BP's total 'oil equivalent' output. By 2000 it was 40 per cent.[26]

Browne's legacy – he resigned in 2007 – was more mixed in other respects. Chemicals were sold in 2005, which may have been overdue, and cost-cutting continued, but there were many who suggested that it went too far. There was a major accident at the Texas City refinery in 2005 and corrosion affected some of the Alaskan facilities, leading to pollution. Both may have been due, in part, to economy measures. Even with cost-cutting, BP seems to have reverted to its old bureaucratic ways with, in the *Financial Times*' words, 'eleven layers of management between the C-suite and the drill bit'. It would be fanciful, however, to see this really as a legacy of the old BP. In terms of efficiency BP seems to have yo-yoed in relation to other oil companies, but of course this partly reflects the fact that they too have gone through ups and downs. All large organizations run the risk of arteriosclerosis and periodic attacks on bureaucracy are probably inevitable. While some of Browne's managerial legacy is now under criticism from within BP as well as outside, his cherished 'Beyond Petroleum' mantra has been retained and with it his focus on alternative energy, although in financial terms this is still only a small part of the company.[27]

BEYOND THE ENVIRONMENT

Eleven years after the *Torrey Canyon*, another tanker disaster was to highlight the continued risk of such incidents. The *Amoco Cadiz* was wrecked off the coast of Brittany in 1978, carrying a cargo of Shell oil. Shell was better known in Europe than Amoco which owned the tanker, and it came under fierce criticism for the resulting pollution even though it was not technically liable.[28] However, criticism of the oil companies' environmental record actually appears to have reached a peak in the 1970–4 period and then fell, remaining relatively low until the late 1980s. Part of this trajectory can probably be accounted for by the prominence achieved by the Trans-Alaska Pipeline in the 1970–4 period (see Chapter 5, 'Wider horizons').[29] Another part of the subsequent decline may have been due to the oil price rise itself, which led to a focus on reducing oil consumption. Of course this was environmentally beneficial but it may have distracted attention from other environmental issues. In addition governments themselves, after a brief spell of environmental consciousness in the late 1960s and early 1970s, were now more concerned with finding alternative sources of energy. Yet another likely reason for the decline in environmental concern is that one of the biggest perceived hazards of the 1970s, lead in petrol, was rapidly phased out in the 1980s. It is also worth noting that climate change was not yet taken seriously by most experts.

Finally, oil companies had themselves become much more aware of the importance of environmental issues and, as suggested in Chapter 6 ('Oil and the environment'), were more proactive in dealing with them. As part of this shift the companies themselves became more conscious of 'corporate responsibility', as the private sector's relationship with the outside world came to be called. The outside world might mean people, such as those living near oil refineries, or it might mean the natural world. Shell and other companies issued statements of Business Principles in the mid-1970s. These tended to be general statements about the importance of upholding ethical principles in business, but the need to disseminate information to third parties and a general concern with the community were acknowledged.[30]

Oil companies had, in fact, been early exponents of one aspect of corporate responsibility – responsibility to their staff. This went back to the inter-war period and strengthened in the 1950s and 1960s. Oil company employees had good benefits, not only in pensions and so forth but also in the security of their employment, and the companies undoubtedly felt an obligation to look after their staff. One reason for this was pragmatic. Good recruits would eventually produce good senior managers, and good recruits could, it was thought, be obtained and retained by good benefits. Shell called it 'growing your own timber'. But at times, as in BP's head office in the 1940s, it appeared that the company was run more for the benefit of the staff than the shareholders. In fact, BP's perennial attempts to rein in its head office numbers seemed doomed to failure. Its historian refers to the 'vast central bureaucracy' of the 1960s and, even after a move towards regionalization in 1971, head office numbers continued to grow. From the 1970s on, this cosy attitude was to change, and the change shows that the concept of 'corporate responsibility' was always constrained in one way or another.[31]

Another facet of staff relations was a gradual move away from the old belief that senior management would be automatically recruited from white males. Back in the 1940s Shell had showed itself advanced in its acceptance of the need to recruit senior staff from natives from all the countries in which it did business. But progress was slow. Most senior staff worked as expatriates at some stage in their career but in 1970 only 22 per cent of expats were other than British or Dutch, and in 1988 only 26 per cent. BP was even slower, and both companies were also slow in recruiting women although in that they were no different from most industrial companies. BP's 'Senior Luncheon Club' for top managers remained all-male until Paula Harris, a senior mathematician in the Computer Department, joined in 1967. But not much changed for years after that, while just two out of Shell's 278 senior management jobs in the London offices in 1978 were occupied by women. Shell was, however, aware of this. It commissioned a report in 1991 which found that the company was not actively discriminatory but that its hiring practices favoured those who already had high academic qualifications and were easily able to mix with others similar to them. Even in the 1990s this tended to favour well-educated white males. Shell clearly wanted to act but reorganization and staff cuts in the mid-1990s impeded change and even in 2000 the proportion of women in top management was less than 8 per cent.[32]

Staff cuts were not new to the oil companies. Shell's staff numbers had actually been falling since the beginning of the 1960s – when its productivity per person was much lower than Exxon's – but the fall accelerated in the 1980s when BP, too, reduced staff numbers sharply. Some areas, such as marine, were cut drastically and, in Shell's case, fairly brutally (see previous section). The decline in both companies continued into the 1990s and Shell's general approach to personnel also changed. In the words of the company history, 'loyalty to the company [became] neither expected nor rewarded'. Shell moved towards more variable payment schemes to reward perceived high-flyers, whilst making redundant substantial numbers of others. In fairness, the company still accepted an obligation by helping those who lost their jobs with alternative careers. But the new approach was no longer so concerned with 'growing your own timber' as with a flexible workforce.[33]

In other areas, corporate responsibility can be seen as a distinct force. In the case of Shell, it influenced the company but intersected with other forces and with commercial imperatives. Thus in Nigeria from 1990 onwards Shell came under sustained criticism from both environmentalists and representatives of the Ogoni people within whose territories lay a proportion of Nigerian oil production. Shell accepted responsibility for some damage to the environment, as many of the facilities were quite old and not in good repair. But it could point to the fact that most pollution was caused by damage to pipelines caused by people siphoning off oil for use or resale, or by sabotage. Insofar as the ultimate causes of such activities were poverty or political grievances, Shell felt that these were essentially issues for the Nigerian government. At that stage it did not believe that, as a private sector company, it should become involved in the politics of a host country.[34]

Criticisms of Shell in Nigeria were partly about the environment although more related to political issues. But they coincided with a resurgence of interest in the environment. This had been originally stirred in 1989 by another major tanker disaster, the *Exxon Valdez* in Alaska where the Trans-Alaska pipeline had

first highlighted environmental issues. British companies were not involved in the
Exxon Valdez incident but soon Shell became caught up in a row over something
much nearer to Britain – the proposed sinking, in 1995, of the Brent Spar. This
was a giant storage tank in the North Sea, which floated vertically rather than
horizontally. The design was originally chosen because it was less likely to cause
environmental damage than the alternative of using a VLCC for storage. So Shell
had cause for anguish when, the Spar having become redundant, the company's
disposal plan became the target of a campaign led by Greenpeace. Shell planned
to sink the Spar in deep water, having cleared out as much as possible of the toxic
residues. The scheme had scientific support as causing less environmental damage
and posing less of a safety risk to personnel than any alternative. Greenpeace, on
the other hand, advanced the reasonable argument that large numbers of offshore
facilities would eventually need to be disposed of and sinking all of them was not
environmentally friendly. However it subsequently lost the moral high ground
when it admitted that it had overestimated the toxic residues one hundredfold.
By that time Shell had aborted its plan, and eventually the Spar was disassembled
successfully.[35]

The Brent Spar episode ended as the Nigerian situation became critical, with
the executions of the Ogoni leader Ken Saro-Wiwa and other tribespeople. The
conjunction of these events exposed Shell to sustained public attack and led to
a rethinking of 'corporate responsibility'. The general principles of 1976 were
extended in 1997 to include the company's responsibility to respect human rights,
'in line with the legitimate role of business' and its commitment to 'contribute
to' sustainable development. Clearly, the responsibilities and commitments were
hedged. Nevertheless they were there and the commitment to human rights
meant that Shell could not in future hide behind its 'no politics' rule in every case
where human rights might have been violated. Subsequently Shell set up a Social
Responsibility Committee and its annual report in 1999 used the phrase 'people,
planet and profits' to describe the company's responsibilities. BP, less exposed to
criticism over human rights issues, continued to emphasize the environment.
In 1997 it became the first major oil company to acknowledge the potential
importance of climate change – an issue with which its then chief executive, John
Browne, has become particularly associated.[36]

'Corporate responsibility' and other mantras invite cynicism. They can seem
the result of whatever idea is fashionable among management gurus. According
to a recent newspaper article, corporate responsibility is no longer used by one
consultancy as a job title because 'The market dropped it'. Now, apparently,
'sustainability' is the new buzzword which companies can flourish to prove that
they are warm and caring.[37] But one can interpret this less cynically as an attempt

to respond to society's changing demands, in which case management gurus might stand accused of inventing irritating neologisms but not of completely wasting everyone's time. It is not cynical but realistic to point out that oil companies were and are commercial firms and in reacting to others, whether those others be staff, environmentalists, or some other group, they have ultimately been constrained by commercial imperatives. In the 1950s and 1960s, however, it was easy for companies to make money and some of that largesse could be diverted from shareholders to staff, if not in pay then in promoting a relatively easy life for everyone, including senior management who did not have to take hard decisions about redundancies. At the same time optimism in the West about the benefits of economic growth prevented much outside criticism of the companies from emerging. From the late 1960s things changed. Environmental challenges became stronger, outside scrutiny more searching, and the commercial climate colder. Companies reacted by moving away from a paternalistic attitude to staff while reaching out more to the outside world. In the end, therefore, corporate responsibility or whatever it may be called is a reaction designed to protect companies' commercial positions. This is not to say that it is just a facade. Oil company executivesare citizens of the world as much as anyone else is and most of them no doubt believe in protecting the environment and helping local communities. Nor is it wrong, unless one is anti-capitalist, to believe in making a profit. In a capitalist economy, profit is a motor which stimulates greater efficiency and therefore higher standards of living. In democracies the media and pressure groups can question and scrutinize companies' activities and thereby put pressure on them and on governments, which ultimately have the power to limit the activities of the private sector. The pure pursuit of profit is therefore itself constrained. All this happens imperfectly, of course. But ultimately the wider interests of society, including the environment, seem better protected in most capitalist democracies than they were in the countries of the old Soviet bloc.

OIL AND GAS IN CHANGING MARKETS

In Cheltenham where I live, a town of about 100,000, I can think of at least eight petrol stations which have closed over the last ten years or so. And these were only in the parts of the town which I regularly travel through. As every British reader will know, there have been replacements – the supermarket filling stations. Over the last 20 years, four have opened in Cheltenham as the big chains have built stores outside the town centre. The rise of the supermarkets is the big story of British petrol retailing over the latter years of the twentieth century, and it has gone along with the closure of large numbers of marginal stations, both company-owned and independents. In the final years of the century, between 1990 and 1998, the total number of stations fell from almost 20,000 to under 15,000, and in 2008 it is little over 9,000.[38]

There were a number of reasons for this. The Shell official history points to the overhang of OPEC capacity from the mid-1980s which increased the availability of oil, but that cannot be the only reason since the growth of supermarket petrol retailing has not occurred in all developed countries. Britain's peculiar planning laws which restrict the supply of new land for housing but allocate vast amounts to new supermarket developments and their associated car parks – on which petrol stations can easily be fitted – must be part of the story. Because of the value of land which can be used for housing, most of the closed petrol stations in Cheltenham have had houses or flats built on their sites and no doubt that has happened frequently elsewhere. It would require a planner or a politician to explain how anything so irrational has come about. One other contributing factor must be the visibility in Britain of a few large supermarket chains, which has established them as 'brands' whose strength rivals and probably surpasses that of traditional producers, including oil companies. As a result, it is unimportant to many people whether they buy petrol from Shell, BP, Tesco or Sainsbury. From a standing start 30 years ago, when Asda pioneered large out-of-town-centre sites, supermarkets had 19 per cent of retail fuel sales in 1997, a figure which has subsequently doubled, to 40 per cent, in 2007.[39]

In spite of the 1970s oil price rises, consumption of petrol and diesel for transport in Britain has continued to grow – by about 90 per cent from 1970 to the end of the century. Average fuel consumption per vehicle improved in the late 1970s and early 1980s, but the number of vehicles on the road increased faster. With the 1986 oil price fall, the stimulus to greater fuel efficiency lessened. However, global warming predictions sparked a Budget commitment to a regular increase in fuel duty at above the rate of inflation from 1994, and subsequently average fuel efficiency improved again. The increase in duty was also, of course, a neat way of raising extra revenue. Part of the recent improvement in fuel efficiency has come from the accelerating switch to diesel-engined cars as technology improved. There is, however, plenty of room for fuel efficiency to improve further, apart from the obvious method of buying smaller cars. Comparing similar models, cars have grown heavier over the past 30 years as extra equipment has been added, so fuel consumption improvements are due largely to better engine technology. Reducing weight will certainly be one target of car designers in the future. Hybrid technology will be another but, if oil prices stay high, the next few years could be the time when battery technology develops to a point at which all-electric cars become an attractive and economic proposition.[40]

While the transport fuel market has continued to grow, the market in Britain for most other oil products has shrunk since the 1970s. Fuel oil use in power stations fell rapidly after the initial oil price rises in 1973–4, and industrial oil and heating oil demand fell more gradually as natural gas became more widely available. The fall in demand was Europe-wide and one oil company response – the closure of refineries – was mentioned earlier ('The rise and rise of BP'). Since 1980 two refineries near Milford Haven, BP's Isle of Grain refinery and the historic Shellhaven site have all closed, as have other smaller refineries. However, there has been expansion in some of the remaining ones and refinery utilization is much higher than it was. Indeed refining remains, as it has been since the 1950s, an important manufacturing industry. As part of the 'de-integration' of the oil market noted in 'Beyond the oil crisis' several British refineries are now independent of the oil majors. For instance a specialist Belgian refiner, Petroplus, now owns refineries at Coryton and Teesside.[41]

Because declines in most market segments have outstripped the growth of transport fuel, oil's share of Britain's total energy supply, 50.5 per cent in 1973, had fallen by 1996 to 36.5 per cent.[42] With coal use also declining, the winner has been gas. In 1980 the gas market in Britain remained firmly under the monopoly control of British Gas, the state-owned corporation. The price paid to North Sea producers, at first very low, had been raised but the market was still essentially an administered rather than a free one and the use of gas for power generation was not allowed. This was partly to protect the coal industry and partly because of the belief that gas was a 'premium' fuel which should be conserved and used only for direct heat and power generation in homes, offices and factories. Between 1980 and 1990 the Conservative government carried out a large-scale experiment in market liberalization. This did not, of course, just involve the gas industry but also the large-scale privatization of other state assets. There were limits to the liberalization process, however. The government wanted to sell assets at good prices and this meant that gas and electricity were sold off in large chunks with limited attempts to bring in competition.

Thus British Gas continued after privatization in 1986 as the monopoly supplier to domestic customers, although competition for large customers in the industrial gas market had been introduced in 1981. The North Sea and Wytch Farm production assets which British Gas had accumulated while a nationalized industry were sold separately. From 1990 a new stage in market liberalization developed with a much more determined attempt to bring in competition. The power generation market was opened to gas in 1990 while the small customer market was opened to competition from 1991, and the domestic market between 1996 and 1998. Liberalization was accompanied by significant price cuts, especially for industrial power users. British Gas itself, once privatized, had been busy accumulating production assets again but in 1997 it decided on another demerger, hiving off its supply business. This retained the Morecambe fields but otherwise production assets remained with the renamed BG Group which has subsequently been extremely successful, accumulating more assets in the years of low prices to become a major international producer of gas and oil.[43]

Energy market liberalization in Britain has accompanied the policy of rapid exploitation of North Sea assets – from the beginning in the case of oil, and from around 1990 in the case of gas. Since North Sea gas production is now falling, liberalization which led to higher consumption can be criticized as accelerating the depletion of a resource which potentially protected the British people from world gas prices if these rose sharply, as they have done at the time of writing (June 2008). Rapid exploitation was discussed in Chapter 8, 'Britain and North Sea oil'. To briefly reiterate the conclusion – it is not clear that there is either an economic or a moral case for freezing the development of natural resources, unless their exploitation would seriously unbalance the national economy. Energy market liberalization has delivered substantial benefits in the past through lower prices. For the future, one can note that successful economies such as Germany and Japan import most of their sources of energy and have done since their coal industries ran down in the 1960s. Producing one's own oil or gas is not a *sine qua non* for prosperity. Perhaps one regret about energy market liberalization is that it was accompanied by a steep fall in government expenditure on research and development in energy, to almost nugatory levels by the late 1990s.[44] One feels that a proportion of the windfall from lower prices might have gone on research into alternative energy. Having said that, the earlier spending did not appear to deliver much benefit, while alternative technology can be imported from elsewhere if needed.

10

Conclusion

THE PAST

In 1900 the international oil industry was still small and dominated by one company, the US-based Standard Oil. By 1914 the industry was growing rapidly and there were a number of major companies. Among them were several European ones – Royal Dutch/Shell, which was already a giant, APOC which became BP and Mexican Eagle. The first was Dutch-British and the others British or British-controlled. How was it that two countries which then had practically no known oil of their own fostered these international oil companies?

As the first chapter showed, some of the founders of these companies had considerable entrepreneurial talent. But entrepreneurial talent was hardly unique to Britain or the Netherlands. The conditions which allowed that talent to flourish were as, or more, important. Both countries had colonial empires, and were in the best position to dominate those empires' economic development. So if there was easily accessible oil, it was likely to be exploited by firms from the parent country. Thus Dutch companies dominated oil production in Sumatra, and British companies in Trinidad and Burma. But possession of an empire was by no means the only factor, since the companies operated in many other places. By 1914 Shell was also a major producer in Russia, Romania and the USA. Other British companies were active in Mexico, Peru, Russia and, of course, Persia. APOC's Persian adventure had a connection with the British Empire, because British interests in India might be threatened by an unstable Persia. But there were limits to how much the British government wished to get involved, so its support of APOC was low key. And the Admiralty's interest in oil fuel was really a side issue. It helped to bale APOC out in 1914 but if the British government had not invested, Shell would almost certainly have stepped in, thus keeping a British interest.

The most important reason why the British were involved in the international oil industry was not the Empire or governmental concerns about the Empire. It was the fact that British citizens invested huge sums of money overseas. On the eve of the First World War Britain was by far the largest international creditor in history. With a constant supply of capital looking for investments, British firms were almost inevitably going to get involved in a new, dynamic and potentially lucrative industry. And by the laws of chance, some of those firms were likely to be successful. That Britain also had an empire covering one-fifth of the world's habitable surface and a supply of entrepreneurs were valuable adjuncts to that underlying factor.

Yet after this period of heady change and expansion, the oil industry for over 50 years after the First World War became a much more staid affair. Production continued to expand rapidly, especially after 1945. But sizeable new firms, certainly British ones, were notable by their absence. The very obscurity for most of their lives of two British start-ups of the 1930s, Ultramar and Premier Oil (originally Caribbean Oil), testifies to the apparent failure of new capital to come into the industry.[1] Although Britain's economic dominance had been seriously weakened after the First World War, it was still a substantial overseas investor. So what had stemmed the flow of new enterprise in oil?

A nexus of factors after 1918 made it hard to challenge the dominance of existing firms. Perhaps paramount was the control that they had established over world-wide distribution networks. Outside the USA, Shell and Jersey Standard's existing strong position was sealed by the high profits they earned during the First World War, which gave them the cash needed to take a lead in European petrol retailing as petrol pumps – expensive and company-owned – became ubiquitous. Apart from state-owned companies in some European countries, the only serious challenge in Europe came from APOC. APOC had itself made good profits during the war, had obtained BP's distribution network in Britain on favourable terms, and as an established company benefited from the easy conditions for raising cash immediately after the war. But most companies lacked such benefits. Regent, the main British challenger in the inter-war petrol market, only made slow progress.

Regent had the benefit of its own crude supplies, but by the inter-war period crude was not that easily available. Downstream independents in Europe had access to Russian and Romanian oil, but both countries were unreliable suppliers. With prices falling throughout the 1920s and early 1930s, investment in crude elsewhere was not as attractive as it had been before the war. And outside the USA there were not many areas available for exploitation. The most rapidly growing producer, Venezuela, was dominated by Shell and Jersey Standard. It offered some possibility for independents – Ultramar started there – but exploration was difficult as were general business conditions. The Middle Eastern countries were difficult to penetrate because of the penchant of rulers for very large concessions. It seems likely that these were related to the lack of governmental capacity, which meant that a sophisticated concession-granting system would have been unworkable. The result was that only large companies were able to bid.

Although conditions seemed to change after the Second World War as rapid growth re-emerged, in actuality there were many continuities with the earlier period. These did not extend to the overt price-fixing which had gone on earlier. But for reasons explained in Chapter 5 ('Cartel or competition?'), competition – not just in Europe but over much of the world oil market – was limited at least until the late 1950s. This kept profits for the established companies high. High profits were theoretically a signal to new independent entrants to the market but, as earlier, the availability of crude was a problem. Only in the USA were there large amounts of crude free from control by the majors. But with US prices high and the US now an importer not an exporter, that was not much use anywhere else. It was only in the 1960s when more giant fields were opened up, particularly in Libya, that some of the larger US independents were able to enter the European market and disrupt the cosy conditions the majors had enjoyed.

So behind the relative stability of the industry over the long period 1914–73 lay the integrated nature of the major companies. Integration meant that entry into any point of the industry was difficult, except in the US where it was structured differently. Downstream operators had to make a heavy investment with no certainty of getting crude; but investment in crude production was difficult for the reasons set out above.

Stability in the structure of the industry and a steady increase in its size meant, of course, great wealth for the majors, which soon became among the largest firms in the world. Such size and wealth has led to many accusations, often contradictory. Those addicted to conspiracy theories have seen oil companies as the outliers of governments, either in some general imperialistic sense or specifically because governments wanted to safeguard their oil supplies. On the other hand, left-wing observers in the inter-war period and beyond saw governments as the tools of oil companies.

It is not within my remit to comment on Western governments and oil companies, apart from Britain. In Britain's case, until 1939 the government only intermittently involved itself with oil, and it was certainly not prepared to act as the oil companies' agent. Its shareholding in APOC was a one-off and after the early 1920s hardly impinged on its relationship with the company. The one big exception to the rule was the Lloyd George period of activism after the First

World War, but this ultimately came to very little. Subsequently Britain opted for a share of Iraqi oil and accepted the Red Line Agreement which limited British claims elsewhere. Then it gave up political control in Iraq and gave way to US pressure for a share of Kuwaiti oil and the right to produce in Bahrain. For this and other reasons T. A. B. Corley, the historian of Burmah Oil, has lambasted the government's oil policy in the inter-war period for 'excessive Foreign Office subservience to the US and other countries', and Brian McBeth has criticized the government's strategic planning, which in his view aimed to secure its supplies from the Middle East but failed.[2]

But as Elizabeth Monroe has pointed out, the background to the government's decisions is that, apart from Lloyd George, British diplomats and politicians saw the Suez Canal as the only vital British interest in the Middle East and recognized that other countries had rights in the area. Oil was not a foreign policy priority. 'Other countries' included those in the region itself, with the exception of Egypt whose autonomy was overridden. Elsewhere, British policy was to behave in the way civilized countries tried to do by the 1920s – that is, to have due regard for the interests of others and for international agreements, notably in the inter-war period the Covenant of the League of Nations. When Iran cancelled APOC's concession in 1932, the British government did intervene; but it did so by turning to the League. Conciliation of the US, both in the Middle East and Latin America, was a more pragmatic policy, which reflected an acceptance of US military and economic power. As a result British companies controlled fewer oil reserves than they might have done. But in 1939 they were still by far the largest Middle East producers, and major players in South America. From a strategic point of view Britain's policy – which was in actuality to rely on diversity of supply – was very effective. Not relying too much on the Middle East proved to be wise, because once the Mediterranean was closed in 1940 hauling most of Britain's oil round the Cape would have been virtually impossible. And although Britain's planners had not assumed they could get US oil in time of war, the earlier conciliation of America paid off as it became Britain's biggest wartime supplier of oil. Other defence-related decisions – not investing much in oil from coal, establishing an effective wartime petroleum control agency – were also good ones.

While the British government usually had an arm's-length relationship with oil companies, of necessity oil companies had to work with foreign governments. Scholars of Latin American history are clear that this did not extend to active interference with countries' internal political affairs, as was often alleged at the time. But undoubtedly oil companies tried to obtain favours over concessions and taxes from ministers and officials and, in Latin America at least, this involved bribery. The best that can be said for this is that it was probably a fairly normal way of doing business in the countries concerned. If oil companies did try to interfere in Romania or the Middle East, the results were poor. Romanian policy in the 1930s was increasingly unfavourable to foreign oil companies, while APOC's negotiations with the Shah in 1932 broke down.

If the British government's policy towards oil before the war was low key, pragmatic and broadly aligned with the norms of ethical international behaviour, for a few years in the 1950s it behaved very differently. In the case of Iran in 1951–3, it initially accepted the difficulty of forcibly opposing the nationalization of AIOC's assets and took the case to the International Court of Justice. But when the Court ruled that it did not have jurisdiction, Britain succumbed to the temptation to support the United States' underhand support of the Shah against Mussadiq. On the British side, the initiative seems to have come mainly from Churchill, and there is no evidence that BP was involved.[3] The short-term result was favourable, the long-term deleterious. In the case of Suez, the oil companies were certainly opposed to forcible intervention. Within the government, oil was only one among a number of motives for Eden, but for Macmillan the potential loss of oil and of oil company's earnings seems to have loomed very large. His concerns were exaggerated and fanciful and helped to precipitate an action which was illegal and counter-productive.

The miserable results of active government intervention emphasize even more the wisdom of the inter-war policy of diplomacy. After 1956, fortunately, the government curbed its tendency to reach for the trigger. Two exceptions both had a number of justifications. Iraqi threats in 1961 led to British military reinforcements for the newly independent Kuwait. In spite of Suez, Britain was still regarded as a significant force in the Persian Gulf, and one broadly welcomed by the Gulf states. And Kuwait was very different to Suez in other ways, in particular because Iraq's claim to the sheikhdom posed a threat to stability in the Arab world. This induced Saudi Arabia and Jordan to give Kuwait military support as well, and in the event there was no fighting. By the late 1960s a variety of factors led to Britain deciding to sever its last formal Middle East ties and pull out of the Gulf. Therefore in 1990–1 Britain was only one actor among many in the coalition against Saddam Hussein, although an important one. Beyond this book's chronological limits is the invasion of Iraq in 2003, which many see as connected with oil in one way or another. If it was – and personally I doubt if oil had any significance for British participation – then the results seem to bear out the lesson of earlier adventures: don't go to war over black gold.

As noted above, the comments of some of the historians who have looked at the UK government and oil over the long term have been critical. This echoes a general trend among historians of twentieth-century Britain. To caricature this slightly but not much, almost everything which its governments have done (an exception is usually made for certain individual administrations of which the historian approves) has been stupid, ill-advised and counter-productive. These mistakes have contributed to Britain starting the present century some way down the pecking order of relative wealth, international influence and other measures of wellbeing and status which she dominated one hundred years ago. Common sense suggests that the conjunction of events which gave Britain such a favourable position in 1900 – namely early industrialization allied to long-standing naval prowess which facilitated the accumulation and retention of a large empire – was likely to end as other countries industrialized. However, this has had only limited effects on many historians' thinking.[4]

My own judgement on the British government and oil in the twentieth century is that policy has usually been quite sensible. This is partly because, in line with civil service practice, it has usually been made by discussion between various departments, ending in a compromise – or possibly in nothing. This means of making policy has often been accused of producing a fudge, and sometimes it has done. But compromise, diplomacy, doing nothing or even fudging may all be better than heedless activism. If Lloyd George's wilder oil-related schemes had come into effect, Britain might have antagonized both France and the USA after the First World War. Fortunately he had so many balls to juggle that these ones fell to the ground, but this did not happen with Churchill's support for the US in Iran in 1953, or with Eden and Suez in 1956. The resulting adventures had deleterious long-term effects in the one case, and disastrous short-term ones in the other.

From the 1970s, the foreign policy imperatives which had dominated government thinking about oil shrank into the background as the North Sea became the focus of attention. But the North Sea did not change the nature of policy-making, instead exemplifying one other characteristic of British oil policy over most of the twentieth century. Because of the substantial civil service input, it has to a considerable extent been bipartisan. Deviations were usually little to do with party, but were rather maverick irruptions, and it is symptomatic that Churchill and Lloyd George were the two leading actors. Only Suez can be regarded as a party issue, and it was hardly a normal one. Oil exhibits many other examples of bipartisanship outside the realms of foreign policy. For the entire period from 1914 until the government shares were sold in the 1980s, both parties kept BP at arm's length. Foreigners often believed that it was an arm of the government, and modern references suggest that journalists sometimes think that too. Anyone who still believes it should wade through the three bulky Treasury files in the National Archives which deal with BP's claim for offsetting the producing countries' taxes against British tax – 'this awful topic' wrote one civil servant as the negotiations dragged on.[5] Another example of bipartisanship is the policy from the 1950s to the 1970s over oil stocks (see Chapter 6, 'Government and oil'). The North Sea is a much more important example, on which Professor Alexander Kemp's forthcoming book will shed more light. Here there have been obvious exceptions to bipartisanship, BNOC and participation being the main ones. But much policy – licensing by allocation, PRT, and rapid depletion, first of oil and then gas – has carried over with variations from one government to another. Clearly North Sea policy-making has not been perfect. While Britain's economic situation in the 1960s and 1970s helps to explain the haste of development, it led to problems – not least a sloppy safety regime. But it is not clear that Norway, the other main North Sea producer, has always done better.

Whether or not there have been fluctuations in government policy, there has been continuity in one thing. Even after the events of the 1970s completely changed the structure of the world oil industry, Shell and BP have remained two of the world's largest oil companies. The pre-eminence of the Western 'Seven Sisters' has, of course, long gone as national oil companies such as Saudi Aramco now control the bulk of the world's reserves, and the composition of the sisters has changed through mergers. But the sisters or their successors are still the world's largest integrated oil companies.[6] Why do integrated companies survive when the oil market was 'de-integrated' in the late 1970s? One answer is that integration provides some hedge against uncertainty as upstream and downstream margins do not move in line, so one part may be profitable when the other is less so. This delivers more stable earnings which investors like. Furthermore the companies' very size gives them vast reserves of cash and expertise to undertake major new investments – and makes them difficult to take over.

Shell continues in its historic position as the second of the sisters, just behind Exxon. Shell has worked quite hard at times to erode this, not by cutting into Exxon's lead but by diminishing its own position through poor decisions, such as a move into coal-mining in the 1970s. Furthermore Shell, surprisingly for a company which was seen in the 1970s as the most cosmopolitan oil major, has become in the last 30 years a target for campaigners over both the environment – the *Amoco Cadiz* and later the Brent Spar – and ethics, particularly its role in Nigeria. Once attention was focused on Shell it became a lightning rod for criticism, some of which may have been unfair. Other parts of Shell's recent record have been more positive, particularly the growth of its gas interests.

It is the rise of BP which is the most striking part of the modern history of British oil companies. Always a relative weakling, in the 1970s it lost its historic area of strength, crude production in the Middle East. But on most measures, it is now almost equal with Shell. What makes the transformation even more striking is the role played in BP's earlier successes by sheer luck. BP's skill, it has often been said, lay in finding crude. But if the company had relied on its own judgement in this, it would never have expanded much outside Iran. In the 1930s it was sceptical of Kuwait and only gained the concession in order to keep others out. Later it looked in the wrong places in Libya and, at first, in Alaska, and it was only discoveries by others which kept it in the game in these areas. It was also sceptical about the North Sea, and only the condition in its licence application that it drilled two wells led it to the Forties field. All this makes its transformation in the 1980s and 1990s, explored in Chapter 9, all the more remarkable, since this was clearly not down to luck. The only valuable legacy of the past was the cash flow from Alaska and Forties, which helped BP transform its downstream operations and make new acquisitions. BP also strengthened its environmental credentials by moving early into solar power and, under John Browne, accepting the likelihood of climate change well before some other major oil companies.[7] The recent problems in Alaska and the Texas City refinery accident have somewhat undermined these initiatives, but high oil prices may give BP and Shell the wherewithal to launch renewed attempts to burnish their environmental record.

Whether oil prices have been high or low, over the twentieth century oil companies have made a lot of money. There are very few industrial companies which have come through almost the whole century, as have Shell and BP, and have ended up so prosperous. So oil companies' long-term rate of return must have exceeded that of most industries. This seems to support those who, from the early days of the industry, have criticized the companies for greed and exploitation. But understanding the context of their profitability suggests that they are less culpable. It was not obvious in 1900 or 1910 that oil would be a winner. An English *rentier*'s portfolio then might well have included loans to South American governments and shares in railways and coalmines, and most of these would turn out to be complete dogs. Oil companies' success over the century should be seen in the context of the total return on all capital invested at the beginning – the bad as well as the good. And even oil companies were not always good investments. The money my grandfather sank into Ural Caspian, and all the other failed or expropriated ventures over the years, must be set against the profits made by the winners.

THE PRESENT AND THE FUTURE

As I write this, the oil price has just set a new peak of $142 per barrel, reached on 27 June 2008. When this book is published . . . who knows what it will be? Rather less uncertainty attaches to some other future oil-related trends, such as likely North Sea production. But even here there are different opinions and the history of previous forecasts suggests that the chances of making an accurate one are pretty low. My only advantage is that knowledge of the past gives one some insight into possible behavioural trends in the future.

As any student of elementary economics knows, barring short-term speculative froth the oil price depends on two things: supply and demand or, since we wish to discuss actual numbers rather than economic concepts, production and consumption. There are basically two schools of thought on world oil production. One holds to the Hubbert peak theory, named after a Shell geologist. According to this oil production in individual fields and, by extrapolation, entire oil provinces follows a bell-shaped curve, rising to a peak and falling at roughly the same rate. Since the majority of really large fields were discovered in the 1960s and 1970s, it follows that global oil production will soon start to decline, since even a multitude of smaller finds cannot make up for the inexorable decline of output from large fields.[8]

According to others, various things can change this scenario. One is that much higher oil prices will call forth new production, both by encouraging exploration in exotic locations and by stimulating technical change. This will enhance recovery rates in existing fields and encourage the finding and exploitation of new small fields in mature provinces such as the North Sea. These are both perfectly reasonable assumptions, but there are various reasons for thinking that they will not make a huge difference. Large amounts of new exploration will be needed simply to replace declining production from older fields. And hoped-for giant new oilfields – offshore Brazil and the Arctic are the current hot favourites – are not going to be cheap and easy to develop, but the very opposite. So production from them will come on stream slowly while, meanwhile, older fields' output falls. Better exploitation of older fields and provinces will also surely happen. But the point here is that it has been happening already. The technological change which drives it has been going on for many years and doesn't seem to be much affected by oil prices. Thus North Sea output, which had been predicted to decline in the 1990s, actually rose to a peak in 1999 – a period of generally low prices. High prices will encourage the exploitation of economically marginal fields, but the North Sea again suggests that they are not going to transform the situation: production has declined significantly since 1999 even though prices have been rising since 2002. One maverick suggestion to mention briefly is 'abiogenic oil' – the idea that oil does not necessarily have an organic origin and therefore a finite supply, but might be manufactured the whole time by geological processes. Unfortunately hardly any geologists seem to give this attractive idea credence.[9]

More tangible is 'non-conventional' oil. Shale oil comes into that category, but even with oil at $142 no one seems to be talking about its revival, in Scotland or elsewhere. More promising is oil from tar sands, but there are numerous problems. The oil is expensive to extract, partly because large amounts of energy are needed to do so, and getting it out is environmentally damaging. Furthermore existing known deposits mainly lie within Canada and Venezuela, the first of which is a wealthy country anyway and the second of which has vast reserves of conventional oil. So in neither case is there a pressing need to exploit the sands rapidly.

Gas is much more promising, being clean and still in abundant supply worldwide. At the moment it is not an economic transport fuel, although Shell is developing a 'gas to liquids' process. But gas is a superior substitute for oil and coal in heating and as a fuel supply for electricity generation. However, gas's very advantages mean that everyone wants it. In particular, Middle Eastern and North African countries which, as with oil, have large reserves of gas, are increasingly using it to generate electricity. Whether gas will fulfil the more optimistic expectations which some such as Peter Odell have for it in the future is not clear.[10]

The Middle East brings us to a different sort of production constraint – OPEC. OPEC is not confined to Middle Eastern and North African countries but they still dominate its output. OPEC currently (June 2008) appears to be keeping production discipline, the secret of its influence, much better than in the early 1980s. Some observers see the national oil companies inside and outside OPEC as another constraint on production because of their inefficiency. In addition, while Iraqi security remains uncertain much potential capacity there is unused. This approach leads to optimism about future world production on the grounds that, if everyone became peaceful and private sector disciplines were applied, a number of countries have the resources to produce more. But military activity, security constraints and inefficiency are likely to remain facts of life, not necessarily in all their present locations but in some of them, and perhaps elsewhere. So to presume a new age of oil abundance when they are removed seems too optimistic. Gradual amelioration may support a slow rise in global production, or reduce the rate of a future decline.

On the other side of the price equation is consumption. In developed countries, consumption fell in 2007 and has continued to fall in 2008, as we would expect given the sharp price rise. Furthermore we know from past experience that the long-term effect of price rises on consumption is greater than the short-term (see Chapter 7, 'The oil crisis and the British economy'). So if prices remain high consumption in the developed world will probably fall for quite some time, irrespective of the future of alternative energy. Other factors besides price will also have an influence. In December 2007 the United States increased its 'Corporate Average Fuel Economy' (CAFE) target for cars and light trucks by over 40 per cent, to be fully effective by 2020.[11] Established during the oil shock of the 1970s, subsequently the scheme had only been slightly modified before this radical tightening. The election of either John McCain or Barack Obama as President will also most likely result in a significant tightening in the US government's attitude towards carbon emissions. Assuming the continued dominance of current scientific views, which largely accept the global warming hypothesis, other governments in developed countries are likely to bear down further on the burning of fossil fuels.

At present, however, most developing countries lie outside the Kyoto Treaty targets on emissions reduction. Many currently subsidize fuel prices and as a result petroleum consumption in such countries continued to increase in 2007. But the expense of subsidies is leading to their reduction and this should restrain consumption. Of course, rapid economic growth in these countries will exert a countervailing upward pressure on consumption so on unchanged policies it is likely to go on growing, if at reduced rates. But it would be naïve to take the current position as fixed. I would be surprised if the Chinese government, for one, does not in the next few years invest huge amounts in alternative energy in order to reduce consumption of hydrocarbons. The Middle East itself, however, is becoming a new focus of alarm for those worried about global energy demand, since domestic fuel prices are far below world levels and energy use per person is extremely high. But political pressure from other countries to restrain consumption is increasingly likely. Perhaps more important, if Middle East production fails to rise much more, its own burgeoning consumption will cut oil exports and earnings and thus exert pressure for policy changes.

Alternative energy is, of course, the greatest unknown of all. 'Biofuels' are a direct substitute for petroleum. At the moment, the main type is ethanol extracted from maize (in American English, corn) or sugar, although there are high hopes for substitutes from agricultural waste products and even algae. However, recent sharp rises in food prices suggest that producing large quantities of such fuels is not an easy solution to oil shortage, and it is certainly not cheap. But even if one is cautious about biofuels, I would guess that within ten years certain types of alternative energy will become competitive with oil – even if its price fell substantially. My own bets would include solar power generated electricity (perhaps not in Britain), which could be stored by battery-driven vehicles. But there are other possible candidates.

I would conclude this guesstimate for the world's oil future as follows. The physical peak of conventional oil output, currently about 82 million bpd, is not far away – assuming there is a market for that oil. Whether that peak is only a little more than present production, as 'peak oil' theorists think, or somewhat higher – Total thinks 95 million bpd, BP 100 million – I don't know. I suspect that non-conventional oil will not make much difference, although gas output will rise for a long time. But assuming prices stay high – and anything over $80 per barrel is high by historical standards – then I think it is entirely possible that the world will not need that volume of oil, either in the medium term or perhaps ever. It is very easy to forget that 30 years ago the world was already consuming 64 million bpd. Because of the long-term effect on consumption of the 1970s oil shocks, growth since then has averaged less than 1 per cent per annum, even though alternative energy has yet to make a serious contribution. Of course, if consumption stagnates and production rises then only one thing can happen – the price will fall again and the incentives to restrict consumption will decline. So I suspect that, if OPEC wishes to keep prices high, it may have to exert production restraint quite soon.

From the Almanack for the world to the Almanack for Britain. North Sea production of both oil and gas will almost certainly continue to fall, but if oil prices stay high the fall may be quite slow. (The waters around the Falkland Islands, however, seem unlikely to become a North Sea in the South Atlantic as some people think. There may be a lot of oil there but drilling for it is very speculative.[12]) Although current oil prices are leading many people to fear an economic rerun of the 1970s, comparisons should not be overdone. Commodity prices generally have risen, as they did in the 1970s, but wage inflation in Britain is far less deeply-rooted now than it was then (see Chapter 7, 'The oil crisis and the British economy'). And much of the income redistribution caused by high prices will be from consumers to all those engaged on North Sea production, and to the government in higher tax receipts, rather than as in 1973–4 from Britain to OPEC countries.

Britain's oil companies, both large and small, will continue to do well. The latter, which are mainly focused on upstream, stand to gain if prices remain high. The majors will benefit from their strength in gas. In boe, Shell's gas reserves are 60 per cent of its total, putting it ahead of all other Western majors; BP's at around 45 per cent are in the middle.[13] BG Group is also a major gas player. The majors' other strengths are technical expertise and cash flow. The biggest clouds on their horizon are the efforts made by national oil companies, particularly China's, to tie up unexploited reserves.

As North Sea production runs down, Britain as a nation will, once more, have to consider security of energy supply. Here John Kay is a source of good advice. There is no point in making detailed plans. Instead, 'The right energy policy is one of diversification – developing as many uncorrelated options as possible'.[14] This is because, unlike the Wizard of Mauritius, none of us can predict the future. So everyone's forecasts (including mine) should be taken with a large pinch of salt. For where the oil industry and the oil price will be in 20 years' time, let alone one hundred, is in truth little more than a guess.

Notes

Notes to Chapter 1: Coming of Age: Oil 1900–18

1 Blainey, *The Rush That Never Ended*, Ch. 20 (quote p. 136).
2 *BP*, Vol. 1, Ch. 1 (quote p. 29).
3 Mitchell, *British Historical Statistics*, pp. 248, 257.
4 Jones, *British Oil Industry*, p. 10.
5 Cable drilling, the usual method until after the First World War, is depicted – realistically so far as I could judge – in the film *There Will be Blood*, which is loosely based on Upton Sinclair's novel *Oil!* (so loosely that it bears hardly any resemblance to the original).
6 *BP*, Vol. 1, Ch. 2 (quote p. 65); Corley, *Burmah Oil*, Vol. 1, Ch. 7 and Ch. 9.
7 *BP*, Vol. 1, p. 88.
8 Corley, *Burmah Oil*, Vol. 1, p. 135.
9 *BP*, Vol. 1, pp. 67, 69; Corley, *Burmah Oil*, Vol. 1, Chs. 7 and 9; Jones, *British Oil Industry*, pp. 26, 99. For a more romantic account see Cook, *MI5's First Spymaster*, pp. 152–5.
10 *BP*, Vol. 1, Ch. 5; Jones, *British Oil Industry*, pp. 143–5.
11 A persistent legend has it that the Admiralty was not interested in oil-firing and that Churchill single handedly effected the switch. Geoffrey Jones (*British Oil Industry*, pp. 10–12) shows that in 1910, before Churchill became First Lord of the Admiralty, the Admiralty purchased 120,000 tons of fuel oil.
12 *Ibid.*, pp. 165–8.
13 Henriques, *Marcus Samuel*, pp. 74–6.
14 Paragraphs above based on *ibid.* and on Howarth, *Shell*, Ch. 2; see also *RDS*, Vol. 1, pp. 37–43.
15 Paragraphs above based on Howarth, *Shell*, Chs. 3 and 4; see also *RDS*, pp. 46–87.
16 Ferguson, *World's Banker*, p. 881; *RDS*, pp. 99–127.
17 Howarth, *Shell*, Ch. 4; Philips, *Oil and Politics*, p. 8 (quote).
18 Middlemas, *Master Builders*, Part 3.

19 Brown, 'Mexican Petroleum', p. 400.

20 *Ibid.*, p 393; Buffington and French, 'The Culture of Modernity', pp. 416–17.

21 Brown, 'Mexican Petroleum', p. 389.

22 *Ibid.*, p. 401.

23 Spender, *Weetman Pearson*, pp. 159, 171.

24 Jones, *British Oil Industry*, p. 70.

25 Knight, *Mexican Revolution*, Vol. 1, p. 186, Vol. 2, pp. 1, 131, 201, 387.

26 *Ibid.*, Vol. 2, p. 386.

27 Schumpeter, *Theory of Economic Development*.

28 Henriques, *Marcus Samuel*, pp. 53–4.

29 Middlemas, *Master Builders*, p. 247.

30 Stockwell, 'British Expansion and Rule in South-East Asia', pp. 389–90; Corley, *Burmah Oil*, Vol. 1, Chs. 1–2.

31 *Ibid.*, p. 39, citing Beeby-Thompson, A., *Oil Pioneer* (1961), p. 80.

32 Two paragraphs above based on Corley, *Burmah Oil*, Vol. 1, Chs. 3–6 and Jones, *British Oil Industry*, pp. 88–105.

33 *Ibid.*, pp. 144–56.

34 *BP*, Vol. 1, citing TNA FO 881/8526.

35 Jones, *British Oil Industry*, pp. 144–56, 160–65.

36 *Ibid.*, pp. 17–26.

37 *Ibid.*, pp. 161–2; Kent, 'Purchase of the British Government's Share', pp. 39–40, 48–9.

38 Jones, *British Oil Industry*, pp. 165–171.

39 Jones, 'Search for an Oil Policy', p. 653.

40 *BP*, Vol. 1, p. 199; Jones, *British Oil Industry*, p. 172.

41 More, *Industrial Age*, p. 139.

42 Jones, *British Oil Industry*, pp. 47–8.

43 *Ibid.*, pp. 50–62.

44 Jones, *Merchants to Multinationals*, pp. 280–85; Middlemas, *Master Builders*, pp. 225–6; Pearton, *Romanian State*, p. 33.

45 Jones, *British Oil Industry*, pp. 107–12.

46 *Ibid.*, pp. 149–50, 155; Kent, *Oil and Empire*, pp. 60–94; *BP*, Vol. 1, pp. 166–9, 197.

47 Dunsterville, *Dunsterforce*, p. 17.

48 *Ibid.*, p. 173 and p. 2.

49 For this paragraph see *Ibid.* and Gokay, 'Battle for Baku'.

50 Strachan, *First World War*, p. 674.

51 *Ibid.*, pp. 780, 787–8.

52 *The Times*, 22 November 1918.

53 *BP*, Vol 1, Appx. 0.1.

54 Pearton, *Romanian State*, pp. 73–5, 80–2, 85.

55 Ludendorff, *War Memories*, pp. 347–8.

56 Jones, *War in the Air*, pp. 274–5, 419–31.

57 Strachan, *First World War*, Vol. 1, p. 240.
58 Howarth, *Shell*, pp. 103–4; Yergin, *The Prize*, p. 175; Strachan, *First World War*, Vol. 1, pp. 1027, 1084–5.
59 Pearton, *Romanian State*, p. 93.
60 See *RDS*, Vol. 1, pp. 175–8 for the argument that lack of oil was important to Germany's war effort.
61 Jones, *British Oil Industry*, p. 179.
62 *Ibid*, p. 185.
63 *RDS*, Vol. 1, p. 94; Howarth, *Shell*, p. 100.
64 *RDS*, Vol. 1, pp. 187–8, 217–18, 267.
65 *BP*, Vol. 1, pp. 217–20, 289 Table 7.4; *RDS*, Vol. 1, p. 199.
66 Jones, *British Oil Industry*, Ch. 7.

Notes to Chapter 2: The World of Oil 1918–39

1 Jackson, 'Harcourt'; Jackson suggests, however, that Harcourt probably died from natural causes; he makes no comment on the truth of the allegations about Harcourt's sexual habits but notes that there had been earlier rumours. Jones, *British Oil Industry*, p. 201.
2 *Ibid.*, pp. 208–13.
3 By 1923 the government share had reduced to 55.87 per cent due to public share offerings (*BP*, Vol. 1, Table 8.2).
4 The above two paragraphs based on Jones, *British Oil Industry*, pp. 222–9.
5 *Ibid.*, p. 223.
6 Kent, *Oil and Empire*, p. 157.
7 Memo presented to Imperial War Conference, 22 July 1918, TNA FO 368/2255, Appx. C, cited in *ibid.*, p. 134.
8 Jones, *British Oil Industry*, pp. 204, 213–17.
9 Venn, *Oil Diplomacy*, pp. 48–53.
10 *Ibid.*, p. 55.
11 Renton, 'Changing Languages of Empire', pp. 647, 653 (quote); 'Middle East' gradually replaced the older 'Near East'; originally it did not include Iran, now often regarded as part of the Middle East.
12 Monroe, *Britain's Moment, passim*.
13 Jones, *British Oil Industry*, p. 181.
14 *Ibid.*, p. 214; Venn, *Oil Diplomacy*, p. 42; Monroe, *Britain's Moment*, p. 102.
15 Kent, *Oil and Empire*, pp. 137–55; Jones, *British Oil Industry*, pp. 216–17; *BP*, Vol. 1, p. 358.
16 Jones, *British Oil Industry*, pp. 237–8.
17 *BP*, Vol. 1, p. 586 (quote).
18 Yergin, *The Prize*, p. 204; *BP*, Vol. 2, p. 168.
19 *BP*, Vol 1, Ch. 9.

20 Venn, *Oil Diplomacy*, p. 58; *BP*, Vol. 2, p. 33.

21 *Ibid.*, Ch. 2 (quote p. 47).

22 Yergin, *The Prize*, p. 204, citing Stivers, William, 'A Note on the Red Line Agreement', *Diplomatic History*, Vol. 7 (1983). The origins of this self-denying ordinance clearly go back to the pre-war TPC negotiations; see Kent, *Oil and Empire*, p. 93.

23 Yergin, *The Prize*, p. 281.

24 *BP*, Vol. 1, p. 427; Vol. 2, p. 148; *RDS*, Vol. 1, p. 283, points out that Shell geologists in the Hague were also sceptical of Saudi Arabia's potential.

25 Yergin, *The Prize*, pp. 286–92.

26 *BP*, Vol. 2, pp. 146–55.

27 This follows the general line of argument in Monroe, *Britain's Moment*.

28 Ambler, Eric, *Uncommon Danger* (London: Penguin, 1960 edn).

29 *Ibid.*, p. 77.

30 Yergin, *The Prize*, pp. 202, 369–70; Deterding seems not to have been anti-Semitic, at least for most of his life; several of the Shell group's top personnel were Jewish; *RDS*, Vol. 1, pp. 477–81.

31 *BP*, Vol. 1, pp. 382–4.

32 Yergin, *The Prize*, p. 260; the oil companies called the agreement the 'Pool Division Agreement'.

33 More, *Britain in the Twentieth Century*, pp. 65–6.

34 Jones, *British Oil Industry*, pp. 238–9.

35 *BP*, Vol. 1, p. 613 Table 13.1.

36 *BP*, Vol. 2, p. 107.

37 *Ibid.*, pp. 109–10 shows that the As-Is agreement was finalized before the Achnacarry meeting; on the other hand, *RDS*, Vol. 1, pp. 278–82 and p. 520, note 128 argues that Deterding must have had a major role in drafting the agreement.

38 For the agreement see *BP*, Vol. 2, pp. 528–34. Contrary to what has sometimes been stated Achnacarry did not impose 'phantom' freight charges, i.e. charges above the normal freight rates payable. It aimed to minimize freight costs by encouraging companies to supply each other from the nearest source of supply – e.g. if Shell supplied APOC in England from the USA, APOC might supply an equal amount from Persia to Shell in Italy. So long as the companies could keep up product prices, then they would make more money that way than by hauling their own oil longer distances. But the Agreement did not specify product prices, although no doubt it hoped for local agreements over these. It relied on maintaining such prices by freezing market share; the standardization of the Gulf Coast price for crude was to facilitate inter-company transfers such as in the example above.

39 *BP*, Vol. 1, p. 613 Table 13.1; Vol. 2, p. 111; Yergin, *The Prize*, pp. 266–8.

40 *BP*, Vol. 2, pp. 116, 119; *RDS*, Vol. 1, pp. 441–5.

41 Yergin, *The Prize*, pp. 65–6; *BP*, Vol. 2, pp. 112–13.

42 Middlemas, *Master Builders*, p. 229; Howarth, *Shell*, p. 120.

43 Yergin, *The Prize*, pp. 272–9.

44 Venn, *Oil Diplomacy*, pp. 65–6.

45 *BP*, Vol. 1, pp. 556–7, 568–70.

46 Yergin, *The Prize*, pp. 234–6; Howarth, *Shell*, pp. 130–2; *BP*, Vol. 1, Appx. 1.

47 McBeth, *Gomez*, pp. 39–40, 44; quote from Venn, *Oil Diplomacy*, p. 65, citing TNA FO 371/A2612/1207/47.

48 McBeth, *Gomez*, pp. 62 and 65; the Middle East royalty figures come from Issawi and Yeganeh, *Middle East Oil*, which may understate them (see note 56 below).

49 McBeth, *Gomez*, pp. 90 and 97.

50 Corley, *Burmah Oil*, Vol. 2, pp. 9–45.

51 Pearton, *Romanian State, passim*, esp. pp. 124, 131–3, 188–9, 207.

52 *Ibid.*; citation on p. 302 and see pp. 132–4, 302–3.

53 Dividends by themselves are not a good measure of profitability for a variety of reasons. Wartime and post-war inflation meant that, all other things being equal, companies would be likely to pay a higher dividend than pre-war. By the mid-1920s, after a fall from their peak, oil prices were still almost double their pre-war level. On the other hand, companies might not pay out all their profits in dividends.

Since the first two volumes of BP's official history did not follow a consistent methodology, I have reconstructed BP's (or APOC/AIOC as it was then) rate of return for 1922–38 as follows below. The reconstruction is quite crude: it is based on share and bond holders' capital after capital raising ceased in the early 1920s, and an average of total profits for the period. A more sophisticated, but more time-consuming, method would be to calculate a net assets figure for each year and then a rate of return for each year based on profits for that year, and then to average the result. My method probably overstates the rate of return.

Total capital raised, including loan capital: £35.3 million (*BP*, Vol. 1, Tables 5.1, 6.1, 8.1, 8.8). Profits comprises dividends plus debenture/loan interest (the latter and preference dividends estimated for 1922–8) (*Ibid.*, Tables 8.3 and 8.12; *BP*, Vol. 2, Table 1.3) plus repayment of loan capital 1929–38 (*Ibid.*, Table 1.4) plus increase in capital employed over the period (*Ibid.*, Table 1.4). The total of the above over 17 years is £69.8 million or an average annual rate of 11.6 per cent.

54 *BP*, Vol. 1, Appx. 8.5.

55 Quote in Yergin, *The Prize*, p. 250; McBeth, *British Oil Policy*, p. 97.

56 Royalties were totalled by adding together *BP*, Vol. 1, Table 13.1 and *BP*, Vol. 2, Table 2.1. The actual figure, having subtracted royalties payable up to 1921 (quite small) is £40.1 million.

The profit and royalty figures above can be compared with those in Issawi and Yeganeh, *Middle Eastern Oil*, Table 34 and Appendix Tables 4 and 6. Until 1947 the great bulk of Middle Eastern output was from Iran, so the figures can be taken as a rough proxy for APOC/AIOC's. From 1913–47 they give a profit/royalty split of 76/24, which appears very different from my estimate above, even allowing for the different period covered. They give a significantly lower figure (about £28 million over the inter-war period, but an exact comparison with 1922–38 is not possible) for royalties. Applying this figure to my calculations would give a profit split much closer to theirs. I suspect their profit figure is estimated as they appear to give no sources before the Second World War. Their royalty figure comes from the International Court of Justice case over the 1951 nationalization. I do not know its ultimate derivation but it seems likely that the BP official history figures are as accurate as is achievable.

57 McBeth, *British Oil Policy*, p. 16.

58 Quote from Philip, *Oil and Politics*, p. 15, citing R. Miller, 'British Business in Peru 1883–1930', Cambridge PhD, 1979, p. 168; *BP*, Vol. 1, pp. 544–5, 560.

59 Philip, *Oil and Politics*, p. 43.

60 *BP Statistical Review.*

61 Brown, 'Mexican Petroleum', pp. 408–10; Issawi and Yeganeh, *Middle Eastern Oil*, pp. 75–6; in Venezuela, however, petrol prices remained extremely high (McBeth, *Gomez*, p. 198).

62 McBeth, *Gomez*, pp. 127, 140, 156; Knight, *Mexican Revolution*, Vol. 2, p. 429; *BP*, Vol. 2, p. 81 and Table 3.6.

63 Philip, *Oil and Politics*, pp. 27 and 28–9; *BP*, Vol. 1, p. 65; Brown, 'Mexican Petroleum', p. 409.

64 Philip, *Oil and Politics*, pp. 408–9.

65 Ambler, *Uncommon Danger*, p. 109; Knight, *Mexican Revolution*, Vol. 1 p. 186, Vol. 2, pp. 1, 131, 201–2, 387; Philip, *Oil and Politics*, p. 40.

66 *Ibid.*, pp. 36–9, 153 and 57 for Mexico.

67 *Ibid.*, p. 57, and Pearton, *Romanian State*, pp. 123–4.

68 *BP*, Vol. 2, p. 54.

69 *Ibid.*, pp. 84 (quote) and 105.

70 McBeth, *Gomez*, pp. 142, 144–50, 156.

71 Philip, *Oil and Politics*, pp. 216–25; Howarth, *Shell*, pp. 177–8; Brown, 'Mexican Petroleum', p. 401.

72 Howarth, *Shell*, p. 126; Yergin, *The Prize*, p. 210; *Petroleum Times*, 10 January 1931 and Pearton, *Romanian State*, p. 125, for Phoenix; *BP*, Vol. 2, pp. 130, 134.

Notes to Chapter 3: Kerosene Lamps and Petrol Pumps: The British People and Oil 1900–39

1 *BP*, Vol. 1, p. 501.

2 Brunner, *Problem of Oil*, pp. 141–2.

3 *Ibid.*, p. 155.

4 Fletcher, 'Coal to Oil', pp. 1–19; Sturmey, *British Shipping*, Ch. IV.

5 Fletcher, 'Coal to Oil', p. 8.

6 *Ibid.*, pp. 10–11; Howarth, *Shell*, p. 137; *BP*, Vol. 1, p. 534.

7 Brunner, *Problem of Oil*, pp. 157, 160, 165, 168 and 169 (quote).

8   *Ibid.*, ch. 10.

9   *Ibid.*, ch. 11. The trade refers to bitumen bound macadam (i.e., road-surfacing material) as bitmac, and in the USA the term 'asphalt' is used; see www.pavingexpert.com (accessed 24 June 2007) for a clear discussion.

10 Brunner, *Problem of Oil*, p. 161; see also Ricardo, *Memories*, pp. 57–8 and 135–6 for early oil engines, including hot-bulbs.

11 Later on, tractors used enriched kerosene (tractor vaporizing oil or TVU) but in low-compression petrol-type engines not hot-bulb engines. TVU was low-octane but adequate for such engines and was untaxed. Payton-Smith, *Oil*, p. 309, refers to such usage as common by the Second World War.

12 Mitchell, *British Historical Statistics*, p. 577.

13 Ricardo, 'Progress of the internal combustion engine', pp. 519–20; Brunner, *Problem of Oil*, p. 164; Rolt, *Landscape with Machines*, Ch. 8.

14 Brown, 'Cultivating a "Green" Image', pp. 348 (quote) and 350.

15 It is sometimes said that 'petrol' was not often used in the early period but a search of *The Times* electronic archive suggests that from the early 1900s it was used as frequently as 'motor spirit', the usual alternative, and rapidly became the standard usage while motor spirit became a more technical term.

16 Dixon, 'Petrol Distribution', pp. 3 and 6; *BP*, Vol. 2, p. 129.

17 Brunner, *Problem of Oil*, pp. 135, 31 and 104; Dixon, 'Petrol Distribution', p. 9; www.ianbyrne.free-online.co.uk (accessed 24 June 2007).

18 *The Times*, 5 April 1935; while Pratts does not seem to have advertised in *The Times* after the 1920s, there were a number of big display advertisements for Esso after the relaunch; see e.g. *The Times* 5 and 12 April, 10 and 30 May, 5 July and 29 August, all 1935.

19 Brunner, *Problem of Oil*, pp. 103–5; Howarth, *Shell*, p. 142.

20 *BP*, Vol. 1, pp. 487–8, Vol. 2, p. 130 Table 4.3.

21 Jones, *British Oil Industry*, pp. 36–7.

22 See e.g. *The Times*, 1, 4 and 7 January 1913; 5–7 February and 11–13 February 1920.

23 Brunner, *Problem of Oil*, pp. 145 and 188–9.

24 Bowden, 'That's the Spirit', p. 643.

25 Brunner, *Problem of Oil*, pp. 39 and 98–9; Dixon, 'Petrol Distribution', p. 6.

26 Brunner, *Problem of Oil*, pp. 93–4 and 97; Bowden, 'That's the Spirit', p. 645.

27 Brown, 'Cultivating a "Green" Image', p. 358; Dixon, 'Petrol Distribution', p. 13; Brunner, *Problem of Oil*, pp. 131–2, suggests that there was still vigorous competition for the control of pumps.

28 *Ibid.*, pp. 40–41; Howarth, *Shell*, p. 164.

29 Bowden, 'That's the Spirit', pp. 644, 648, 661, 658; MI5 was interested in ROP for obvious reasons (*The Times*, 4 March 2008).

30 Brunner, *Problem of Oil*, pp. 36–7; Dixon, 'Petrol Distribution', p. 15.

31 *BP*, Vol. 2, p. 130 Table 4.3.

32 Brown, 'Cultivating a "Green" Image', pp. 348, 350 (quote), 353–4.

33　*BP*, Vol. 1, p. 500.

34　Brunner, *Problem of Oil*, p. 129; Brown, 'Cultivating a "Green" Image', p. 356.

35　*Ibid.*, pp. 350 and 357; Howarth, *Shell*, p. 167; *BP*, Vol. 2, p. 128.

36　Fitzgerald, *British Labour Management*, Ch. 1 and pp. 184–6.

37　Howarth, *Shell*, pp. 161 and 135.

38　*BP*, Vol. 1, Ch. 8; *BP*, Vol. 2, p. 269.

39　Johnson, 'Women in the History of BP', p. 16.

40　*BP*, Vol. 2, pp. 84–92.

41　Johnson, 'Women in the History of BP', pp. 17–18.

42　*BP*, Vol. 2, p. 83.

43　Howarth, *Shell*, pp. 239–40.

44　Brunner, *Problem of Oil*, pp. 66–7; *Fifth Census of Production*, Part III.

45　Corley, *Burmah Oil*, p. 6; *BP*, Vol. 1, p. 67; Howarth, *Shell*, p. 127.

46　Howarth, *Shell*, p. 126; *BP*, Vol. 1, p. 427; Yergin, *The Prize*, pp. 218–19.

47　Howarth, *Shell*, p. 127; Yergin, *The Prize*, Ch. 13; *BP*, Vol. 1, pp. 409–10 and 420 (quote).

48　Yergin, *The Prize*, p. 83; *BP*, Vol. 1, pp. 414 (quote)–417; Howarth, *Shell*, p. 130.

49　*BP*, Vol. 1, p. 417; www.dukeswoodoil.co.uk/Sherwood_forest.htm (accessed 10 July 2007); Woodward and Woodward, *Secret of Sherwood Forest*, esp. Ch. 12 and pp. 246–7; *RDS*, Vol. 1, pp. 200–1.

50　Yergin, *The Prize*, pp. 111–12.

51　*BP*, Vol. 1, pp. 430 (quote) and 438.

52　Howarth, *Shell*, pp. 146, 171; Ricardo, *Memories*, pp. 187–90, 207.

53　*BP*, Vol. 1, p. 280; *BP*, Vol. 2, pp. 182, 203–4; Howarth, *Shell*, p. 169; *RDS*, Vol. 1, p. 366.

54　McKay, 'Pumpherston', *passim*; Saville, *Industrial Archaeology*, pp. 10–11; Payton-Smith, *Oil*, pp. 19, 23; *BP*, Vol. 1, p. 483.

55　Jones, *British Oil Industry*, pp. 191, 202–3, 208, 218; Payton-Smith, *Oil*, p. 17 suggests 1921 as the year when exploration ceased and puts the grant at £560,000.

56　*Ibid.*, p. 17.

57　*Ibid.*, pp. 22–3; www.theaa.com/publicaffairs/reports/Petrol_Prices_1896_todate_gallons. pdf; 4d (four pence) is about 1.65p; one shilling and sixpence equals 7.5p; values should be multiplied by about 50 to arrive at modern-day equivalents.

58　*BP*, Vol. 2, pp. 178–9; www.dukeswoodoil.co.uk/Sherwood_forest.htm (accessed 10 July 2007).

59　www.mineralsuk.com/britmin/mpf oil_gas.pdf (accessed 10 July 2007); *Petroleum Times*, Vol. XLI, 28 January 1939, p. 110.

60　Reader, *Imperial Chemical Industries*, pp. 164, 178–9, 181; *BP*, Vol. 2, p. 180; *RDS*, Vol. 1, p. 340.

61　Reader, *Imperial Chemical Industries*, pp. 263–5; Payton-Smith, *Oil*, pp. 23–4.

62　*Ibid.*, pp. 95–7; Dixon, 'Petrol Distribution', p. 9; *BP*, Vol. 2, p. 131.

63　More, *Britain in the Twentieth Century*, p. 75.

64　Payton-Smith, *Oil*, pp. 39 and 52 ff.

65　Kent, 'British Government Oil Policy', pp. 148, 154–6, 163 n. 3.

66 Kennedy, *Freedom from Fear*, pp. 394–6, 400–1.
67 Payton-Smith, *Oil*, pp. 52, 57–64.
68 McBeth, *British Oil Policy*, pp. 79–80, 148–9.
69 Kennedy, *Freedom From Fear*, p. 433.

Notes to Chapter 4: Britain, Oil and the Second World War

1 Hastings, *Bomber Command*, pp. 65 (quote)–66.
2 Cooke and Nesbit, *Hitler's Oil*, pp. 71–7 (quote p. 76).
3 Gunther, 'German War', p. 1273 (crude); Muller; 'Albert Speer', p. 475 (synthetic).
4 Pearton, *Romanian State*, pp. 258–9.
5 Payton-Smith, *Oil*, p. 483 Table 52.
6 Tooze, *Wages of Destruction*, p. 412.
7 Imlay, 'Anglo-French Strategy', pp. 334–5, 345–52, 363–70; Cooke and Nesbit, *Hitler's Oil*, Ch. I.
8 Butler, *Grand Strategy*, pp. 343–4; Webster and Frankland, *Strategic Air Offensive*, Vol. 1, p. 146.
9 *Ibid.*, pp. 152, 156–7, 169.
10 Payton-Smith, *Oil*, pp. 143–4, 159–60.
11 *Ibid.*, pp. 128–30, 161, 178, 195–6. Lend-Lease was the provision for the US to 'lend' Allied countries war material, in return for various vaguely specified future considerations.
12 *Ibid.*, pp. 142 Table 6, 145–6, 155–7.
13 *Ibid.*, pp. 77–8. Lubricating oil was within a separate pool.
14 *Ibid.*, pp. 143–4, 331.
15 *Ibid.*, pp. 134–40.
16 Howarth, *Shell*, pp. 198–9.
17 Payton-Smith, *Oil*, pp. 162, 199–201.
18 *Ibid.*, pp. 206–8, 299.
19 *Ibid.*, pp. 379–401.
20 *Ibid.*, p. 393 Table 32, and p. 433 Table 41, pp. 439–40.
21 *Ibid.*, pp. 172, 185–6, 313, 482–3 Tables 49 and 52; www.dukeswoodoil.co.uk/Sherwood_forest.htm (accessed 7 August 2007); for American drillers see also Woodward and Woodward, *Secret of Sherwood Forest*.
22 Payton-Smith, *Oil*, pp. 85–93, 288–93, 483–4 Tables 52 and 53.
23 *Ibid.*, p. 483 Table 52.
24 *Ibid.*, pp. 54–7, 260–82, 385–8, p. 384 Table 31; *RDS*, Vol. 1, p. 366; Vol. 2, p. 72; also Chapter 3, 'Scientists and practical men'.
25 Payton-Smith, *Oil*, pp. 225–7, 332–5, 408–9, map facing p. 213. The pipelines still exist as the Government Pipeline and Storage System (GPSS); www.linewatch.co.uk/htm (accessed 9 August 2007) has a map which suggests that the lines are pretty much the same although the Scottish ones no longer appear on it.

26 Payton-Smith, *Oil*, uses the first name; a post-war press release used the more familiar term although it is not clear when it became current (TNA CAB 106/1129, 24 May 1945).

27 Payton-Smith, *Oil*, pp. 334–5, 410–11, 446–9.

28 Murray and Millett, *A War to be Won*, pp. 437–8; Bennet, *Ultra in the West*, pp. 140–45.

29 Manning, *The Danger Tree*, p. 139. I use the term Middle East in this section in the sense it was used during the war, that is the older sense which excludes Iran; Egypt, however, was often included.

30 Venn, *Oil Diplomacy*, p. 171 Table A1.

31 Farrell, *British Grand Strategy*, p. 37.

32 Butler, *Grand Strategy*, Vol. II, pp. 460 ff and pp. 520 ff; Beaumont, J., 'Britain and the rights of neutral countries'.

33 Farrell, *British Grand Strategy*, pp. 280–81.

34 *Ibid.*, p. 321 for references to frequent concern about oil in the summer of 1942; Danchev and Todman (eds), *War Diaries 1939–45*, p. 290 (quote).

35 Bryant, *Turn of the Tide*, p. 457; this was from Brooke's later notes, not from his diary.

36 Butler, *Grand Strategy*, Vol. III, Pt. II, pp. 652–5.

37 Payton-Smith, *Oil*, p. 233 Table 14, p. 454 Table 46.

38 Schreiber, 'Political and military developments', pp. 165 ff, 182, 186–7, 198–9, 203; Schwanitz, 'German Middle Eastern Policy' confirms Hitler's lack of interest in the area.

39 Schreiber, 'Political and military developments', pp. 212–13, 232; Schreiber, 'Politics and Warfare in 1941', pp. 593–4; Stegemann, 'The Italo-German Conduct', p. 657.

40 *Ibid.*, p. 657; Kershaw, *Hitler*, pp. 530, 537.

41 Greene and Massignani, *Naval War*, p. 273.

42 Stumpf, 'War in the Mediterranean area', pp. 838–9; Crefeld, *Supplying War*, Ch. 6, esp. pp. 199–200.

43 Greene and Massignani, *Naval War*, p. 144; Schreiber, 'Political and Military Developments', p. 26, suggests slightly higher Italian reserves.

44 Greene and Massignani, *Naval War*, pp. 143–4, 204.

45 *Ibid.*, pp. 96, 144.

46 Crefeld, *Supplying War*, p. 185.

47 Stumpf, 'War in the Mediterranean Area', p. 837; Schreiber, 'Political and Military Developments', pp. 26–7.

48 Corley, *Burmah Oil*, Vol. 2, p. 99.

49 Goralski and Freeburg, *Oil and War*, p. 152 (quote); Murray and Millett, *A War to be Won*, Ch. 7.

50 *Ibid.*, Ch. 7; Goralski and Freeburg, *Oil and War*, pp. 99–102.

51 Murray and Millett, *A War to be Won*, pp. 224–6; Goralski and Freeburg, *Oil and War*, pp. 195–9, 308–9.

52 Harrison, 'Economics of World War II', p. 10 Table 1.3, pp. 15–16 Table 1.6.

53 *Ibid.*, Table 1.6; Italian production of most weapons was negligible.

54 Overy, *Goering*, Ch. 6, pp. 189–93, 208–15; Tooze, *Wages of Destruction*, pp. 413, 497; TNA CAB 146/463, p. 86 (quote).

55 Overy, *The Battle*, *passim*; Goralski and Freeburg, *Oil and War*, Ch. 3.

56 *Ibid.*, pp. 81–2, 177–9.

57 Muller, 'Albert Speer and Armaments Policy', p. 475, for total German petroleum supply (1940 and 1943 were averaged).

58 Goralski and Freeburg, *Oil and War*, pp. 245–9, 268–71, 279; Murray and Millett, *A War to be Won*, pp. 330–31.

59 Goralski and Freeburg, *Oil and War*, pp. 75–6, 180–83; Gunther, 'German War', Vol. LII, pp. 117, 170.

Notes to Chapter 5: The World of Oil 1945–1973

1 Yergin, *The Prize*, pp. 518, 532; *BP*, Vol. 3, Fig. 12.3; Issawi and Yeganeh, *Middle Eastern Oil*, pp. 100–102 and Table 33.

2 Venn, *Oil Diplomacy*, p. 166 Table 8.1.

3 Yergin, *The Prize*, p. 445.

4 TNA, T 236/4237, 4238, 4239; the concession depended on various producing states adjusting their tax laws to the satisfaction of the Inland Revenue, so it took several years to agree for all of them.

5 Sampson, *Seven Sisters*, pp. 157–8; *BP*, Vol. 3, pp. 147, 150; Yergin, *The Prize*, p. 518.

6 *RDS*, Vol. 2, pp. 99, 106–9, 131, 136; *RDS*, Vol. 3, p. 265; *BP*, Vol. 3, Table 20.1 and Fig. 8.2; Sampson, *Seven Sisters*, p. 189.

7 *BP*, Vol. 3, Tables 20.1 and 11.2; Fig. 8.2.

8 Cited in *BP*, Vol. 2, p. 413.

9 *Ibid.*, p. 413 (quote).

10 *Ibid.*, pp. 324–5.

11 *Ibid.*, p. 256.

12 *Ibid.*, p. 417.

13 Sampson, *Seven Sisters*, p. 119; Marsh, 'Anglo-Iranian Oil Crisis', p. 160; *BP*, Vol. 2, p. 411; Monroe, *Britain's Moment*, p. 171 citing Lambton, A. K., 'The Impact of the West on Persia', *International Affairs* (Jan. 1957), p. 24.

14 *BP*, Vol. 2, pp. 384, 418; Sampson, *Seven Sisters*, p. 117; Bill and Louis, *Mussadiq*, pp. 252–5, 274–5, 282–5.

15 Yergin, *The Prize*, p. 471.

16 The estimate of 60 per cent is taken from Burn, 'Oil Industry', Table 9, p. 182. I have subtracted western hemisphere imports and Iraqi oil (most of which would have come through the pipeline) from total imports of both crude and products, and assumed that the remainder was Middle Eastern oil and came through the Canal. I suspect the figure of 80 per cent sometimes mentioned includes Iraqi oil.

17 *BP*, Vol. 3, p. 81, citing Eden, *Full Circle*, p. 426.

18 *BP*, Vol. 3, p. 81, citing TNA PREM 11/1135, EC (56) 35 (quote); Catterall, *The Macmillan Diaries*, pp. 590, 607.

19 Hennessy, *Having It So Good*, p. 430; Howarth, *Shell*, pp. 251 (quote), 252–4; TNA, PREM 11/1117.

20 Paragraphs above based on Hennessy, *Having It So Good*, pp. 421–52, and More, *Britain in the Twentieth Century*, pp. 206–7.

21 Worrall, 'Coping', p. 186.

22 *BP*, Vol. 3, Figs. 7.1 and 9.1; *RDS*, Vol. 2, pp. 219–20; Smith, 'Power Transferred?', p. 3.

23 Worrall, 'Coping', pp. 184 and 189 citing TNA FO 371/156883.

24 Podeh, 'Arab Response', p. 105.

25 Worrall, 'Coping', p. 193.

26 Yergin, *The Prize*, p. 524.

27 Thorpe, 'Forgotten Shortage', p. 203.

28 Yergin, *The Prize*, p. 556.

29 Klantschnig, 'Oil and Sterling Reserves', p. 139.

30 *BP*, Vol. 3, p. 294; *RDS*, Vol. 2, pp. 285–6.

31 Klantschnig, 'Oil and Sterling Reserves', p. 146; Wilson, *The Labour Government*, p. 400 devotes just two paragraphs to his argument which suggests that he thought it was pretty weak.

32 Thorpe, 'Forgotten Shortage', pp. 214–16; see also this volume Chapter 6, 'Government and oil'.

33 Sampson, *Seven Sisters*, p. 240.

34 Howarth, *Shell*, pp. 218, 243–5; *RDS*, Vol. 4, Table 1.3 and Venn, *Oil Diplomacy*, pp. 172–6 (Venezuelan production); *RDS*, Vol. 2, pp. 195–9.

35 *BP*, Vol. 3, pp. 109–10; Venn, *Oil Diplomacy*, p. 174.

36 *BP*, Vol. 2, p. 172, Vol. 3, p. 118; *RDS*, Vol. 2, p. 220.

37 *Trinidad Oil Company*; Corley, *Burmah Oil*, Vol. 2, pp. 275–9, 370; Burmah also bought Atlas Preservatives in 1965, and thus acquired the services of its owner Denis Thatcher, Margaret Thatcher's husband, who became a Burmah director.

38 *BP*, Vol. 3, pp. 261–3, 267; Howarth, *Shell*, p. 294; *RDS*, Vol. 2, pp. 197–219.

39 *RDS*, Vol. 4, Table 3.1 and *BP*, Vol. 3, Figs. 9.1–9.3; the latter actually puts Shell ahead on product sales.

40 *BP*, Vol. 3, pp. 236, 242, 247.

41 *Ibid.*, pp. 271–5.

42 *Ibid.*, Fig. 9.1 and p. 270.

43 *Ibid.*, pp. 188, 205–6.

44 *Ibid.*, pp. 189–93; Humble Oil was a subsidiary of Jersey Standard.

45 Material above from Coates, *Trans-Alaska Pipeline Controversy*, Ch. 7.

46 *Ibid.*, Ch. 8.

47 *Ibid.*, p. 195.

48 *Ibid.*, pp. 267–8.
49 'f.o.b.' usually means 'free on board' – in other words, the price before freight charges to the destination.
50 Yergin, *The Prize*, pp. 472–6; Sampson, *Seven Sisters*, pp. 122–5.
51 Penrose, *Oil Industry*, pp. 183–4; Issawi and Yeganeh, *Middle Eastern Oil*, pp. 65, 202 n. 15 and Table 21.
52 Issawi and Yeganeh, *Middle Eastern Oil*, p. 18.
53 Penrose, *Oil Industry*, pp. 176, 180, 188–9.
54 *Ibid.*, pp. 156–73; *RDS*, Vol. 2, p. 172; Sampson, *Seven Sisters*, pp. 131–2.
55 *Ibid.*, p. 133; Yergin, *The Prize*, pp. 473–8.
56 Penrose, *Oil Industry*, pp. 186–7.
57 *Ibid.*, pp. 190–2; *BP*, Vol. 3, pp. 299–300.
58 Penrose, *Oil Industry*, p. 156; *BP*, Vol. 3 pp. 175, 179.
59 Issawi and Yeganeh, *Middle Eastern Oil*, Table 33; the figures relate to US oil companies only but the authors suggest (p. 111) that European majors were comparable.

Notes to Chapter 6: Age of Optimism: The British People and Oil 1945–73

1 *UK Annual Abstracts*, No. 84, Table 230; No 108, Table 243.
2 www.theaa.com/public affairs/reports/Petrol_Prices_1896_todate_gallons.pdf (petrol prices; accessed 11 October 2007); www.statistics.gov.uk.
3 Burn, 'Oil industry', p. 177; *UK Energy Statistics* (1971), Table 44.
4 Mitchell, *British Historical Statistics*, p. 556.
5 Burn, 'Oil Industry', p. 177.
6 *UK Energy Statistics* (1971), Table 39 (naphtha consumption taken as a proxy for input to petrochemicals); *ibid.* (1975), Table 46; Chick, 'Making of fuel policy', p. 145.
7 *BP*, Vol. 3, pp. 340, 351, 380; Howarth, *Shell*, p. 230.
8 *Ibid.*, p. 276; *BP*, Vol. 3, pp. 370, 372, 375, 385–6.
9 *BP*, Vol. 3, pp. 229–30.
10 Dixon, 'Solus System', pp. 41–3; Burn, 'Oil industry', pp. 196–7.
11 Dixon, 'Solus System', pp. 43–6.
12 *BP*, Vol. 3, pp. 231–2, 234–6, Fig. 9.6.
13 *Ibid.*, Fig. 9.6; Dixon, 'Solus System', pp. 46–7; Burn, 'Oil industry', p. 190; *Trinidad Oil Company*. Caltex was a joint venture between Texaco and Chevron (ex Standard of California or Socal). They split up their European operations in 1967.
14 Catterall, *Macmillan Diaries*, pp. 563–7.
15 *BP*, Vol. 3, Fig. 9.6 and p. 232.
16 *BP*, Vol. 3, p. 232.
17 *Ibid.*, pp. 231–2.
18 Burn, 'Oil industry', p. 192.

19 *BP*, Vol. 3, pp. 238–9; Howarth, *Shell*, p. 274.

20 www.ianbyrne.free-online.co.uk/.

21 *BP*, Vol. 3, p. 230; Howarth, *Shell*, p. 242.

22 *Ibid.*, pp. 241–2 has some examples of Shell advertisements.

23 Various websites give details of the 'Tiger' campaign; *BP*, Vol. 3, p. 236.

24 *Ibid.*, pp. 231–4, 239–40.

25 *Ibid.*, pp. 238–40.

26 The term 'jobbers' for wholesalers is more often used in the US, although it is sometimes used in Britain for wholesalers of petrol to small independent garage chains.

27 Burn, 'Oil Industry', p. 201.

28 *BP*, Vol. 3, pp. 375, 390.

29 Company websites.

30 *BP*, Vol. 3, pp. 435–44 (quote pp. 438–9).

31 Buncefield Investigation, 'Initial Report', 13 July 2006, www.buncefieldinvestigation.gov.uk (accessed 14 February 2008).

32 Burn, 'Oil industry', pp. 183–4; *BP*, Vol. 2, pp. 289–90.

33 TNA, POWE 33/2211, T 256/2891, CAB 130/27.

34 Burn, 'Oil industry', Tables 7, 8 and 10.

35 Howarth, *Shell*, p. 218; Burn, 'Oil industry', Table 12.

36 *BP*, Vol. 3, pp. 287–8; *RDS*, Vol. 2, p. 278; UK Petroleum Industry Association (UKPIA) website, www.ukpia.com/home.aspx (accessed 18 October 2007); *UK Energy Statistics* (1970), Table 38.

37 Tonnage is deadweight, i.e. carrying capacity; *BP*, Vol. 3, pp. 290–98; Howarth, *Shell*, pp. 254–6, 291, 297. Giant tankers were conceived well before the Canal closure; the *Torrey Canyon*, for instance, was too large for the Canal (see this chapter, 'Oil and the environment').

38 *BP*, Vol. 3, p. 297; Howarth, *Shell*, p. 290.

39 *The Times*, 4 January 1960 and 22 April 1961 (Fawley and BP pipelines); *ibid.*, 20 October 1961 and 5 July 1962 (government bill); *ibid.*, 28 November 1962, 31 January 1963, 19 July 1963, 3 November 1965 (cross-country pipeline); www.linewatch.co.uk; www.ukpia.com/home.aspx; www.buncefieldinvestigation.gov.uk (accessed 14 February 2008).

40 Cowan, *Oil and Water*, Chs. 1–6.

41 TNA, CAB 130/318.

42 Cowan, *Oil and Water*, pp. 75–6, 97–9.

43 TNA, TS 68/73 (quote p. 20); Cowan, *Oil and Water*, p. 116 for estimate – other sources put the amount released higher.

44 *RDS*, Vol. 2, pp. 5–6; www.imo.org/Environment (accessed 18 December 2007).

45 *RDS*, Vol. 2, pp. 399, 401, 417–19, 422–3.

46 *Ibid.*, pp. 423–4.

47 *Ibid.*, pp. 427–37, which has a résumé of the issues and further references.

48 Cowan, *Oil and Water*, Chs. 15–18.

49 TNA, FT 3/663; Cowan, *Oil and Water*, Ch. 19; obituary of Professor Alan Southward, *The Times*, 11 November 2007; 'Prevention of pollution by oil', www.imo.org/Environment (accessed 19 February 2008).

50 Cowan, *Oil and Water*, Chs. 22–3; Union Oil was a medium-sized American company. It was taken over by Chevron in 2005.

51 *The Times*, 26 October 1970, 12 November 1970, 14 November 1970; www.Shetlapedia. com/The_Braer_Disaster (accessed 18 December 2007).

52 'Report of the Chief Inspector of Marine Accidents into the grounding and subsequent salvage of the tanker Sea Empress', www.archive.officialdocuments.co.uk/document/dot/ seaemp (accessed 19 December 2007); 'The Environmental Impact of the Sea Empress Oil Spill', www.archive.officialdocuments.co.uk/document/seeeec/impact.1998seaemp. htm (accessed 19 February 2008).

53 www.imo.org/Environment (accessed 19 February 2008).

54 Owen, D. *Time to Declare*, (London: Peguin, 1992) p. 293.

55 Bingham Report, pp. 11, 50–2, 86–8, 284, 316–17.

56 *Ibid.*, pp. 27, 235, 238.

57 *Ibid.*, pp. 163–4, 176, 184–9, 250–3, 300, 375–85.

58 Owen, *Time to Declare*, pp. 292–5.

59 Bingham Report, pp. 276–7, 288–9, 342, 405–10. The companies continued to operate in Rhodesia itself but with virtually no control from the parents and with entirely local management; the arrangement was known about and accepted since if they had refused to operate, they would have been taken over by the Rhodesian government (*ibid.*, pp. 335–9, 397). The oil which went to Rhodesia was not consigned directly to these subsidiaries, but was bought centrally by the Rhodesian government and then distributed to the various local companies (*ibid.*, pp. 343–4).

60 Owen, *Time to Declare*, p. 296.

61 Chick, 'Marginalist approach', pp. 147–58.

62 *Ibid.*, p. 147 Tables 3 and 4.

63 TNA CAB 21/4452; CAB 134/1086, Memo 20.

64 TNA CAB 21/4452 paper, 18 March 1957.

65 TNA POWE 57/13. A retrospective paper (24 February 1967) suggests that in 1959 the plan was for companies to have about 15 weeks' consumption on hand and the government 10 days; however a draft (22 July 1959) of a brief to the OEEC explicitly states a four-week government reserve target, which at the time was estimated at about 1.7 million tons; in practice only about one million seems to have been accumulated. These stocks were separate from military reserves of about two million tons (POWE 63/413, p. 20).

66 TNA POWE 61/293; POWE 57/13.

67 TNA POWE 57/13, 24 February 1967; POWE 63/309, 4 August 1967; POWE 63/413, pp. 20, 23; Thorpe, 'The Forgotten Shortage', p. 215; Ch. 5 in this volume, 'The moment passes: the Arabs, Israel and oil'.

68 TNA POWE 63/999, Graph 3; FV 191/4 (19 January 1973, 6 March 1973, 22 March 1973); POWE 63/1005.
69 Thorpe, 'The Forgotten Shortage', pp. 215–16.

Notes to Chapter 7: Crisis: Oil in the 1970s

1 *The Times*, 12 October 1973.
2 *BP*, Vol. 3, p. 478.
3 *Ibid.*, p. 481.
4 Account and quote from Yergin, *The Prize*, p. 624, based on interviews with and letters from Drake and McFadzean.
5 *BP*, Vol. 3, p. 484, which also cites the Heath quote (*Course of My Life*, p. 503).
6 Stuttaford, T., 'The Telltale Loss of Power', *The Times*, 4 November 2007.
7 Yergin, *The Prize*, pp. 516, 522.
8 *BP*, Vol. 3, p. 450; Yergin, *The Prize*, p. 548.
9 *BP*, Vol. 3, pp. 452–3.
10 *Ibid.*, pp. 454, 456–7.
11 *Ibid.*, pp. 459–60; Yergin, *The Prize*, p. 644.
12 *BP*, Vol. 3, p. 465.
13 Sampson, *Seven Sisters*, p. 234.
14 *Ibid.*, p. 231; *BP*, Vol. 3, pp. 468–73.
15 *Ibid.*, p. 468 (first quote from *BP*, second a citation).
16 Yergin, *The Prize*, p. 586; *BP*, Vol. 3, p. 476.
17 Yergin, *The Prize*, pp. 604–5.
18 *BP*, Vol. 3, p. 477.
19 *Ibid.*, p. 479.
20 *Ibid.*, pp. 480–84; Yergin, *The Prize*, p. 634.
21 *BP*, Vol. 3, pp. 485–6; Yergin, *The Prize*, pp. 646–8, 652.
22 TNA, T 317/2382, Meeting 23 December 1974.
23 Corley, *Burmah Oil*, Vol. 2, p. 377; TNA T 317/2382, Meeting 26 December 1974.
24 TNA, POWE 64/2; TNA, T 317/2384; Corley, *Burmah Oil*, pp. 387–8; Burmah Oil, *Chairman's Statement and Directors' Report* (1974, 1976, 1979).
25 *RDS*, Vol. 4, Table 1.2.
26 Heal and Chichilnisky, *Oil and the International Economy*, pp. 27–9.
27 *Ibid.*, pp. 32–3.
28 *Ibid.*, pp. 32–3; more recent figures suggest that the price elasticity for gasoline or petrol alone is lower; since it is a larger proportion of Western oil demand than in the 1970s, the overall price elasticity for oil is probably now lower.
29 *RDS*, Vol. 3, pp. 55–6, 60, and Fig. 1.3, p. 56; Venn, *Oil Diplomacy*, Table A.2.
30 *RDS*, Vol. 3, p. 270 Fig. 4.2.

31 WRTG Economics, www.wrtg.com/prices.htm (accessed 29 November 2007).

32 More, *Industrial Age*, pp. 261–2 and Table 28.1.

33 Heal and Chichilnisky, *Oil and the International Economy*, p. 75; Kennedy, 'The Economy' (1972), p. 40.

34 Kennedy, 'The Economy' (1974), p. 42, (1976), pp. 45–7, (1982), p. 41.

35 Heal and Chichilnisky, *Oil and the International Economy*, p. 81. To obtain proportions for Britain I divided the value of net petroleum imports by GNP for 1970, before any significant oil price rises (£750 million and £44.0 billion), and 1974 (£3.84 billion and £75.5 billion); domestic production was insignificant in both years. 1982 was more complicated because by then Britain was a net exporter but I derived an imputed value for oil consumed by extrapolating from the tonnage and value of gross imports, and then divided the imputed value by GNP (*UK Annual Abstract* (1980), Tables 12.6 and 14.1; *ibid.* (1984), Tables 12.4 and 14.1).

36 More, *Britain in the Twentieth Century*, pp. 160–62.

37 More, *Industrial Age*, p. 263 Table 28.2, and p. 266; 'Thatcherite' policy was not actually as simple as this rather bald explanation suggests – and hence its exact responsibility for unemployment is not simple to establish.

Notes to Chapter 8: The North Sea

1 Harris, *Offshore Oil and Gas*, pp. 5–6, 18–19; Cooper and Gaskell, *Adventure*, p. 20.

2 *Ibid.*, pp. 22–3, 88; Noreng, *Oil Industry*, pp. 39–40.

3 *Ibid.*, pp. 43, 115–16, 117–19.

4 Cooper and Gaskell, *Adventure*, pp. 24–5, 130–32.

5 Woodward, *Offshore Oil and Gas*, p. 47.

6 Cooper and Gaskell, *Adventure*, pp. 26–8.

7 *UK Annual Abstracts*, various years.

8 Harris, *Offshore Oil and Gas*, pp. 20–25; Noreng, *Oil Industry*, p. 43.

9 Cooper and Gaskell, *Adventure*, pp. 64–5; *BP*, Vol. 3, pp. 202–3.

10 *Ibid.*, pp. 202–3.

11 *Ibid.*, p. 202 (quote); Cooper and Gaskell, *Adventure*, p. 76; *RDS*, Vol. 3, p. 39.

12 Cooper and Gaskell, *Adventure*, pp. 76, 112–13; Woodward, *Offshore Oil and Gas*, p. 28.

13 *Ibid.*, pp. 39, 42.

14 *UK Annual Abstracts*, various years; Woodward, *Offshore Oil and Gas*, p. 47 (estimates of future production). Note that production is crude only; including oil extracted from condensates increases the total by about 10 per cent.

15 *RDS*, Vol. 3, p. 43; Harvie, *Fool's Gold*, pp. 78–9, 335.

16 *Ibid.*, pp. 135, 138, 143, 335; Woodward, *Offshore Oil and Gas*, pp. 24–8.

17 *Petroleum Economist*, Vol. LVII (June 1990), pp. 178–9; Vol. LIX (April 1992), pp. 5–8; *UK Annual Abstracts*, various years.

18 *Petroleum Economist*, Vol. LVII (April 1990), p. 114; www.oilandgas.org.uk (accessed 7 April 2008); Harris, *Offshore Oil and Gas*, pp. 52–3.

19 www.bp.com/liveassets/bp; www.bp/nsi (accessed 8 April 2008).

20 Woodward, *Offshore Oil and Gas*, p. 12; www.mineralsuk.com/britmin/mpfoil_gas.pdf; www.offshore-technology.com; www.bbc.co.uk/1/hi/england/2389223.stm (accessed 8 April 2008).

21 *The Times*, 30 September 1988, citing interim technical report on the disaster.

22 *The Times*, 13 November 1990, citing *The Public Enquiry into the Piper Alpha Disaster* (London: HMSO, 1990) (quotes).

23 *The Times*, 8 July 1988; 13 November 1990 (quote); 20 December 1990; Hall, 'Survivors of Piper Alpha'.

24 Kevin Topham interview.

25 *Ibid.*; Maurice White interview.

26 Maurice White interview.

27 Kevin Topham and Maurice White interviews.

28 Maurice White interview; Harvie, *Fool's Gold*, pp. 237–9.

29 Cooper and Gaskell, *Adventure*, pp. 168–72; Harvie, *Fool's Gold*, pp. 136–7; Harris, *Offshore Oil and Gas*, p. 56.

30 TNA, T 171/98, 'Taxation of the Oil Industry' (25 February 1972); TNA, CAB 184/111 (note 26 July 1973); Harvie, *Fool's Gold*, pp. 181–2, 270; Toye, 'New Commanding Height', p. 105.

31 TNA, CAB 184/110, 111, 112; *The Times*, 14 November 1974; Noreng, *Oil Industry*, pp. 169–70.

32 Andersen, *Struggle*, p. 132; *Petroleum Economist*, Vol. LIX (April 1992), pp. 5–8, *ibid.* (June 1992), p. 20; www.hmrc.gov.uk/international/ns.fiscal3; *Energy Policies of IEA Countries*, p. 73.

33 Cooper and Gaskell, *Adventure*, pp. 26–30; Toye, 'New Commanding Height', p. 92

34 Harvie, *Fool's Gold*, p. 68; Noreng, *Oil Industry*, pp. 54–5.

35 Harvie, *Fool's Gold*, pp. 117–18, 158–9.

36 Noreng, *Oil Industry*, pp. 54–5; *Financial Times*, 5 March 2008; Harvie, *Fool's Gold*, p. 149; company websites.

37 Cumbers, 'Aberdeen Oil Complex', pp. 376, 378–80; Harvie, *Fool's Gold*, pp. 167–74.

38 Noreng, *Oil Industry*, p. 202 (quote); Harvie, *Fool's Gold*, pp. 222–3; Cumbers, 'Aberdeen Oil Complex', pp. 372–3.

39 Cumbers, 'Aberdeen Oil Complex', pp. 374–5.

40 Cable, 'Industry', p. 205.

41 Harvie, *Fool's Gold*, pp. 129–30.

42 *Ibid.*, Ch. 6, pp. 225–7, 291–4, 355, 370.

43 Noreng, *Oil Industry*, pp. 53, 116, 118–19, 173–4, 247–8.

44 *Ibid.*, pp. 52, 147 ff; Andersen, *Struggle*, pp. 132–6.

Notes to Chapter 9: Age of Uncertainty: Oil After the Oil Crisis 1980–2000

1 *BP Annual Report* (1982), p. 13.
2 *RDS*, Vol. 4, Table 1.2.
3 Venn, *Oil Diplomacy*, Table A.2; Yergin, *The Prize*, p. 721.
4 *Ibid.*, pp. 689, 722, 745–6; *RDS*, Vol. 3, pp. 59–60.
5 Yergin, *The Prize*, pp. 748–50, 763–4; WRTG website (accessed 3 November 2007); *RDS*, Vol. 3, p. 159.
6 WRTG website (accessed 3 November 2007); *RDS*, Vol. 4, Table 1.2.
7 *BP*, Vol. 3, pp. 307, 496.
8 *Ibid.*, p. 289.
9 *RDS*, Vol. 3, pp. 74, 199–201 and Fig. 3.7.
10 *Ibid.*, pp. 63–8, 220.
11 *Ibid.*, pp. 166, 182–3, 195–8; *BP Annual Reports*: (1993), p. 13; (1994), p. 15.
12 Harvie, *Fool's Gold*, pp. 108–9; company websites and (LASMO and Ultramar) diverse websites located through Google.
13 *RDS*, Vol. 3, pp. 231–7.
14 *Ibid.*, pp. 129–53 for chemicals (p. 149 'building on basics'), p. 225; company websites; see also Chapter 6 in this volume, 'Selling oil' for petrochemicals.
15 *BP Annual Report* (1983), p. 5.
16 Yergin, *The Prize*, p. 696; *BP Annual Report* (1984), p. 6.
17 *BP Annual Reports*: (1976), p. 38; (1979), p. 22; (1981) 'Chairman's Report'; (1982), p. 12; (1983), p. 18.
18 *BP Annual Reports*: (1976), p. 38; (1978), p. 18; Yergin, *The Prize*, pp. 722–3.
19 *BP Annual Reports*: (1978), p. 26; (1980), p. 9; (1985), p. 2; (1986), p. 2; (1987), p. 22; (1988), p. 2; (1989), p. 2; (1993), p. 6; *RDS*, Vol. 3, p. 271, Fig. 4.3 (companies' net income).
20 *Petroleum Economist*, Vol. LIX (July 1992), p. 4; *BP Annual Reports*: (1993), pp. 5 and 13; (1994), pp. 13 and 19.
21 *BP*, Vol. 3, pp. 236, 242, 247.
22 *BP Annual Reports* (1979), p. 22; (1980), p. 15; (1981), p. 14; (1986), pp. 13 and 15; (1987), p. 29; *RDS*, Vol. 3, p. 211.
23 *BP Annual Reports*: (1992), p. 23; (1993), p. 19; (1996), pp. 17–18; BP purchased the joint venture with Mobil outright in 1999.
24 *BP Annual Reports*: (1981), 'Chairman's Report'; (1988), p. 18.
25 *Ibid.* (1998), p. 5.
26 *BP Annual Reports*: (1989), p 13; (2000), p. 2.
27 *BP Annual Reports*: (1987), p. 14; (1995), p. 16; (1998), p. 19; *Financial Times*, 18 December 2006, 19 December 2006, 1 February 2008, 28 February 2008 (quote).
28 *RDS*, Vol. 3, p. 66.
29 *Ibid.*, p. 331; the estimate was apparently made by counting articles in US trade journals which may, because of the prominence of the Alaska issue in the US, skew the results.

30 *BP Annual Report* (1975), p. 17; *RDS*, Vol. 3, pp. 307–9, 311–13.

31 *Ibid.*, pp. 242–3; *BP*, Vol. 3, pp. 328–9 (quote), 336.

32 *RDS*, Vol. 3, pp. 256–60, 265; few Shell expatriates would be American because Shell Oil in the USA operated more or less autonomously. *BP*, Vol. 3, pp. 326 and 330.

33 *RDS*, Vol. 3, p. 242 Fig. 4.1 (numbers employed); p. 288 (quote).

34 *Ibid.*, pp. 348–55.

35 Yergin, *The Prize*, p. 778, for the *Exxon Valdez*; Howarth, *Shell*, pp. 320–3; *RDS*, Vol. 3, pp. 335–9.

36 *Ibid.*, pp. 357–62 (quotes on p. 358); *BP Annual Reports*: (1997), p. 18; (1999), pp. 24–5.

37 Stefan Smith, 'Cutting edge innovators must avoid costing the earth', *Financial Times*, 27 November 2007.

38 *Energy Policies of IEA Countries*, p. 75; *UKPIA Statistical Review* (www.ukpia.com/home. aspx).

39 *RDS*, Vol. 3, p. 212; www.ukpia.com/home.aspx.

40 *Energy Policies of IEA Countries*, p. 33; Daniel Yergin, 'Oil has reached a turning point', *Financial Times*, 28 May 2008.

41 *Energy Policies of IEA Countries*, pp. 73, 74, Fig. 17; www.ukpia.com/home.aspx.

42 *Energy Policies of IEA Countries*, p. 23; by 2005 gas's share was a little over 35 per cent, and oil's a little over 30 per cent ('2005 Energy Balances for the UK', *IEA Statistics*), www.iea. org.

43 *Energy Policies of IEA Countries*, pp. 78, 81, 85; BG Group website.

44 *Energy Policies of IEA Countries*, p. 97.

Notes to Chapter 10: Conclusion

1 Atterbury and MacKenzie, *Golden Adventure*; Premier Oil website.

2 Corley, 'Oil companies', p. 166, and see Ch. 3 'Preparing for war'.

3 *BP*, Vol. 2, pp. 469, 518–19, n. 115.

4 I expanded on these points in *Britain in the Twentieth Century*, pp. 252–3; there are signs that this congenital pessimism is being chipped away; see e.g. Peden, G. *Arms, Economics and British Strategy* (Cambridge: CUP, 2007), and references in this.

5 TNA T236/4237, 4238, 4239 (quote in 4239, minute of 17 March) and see Chapter 5 in this volume, 'Seven Sisters'; for the government and BP see also (e.g.) the company history and Marsh, 'Anglo-Iranian oil crisis'.

6 *Financial Times*, 12 March 2007, 'The New Seven Sisters'.

7 *BP Annual Report* (1997), pp. 17–18.

8 *The Times*, 9 June 2008, p. 48; a mass of material on 'peak oil' can be found on the internet.

9 *Financial Times*, 5 May 2008; *The Times*, 9 June 2008; for abiogenic oil see Odell, *Carbon Fuels*, Ch. 6; Mello and Moldowan, 'Petroleum', is a critique.

10 *Financial Times*, 2 April 2008; Odell, *Carbon Fuels*, p. 71.

11 *Financial Times*, 3 December 2007.

12 *Ibid.*, 18 October 2007.

13 *Ibid.*, 4 March 2008.

14 *Ibid.*, 29 May 2007, 'Energy wisdom is knowing that you do not know'.

Sources and Bibliography

ARCHIVAL SOURCES

The National Archives (TNA) of the United Kingdom, London
Records of the following:
Cabinet Office (CAB)
Foreign Office (FO)
Ministry of Power/Department of Energy (POWE)
Nature Conservancy (and related bodies) (FT)
Prime Minister's Office (PREM)
Treasury (T)
Treasury Solicitor (TS)
The British Library Sound Archive: 'Lives in the Oil Industry'
Interviews with: Kevin Topham; Christine Wheeler; Maurice White

PUBLISHED PRIMARY MATERIAL

BP Annual Report (© BP), various years (BP Archives).
Burmah Oil Chairman's Statement and Director's Report (© Burmah Oil),
    various years (BP Archives).
Catterall, Peter (ed.), *The Macmillan Diaries: The Cabinet Years 1950–1957*
    (London: Macmillan, 2003).
Danchev, A. and Todman, D., *War Diaries 1939–45: Field Marshal Lord
    Alanbrooke* (London: Weidenfeld & Nicolson, 1957).
Dunsterville, Lionel, *The Adventures of Dunsterforce* (London: Edward Arnold,
    1920).

Ludendorff, Erich, *My War Memories* (Vol. 1) (London: Hutchinson, n.d.).
Ricardo, Harry R., *Memories and Machines: The Pattern of My Life* (London: Constable, 1968).
Rolt, L. T. C., *Landscape with Machines* (Stroud: Alan Sutton, 2nd edn, 1984).
Wilson, Harold, *The Labour Government 1964–1970: A Personal Record* (London: Weidenfeld & Nicolson, 1971).

OFFICIAL PUBLICATIONS

Bingham, T. H. and Gray, S. M., *Report on the Supply of Petroleum and Petroleum Products to Rhodesia* (London: HMSO, 1978) (The Bingham Report).
Energy Policies of IEA Countries: the United Kingdom 1998 Review (Paris: IEA, 1998) (www.iea.org).
Final Report, Fifth Census of Production, Part III (London: HMSO, 1940).
IEA Statistics (www.iea.org).
Trinidad Oil Company: Proposed Purchase by the Texas Oil Company, Cmd 9790 (1956).
United Kingdom Annual Abstract of Statistics, various years (London: HMSO).
United Kingdom Digest of Energy Statistics, various years (London: HMSO).

JOURNALS AND NEWSPAPERS

Financial Times
Petroleum Economist
Petroleum Times
The Times

OTHER BOOKS AND ARTICLES

ABBREVIATIONS

CBH = *Contemporary British History*
BP (in notes) = History of British Petroleum: volumes can be found under Bamberg and Ferrier
DS = *Diplomacy and Statecraft*
RDS (in notes) = History of Royal Dutch Shell: volumes can be found under Howarth; Jonker; Luiten van Zanden; Sluyterman

OUP = Oxford University Press
CUP = Cambridge University Press

Andersen, Svein, *The Struggle over North Sea Oil and Gas: Government Strategies in Denmark, Britain and Norway* (Oslo: Scandinavian University Press, 1993).

Atterbury, Paul and MacKenzie, Julia, *A Golden Adventure: The First Fifty Years of Ultramar* (London: Hurtwood Press, 1985).

Balfour-Paul, Glen, 'Britain's Informal Empire in the Middle East', in Brown, Judith M. and Louis, W. R. (eds), *The Oxford History of the British Empire: The Twentieth Century* (Oxford: OUP, 1999).

Bamberg, James, *The History of the British Petroleum Company: The Anglo-Iranian Years, 1928–54*, Vol. 2 (Cambridge: CUP 1994).

Bamberg, James, *British Petroleum and Global Oil 1950–1975: The Challenge of Nationalism*, Vol. 3 (Cambridge: CUP, 2000).

Beaumont, Joan, 'Great Britain and the rights of neutral countries: the case of Iran, 1941', *Journal of Contemporary History*, Vol. 16, pp. 213–28 (1981).

Bennet, Ralph, *Ultra in the West: the Normandy Campaign 1944–5* (London: Hutchinson, 1979).

Bill, J. A. and Louis, W. R. (eds), *Mussadiq, Iranian Nationalism and Oil* (London: I. B. Tauris, 1988).

Blainey, Geoffrey, *The Rush That Never Ended: A History of Australian Mining* (Melbourne: Melbourne University Press, 1963).

Boog, H. *et al.*, *Germany and the Second World War*, Vol. VI (Oxford: Clarendon, 2001).

Bowden, Julian, ' "That's the Spirit"; Russian Oil Products Ltd (ROP) and the British Oil Market, 1924–39', *Journal of European Economic History*, Vol. 17, pp. 641–63 (1988).

BP Statistical Review of World Energy (2007 & 2008) (www.bp.com).

Brown, J. C., 'British Development of Mexican Petroleum 1889–1911', *Business History Review*, Vol. 61, pp. 387–416 (1987).

Brown, Robert, 'Cultivating a "Green" Image: Oil Companies and Outdoor Publicity in Britain and Europe, 1920–1936', *Journal of European Economic History*, Vol. 22, pp. 347–65 (1993).

Brunner, Christopher T., *The Problem of Oil* (London: Ernest Benn, 1930).

Bryant, Arthur, *The Turn of the Tide 1940–43* (London: Collins, 1957).

Buffington, R. M. and French, W. E., 'The Culture of Modernity', in Meyer, M. C. and Beezley, W. H., *The Oxford History of Mexico* (Oxford: OUP, 2000).

Burn, Duncan, 'The Oil Industry', in Burn, Duncan (ed.), *The Structure of British Industry*, Vol. 1 (Cambridge: CUP, 1958).

Butler, J. R. M., *Grand Strategy*, Vol. II (London: HMSO, 1957).

Butler, J. R. M., *Grand Strategy*, Vol. III, Pt. II (London: HMSO, 1964).

Cable, J. R., 'Industry', in Artis, M. J. (ed.), *The UK Economy* (London: Weidenfeld & Nicolson, 1986).

Chick, Martin, 'The marginalist approach and the making of fuel policy in France and Britain, 1945–72', *Economic History Review*, Vol. LIX, pp. 143–67 (2006).

Coates, Peter A., *The Trans-Alaska Pipeline Controversy: Technology, Conservation and the Frontier* (Bethlehem: Lehigh University Press, 1991).

Cook, Andrew, *M: MI5's First Spymaster* (Stroud: Tempus, 2004).

Cooke, Ronald and Nesbit, Roy, *Target: Hitler's Oil* (London: William Kimber, 1985).

Cooper, Bryan and Gaskell, T. F., *The Adventure of North Sea Oil* (London: William Heinemann, 1976).

Corley, T. A. B., *A History of the Burmah Oil Company 1886–1924*, Vol. 1 (London: Heinemann, 1983).

Corley, T. A. B., *A History of the Burmah Oil Company 1924–1966*, Vol. 2 (London: Heinemann, 1988).

Corley, T. A. B., 'Oil companies and the role of government: the case of Britain 1900–1975', in Jones, G. and Kirby, M., *Competitiveness and the State: Government and Business in Twentieth Century Britain* (Manchester: Manchester University Press, 1991).

Cowan, Edward, *Oil and Water: The Torrey Canyon Disaster* (London: William Kimber, 1969).

Crefeld, Martin van, *Supplying War: Logistics from Wallenstein to Patton* (Cambridge: CUP, 1977).

Cumbers, Andrew, 'Globalisation, Local Economic Development and the Branch Plant Region: the Case of the Aberdeen Oil Complex', *Regional Studies*, Vol. 34, pp. 1–19 (2000).

Dixon, D. F., 'The Development of the Solus System of Petrol Distribution in the United Kingdom 1950–1960', *Economica*, Vol. XXIX, pp. 40–52 (1962).

Farrell, Brian, *The Basis and Making of British Grand Strategy 1940–43*, Vol. 1 (Lampeter: Edwin Mellen, 1998).

Ferguson, N., *The World's Banker: The History of the House of Rothschild* (London: Weidenfeld Nicolson, 1998).

Ferrier, R. W., *The History of the British Petroleum Company: The Developing Years 1901–32*, Vol. 1 (Cambridge: CUP, 1982).

Fitzgerald, Robert, *British Labour Management and Industrial Welfare 1864–1939* (London: Croom Helm, 1988).

Fletcher, Max E., 'From Coal to Oil in British Shipping', *Journal of Transport History*, Vol. III, pp. 1–19 (1975).

Gokay, Bulent, 'The Battle for Baku: A Peculiar Episode in the History of the Caucasus', *Middle Eastern Studies*, Vol. 34, pp. 30–50 (1998).

Goralski, Robert and Freeburg, Russell, *Oil and War* (New York: William Morrow, 1987).

Greene, Jack and Massignani, Alessandro, *The Naval War in the Mediterranean 1940–43* (Rochester: Chatham Publishing, 1998).

Gunther, A. E., 'The German War for Crude Oil Production in Europe 1934–45', *Petroleum Times*, Vols. LI, LII, Chs. IV, VII, VIII (1947 and 1948).

Hall, A. *et al.*, 'Survivors of the Piper Alpha oil platform disaster: long-term follow-up study', *British Journal of Psychiatry*, Vol. 181, pp. 433–8 (2002).

Harris, Steve, *et al.* (eds), *Britain's Offshore Oil and Gas* (2nd edn; London: UK Offshore Operators Association, 2002).

Harrison, Mark, 'The economics of World War II', in Harrison, Mark (ed.), *The Economics of World War II* (Cambridge: CUP, 1998).

Harvie, Christopher, *Fool's Gold: The Story of North Sea Oil* (London: Hamish Hamilton, 1994).

Hastings, Max, *Bomber Command* (London: Pan, 1999; 1st edn 1979).

Heal, Geoffrey and Chichilnisky, Graciela, *Oil and the International Economy* (Oxford: OUP, 1991).

Hennessy, Peter, *Having It So Good: Britain in the Fifties* (London: Allen Lane, 2006).

Henriques, Robert, *Marcus Samuel* (London: Barrie and Rockliff, 1960).

Howarth, Stephen, *A Century in Oil: The Shell Transport and Trading Co. 1897–1997* (London: Weidenfeld & Nicolson, 1997).

Howarth, Stephen and Joost, Jonker, *Powering the Hydrocarbon Revolution, 1939–1973: A History of Royal Dutch Shell*, Vol. 2 (Oxford: OUP, 2007).

Imlay, T. C., 'A Reassessment of Anglo-French Strategy during the Phoney War, 1939–40', *English Historical Review*, Vol. CXIX, pp. 333–72 (2004).

Issawi, Charles and Yeganeh, Mohammed, *The Economics of Middle Eastern Oil* (London: Faber & Faber, 1962).

Jackson, Patrick, 'Harcourt, Lewis Vernon', in Matthews, H. C. G. and Harrison, Brian, *The Oxford Dictionary of National Biography* (Oxford: OUP, 2004).

Johnson, Valerie, 'Making the Invisible Visible: Women in the History of BP', *Business Archives*, 90, pp. 15–24 (2005).

Jones, Geoffrey, *The State and the Emergence of the British Oil Industry* (London: Macmillan, 1981).

Jones, Geoffrey, 'The British Government and the Oil Companies 1912–1924: the Search for an Oil Policy', *Historical Journal*, Vol. 20, pp. 647–72 (1977).

Jones, Geoffrey, *Merchants to Multinationals: British Trading Companies in the Nineteenth and Twentieth Centuries* (Oxford: OUP, 2000).

Jones, H. A., *The War in the Air*, Vol. 4 (Oxford: Clarendon, 1934).

Jonker, Joost and Luiten van Zanden, Jan, *From Challenger to Joint Industry Leader, 1890–1939: A History of Royal Dutch Shell*, Vol. 1 (Oxford: OUP, 2007).

Kennedy, David, *Freedom from Fear: The American People in Depression and War, 1929–1945* (Oxford: OUP, 2005).

Kennedy, M. C., 'The Economy as a Whole', in Prest, A. R. and Coppock, D. J., *The UK Economy* (London: Weidenfeld and Nicolson, 1972, 1974, 1976, 1982).

Kent, Marion, 'Developments in British Government Oil Policy in the Inter-War Period', in Kent, Marion, *Moguls and Mandarins: Oil, Imperialism and the Middle East in British Foreign Policy 1900–1940* (London: Frank Cass, 1993).

Kent, Marion, 'The Purchase of the British Government's Share in the British Petroleum Company 1912–1914' in *ibid*.

Kent, Marion, *Oil and Empire: British Policy and Mesopotamian Oil, 1900–1920* (London: Macmillan, 1976).

Kershaw, Ian, *Hitler 1936–45: Nemesis* (London: Allen Lane, 2000).

Klantschnigg, G., 'Oil, The Suez Canal, and Sterling Reserves: Economic Factors Determining British Decisionmaking during the 1967 Arab-Israeli Crisis', *DS*, Vol. 14, pp. 131–50 (2003).

Knight, Alan, *The Mexican Revolution* (Vols. 1 and 2) (Cambridge: CUP, 1986).

Kroener, B. (ed.), *Germany and the Second World War*, Vol. V.2 (Oxford: Clarendon, 2003).

Luiten van Zanden, Jan, *Appendices etc: A History of Royal Dutch Shell*, Vol. 4 (Oxford: OUP, 2007).

Manning, Olivia, *The Danger Tree* (first published 1977) in *Fortunes of War*, Vol. II (London: Penguin, 1982).

Marsh, Steve, 'HMG, AIOC and the Anglo-Iranian Oil Crisis: In Defence of Anglo-Iranian', *DS*, Vol. 12, pp. 143–74 (2001).

McBeth, B. S., *Juan Vicente Gomez and the Oil Companies in Venezuela, 1908–1935* (Cambridge: CUP, 1983).

McBeth, B. S., *British Oil Policy 1919–1939* (London: Frank Cass, 1985).

McKay, John, 'Pumpherston and the Shale Oil Industry', in Cavanagh, Sybil (ed.), *Pumpherston: The Story of a Shale Oil Village* (Edinburgh: Luath Press, 2002).

Mello, M. R. and Moldowan, J. M., 'Petroleum: to be or not to be abiogenic' (abstract found via Google).

Middlemas, R. K., *The Master Builders* (London: Hutchinson, 1963).

Mitchell, B. R., *British Historical Statistics* (Cambridge: CUP, 1988).

Monroe, Elizabeth, *Britain's Moment in the Middle East 1914–1971* (London: Chatto & Windus, 1981).

More, Charles, *The Industrial Age: Economy and Society in Britain 1750–1995* (London: Longman, 2nd edn 1997).

More, Charles, *Britain in the Twentieth Century* (London: Longman, 2007).

Muller, R. D., 'Albert Speer and Armaments Policy in Total War', in Kroener, *Germany and the Second World War*.

Murray, Williamson and Millett, Allan, *A War to be Won: Fighting the Second World War* (Cambridge, Mass.: Belknap Press, 2000).

Noreng, Oystein, *The Oil Industry and Government Strategy in the North Sea* (London: Croom Helm, 1980).

Odell, Peter, *Why Carbon Fuels Will Dominate the 21st Century Energy Economy* (Brentwood: Mullin Science Publishing, 2004).

Overy, Richard, *Goering: The 'Iron Man'* (London: Routledge and Kegan Paul, 1984).

Overy, Richard, *The Battle* (London: Penguin, 2000).

Payton-Smith, D. J., *Oil: A Study of Wartime Policy and Administration* (London: HMSO, 1971).

Pearton, Maurice, *Oil and the Romanian State* (Oxford: OUP, 1971).

Penrose, Edith, *The Large International Firm in Developing Countries: The Oil Industry* (London: George Allen and Unwin, 1968; reprint Westport: Greenwood Press, 1976).

Philip, George, *Oil and Politics in Latin America* (Cambridge: CUP, 1982).

Podeh, Elie, ' "Suez in Reverse": the Arab Response to the Iraqi Bid for Kuwait, 1961–63', *DS*, Vol. 14, pp. 103–28 (2003).

Reader, W. J., *Imperial Chemical Industries: A History*, Vol. 2 (Oxford: OUP, 1975).

Renton, James, 'Changing Languages of Empire and the Orient: Britain and the Invention of the Middle East 1917–18', *Historical Journal*, Vol. 50, pp. 645–67 (2007).

Ricardo, Harry R., 'Progress of the Internal Combustion Engine during the Last Twenty Years', *Petroleum Times*, Vol. XLI, pp. 485–8 and 519–22 (1939).

Sampson, Anthony, *The Seven Sisters: the Great Oil Companies and the World They Made* (London: Hodder and Stoughton, 1975).

Saville, R. J., *The Industrial Archaeology and Transport of Purbeck* (Basingstoke: Globe Education, n.d).

Schreiber, G., Stegemann, B. and Vogel, D., *Germany and the Second World War*, Vol. III (Oxford: Clarendon, 1995).

Schreiber, G., 'Political and Military Developments in the Mediterranean Area 1939–40', in Schreiber *et al.*, *Germany and the Second World War*.

Schreiber, G., 'Politics and Warfare in 1941', in Schreiber *et al.*, *Germany and the Second World War*.

Schumpeter, J., *The Theory of Economic Development* (Cambridge, Mass.: Harvard University Press, 1934).

Schwanitz, Wolfgang., 'The German Middle Eastern Policy 1871–1945', in Schwanitz, W. (ed.), *Germany and the Middle East 1871–1945* (Princeton: Princeton University Press, 2004).

Sluyterman, Keetie, *Keeping Competitive in Turbulent Markets: A History of Royal Dutch Shell*, Vol. 3 (Oxford: OUP, 2007).

Smith, Simon, 'Power Transferred? Britain, the United States and the Gulf 1956–71', *CBH*, Vol. 21, pp. 1–23 (2007).

Spender, J. A., *Weetman Pearson, First Viscount Cowdray 1856–1927* (London: Cassell, 1930).

Stegemann, B., 'The Italo-German Conduct of the War in the Mediterranean and North Africa', in Schreiber *et al.*, *Germany and the Second World War*.

Stockwell, A. J., 'British Experience and Rule in South-East Asia', in Porter, Andrew (ed.), *The Oxford History of the British Empire: The Nineteenth Century* (Oxford: OUP, 1999).

Strachan, Hew, *The First World War: To Arms*, Vol. 1 (Oxford: OUP, 2001).

Stumpf, Reinhard, 'The War in the Mediterranean Area 1942–3', in Boog, H. *et al.*, *Germany and the Second World War*.

Sturmey, S. G., *British Shipping and World Competition* (London: Athlone Press, 1962).

Thorpe, Keir, 'The Forgotten Shortage: Britain's Handling of the 1967 Oil Embargo', *CBH*, Vol. 21, pp. 201–22 (2007).

Tooze, Adam, *The Wages of Destruction: the Making and Breaking of the Nazi Economy* (London: Allen Lane, 2006).

Toye, Richard, 'The New Commanding Heights: Labour Party Policy on North Sea Oil and Gas 1964–74, *CBH*, Vol. 16, pp. 89–118 (2002).

UK PIA Statistical Review (2008) (www.ukpia.com/home/aspx).

Venn, Fiona, *Oil Diplomacy in the Twentieth Century* (Basingstoke: Macmillan, 1986).

Webster, C. and Frankland, N., *The Strategic Air Offensive against Germany 1939–45*, Vol. 1 (London: HMSO, 1961).

Woodward, C. (ed.), *Britain's Offshore Oil and Gas* (London: Natural History Museum, 1988).

Woodward, G. H. and Woodward, G. S., *The Secret of Sherwood Forest: Oil Production in England during World War 2* (Norman: University of Oklahoma Press, 1973).

Worrall, Richard J., ' "Coping with a Coup d'Etat": British Policy towards Post-Revolutionary Iraq, 1958–63', *CBH*, Vol. 21, pp. 173–99 (2007).

Yergin, Daniel, *The Prize: The Epic Quest for Oil, Money and Power* (New York: Simon and Schuster, 1991).

WEBSITES

www.theaa.com/public affairs/reports/Petrol_Prices_1896_todate_gallons.pdf

www.archive.officialdocuments.co.uk/document/dot/seaemp

www.archivesnetworkwales.info

www.bbc.co.uk/1/hi/england/2389223.stm

www.bp.com/liveassets/bp

www.bp/nsi

www.buncefieldinvestigation.gov.uk

www.dukeswoodoil.co.uk/Sherwood_forest.htm

www.hmrc.gov.uk/international/ns.fiscal3

www.ianbyrne.free-online.co.uk/

www.imo.org/Environment

www.linewatch.co.uk/htm

www.mineralsuk.com/britmin/mpfoil_gas.pdf

www.offshore-technology.com

www.oilandgas.org.uk

www.pavingexpert.com/

www.Shetlapedia.com/The_Braer_Disaster

www.ukpia.com/home.aspx

www.wrtg.com/prices.htm

Index